Maria D. Weston

Bessie and Raymond

Or, Incidents Connected With the Civil War in the United States

Maria D. Weston

Bessie and Raymond
Or, Incidents Connected With the Civil War in the United States

ISBN/EAN: 9783337009205

Printed in Europe, USA, Canada, Australia, Japan

Cover: Foto ©ninafisch / pixelio.de

More available books at **www.hansebooks.com**

BESSIE AND RAYMOND;

OR

INCIDENTS CONNECTED WITH THE CIVIL WAR

IN

THE UNITED STATES.

BY THE AUTHOR OF

'"Kate Felton," "Elfie Grafton," &c. &c. &c.

———◆———

BOSTON:
PUBLISHED BY EDWARD PAYSON WESTON,
FOR SALE BY CROCKER AND BREWSTER,
51 WASHINGTON STREET.
1866.

TO THE PATRONS OF THIS WORK.

THE AUTHOR

RESPECTFULLY INSCRIBES IT.

SHE does so, with the hope that it may be read with interest and profit by such as sympathize with her in loving the dear old "Stars and Stripes." A deep-plotted romance need not be expected; therefore, such as are looking for a number one novel will be disappointed. The work is calculated to exhibit life as it was in our country during the late Rebellion. We have used fictitious names in stating facts, and have endeavored to write so as to avoid giving offence to any who may recognize incidents in which their words and act have been given to the public. The author loves her country, a united North and South; such she would ever have it, by the blessing of God.

PROVIDENCE, OCTOBER 1, 1865.

BESSIE AND RAYMOND.

CHAPTER I.

" I did not know she could be so brave."

"MOTHER, I am going to enlist under our dear old flag. I am ashamed to stay here at home, when my country needs the services of her sons, as she does at this hour."

"Are you sure, Frederic, that the Government needs you? Many thousands of soldiers have gone forth, already; perhaps it will not be necessary for more to go."

"I hope it will not be; still, there is little foundation upon which to build such a hope. Mother, this is a gigantic Rebellion; it will require a great force to crush it; I want to do something towards it myself. I must go forth to battle, and I desire your help in reconciling my wife to the parting. I believe you will not try to hold me back yourself, much as you love me."

"You judge rightly, my son; much as I dread the horrors of war that must surround you, I dare not withhold my consent to your taking up arms in defence of our Government. I will do all in my power to make it easy for you to go. Julia, I trust, will not oppose you, in doing what you feel to be your duty. She can come and stay with me while you are away, and

I will assist her, in taking care of her children. Have you told her your intentions in regard to enlisting?"

"I have not yet told her my decision; I have merely told her I felt inclined to join the army. I dont know what she will say, when she knows that I have determined to go. I hate to tell her myself; I wish, mother, that you would do the disagreeable job for me."

"I will, my son."

"Will you do so to-day, mother?"

"Yes, Frederic, I will go to Julia, immediately." And Mrs. Sedgwick went, on the wings of love and sympathy, to the home of her son. When she entered his dwelling, and beheld his wife seated in her cheerful sitting-room, with busy fingers and a happy countenance, working for the comfort of her husband, while two sweet children were at play near her, a pang shot through the heart of the kind mother, as she thought of her errand. There was, too, something like restraint in her manner, as she reciprocated the affectionate greeting of Julia, and Julia saw at once that something troubled her mother, and kindly asked her if anything had occurred to cause her uneasiness.

"No, Julia," she replied, "I cannot say that the occurrence of any recent event has caused me pain, but the anticipation of future trial has cast a shade of sadness over my heart. I didn't intend, however, to sadden you with my sorrow, I must not be so selfish."

Mrs. Sedgwick had taken a seat, and lifted the youngest of Julia's children into her lap, while she was uttering the words above quoted.

Little Alice, the pet of the whole family, peeped into the face of her grandmother, with a loving look, saying, as she did so, "I wont let grandma feel sorry."

"I know you wouldn't, my little darling, and grandma mustn't do, say, or look anything, to pain your infant heart."

"Mother," asked her daughter-in-law, "has Frederic been saying anything to you, to give you pain?"

"Why ask me such a question, Julia?"

"Because I didn't know but he had told you, as he has me, that he felt almost certain he ought to enlist under the stars and stripes."

The tone in which Julia uttered these words was cheerful, and Mrs. Sedgwick experienced a feeling of relief, as she listened to them.

"Do you feel, daughter, that you could submit cheerfully to the trial of parting with Frederic, if he should take up arms, and go forth to fight for his country?"

"I have not yet been tried, so I don't know how I should feel. I know what my duty would be in such a case, and I will pray for strength, to bear whatever of ill this war may bring upon me. I will try, if Frederic feels, either now or at some future time, that he must go, to help him all I can to do his duty."

"You are a dear, good girl," said her mother-in-law; "my heart misgave me, when I first came in, and saw you so happy in your little family. I almost repented of the promise I had made Frederic, to tell you, what he shrunk from telling you himself, that he is going to the war; but now I feel that you will not be shocked, or go into hysterics, at learning the fact."

Julia looked earnestly into her mother's face while she was speaking, then remarked thoughtfully, "He has, then, decided to go. I thought it was more than possible that he would go, and I have been preparing myself for the trial. I have thought of you, too, dear mother, in regard to the liabilities of your son's going forth to battle, and have dreaded the trial as much for you as for myself."

"We will sympathize with each other, Julia, in this mutual trial that is near us now."

Here these two friends were interrupted by the entrance of a young lady, who was ushered into the room by a servant; her name was Bessie Jenkins, and she had for some years been an intimate acquaintance of Julia's. Miss Jenkins greeted the two ladies politely, then having taken a seat, she abruptly introduced a subject that seemed to engross all her thoughts.

"I am so nervous I could *not* stay at home," said she, addressing Julia, "or I should n't have called on you to-day."

"Indeed," replied Julia, smiling as she spoke, "what has occurred to affect you thus? You are not wont to complain of your nerves."

"I know I am not, but at present Raymond seems determined to trouble me all he can."

"Raymond trouble you, Bessie? What about, I wonder. I thought it was just the reverse of that; that you tried to vex him."

Bessie laughed at this remark of her friend. "I don't think you ought to say that, Mrs. Sedgwick," answered she, "and yet I suppose you feel that you have reason to think I am a teasing girl." Here she paused, for memory was busy at this moment displaying many little acts of coquetry of which she had been guilty. After a moment's silence, she said in a disdainful tone, "Mrs. Sedgwick, Raymond has resolved to go to the war; is n't it ridiculous?"

"Ridiculous, to go out to defend our dear old flag? why, no, it is brave and glorious, I am sure."

"Let it be brave and glorious, as you say," responded Bessie, in an offended tone; "If your husband were to go, you wouldn't see the glory. Mr. Sedgwick hasn't gone, and perhaps never will go."

"Yes, Bessie, Mr. Sedgwick intends going soon; this very hour I have learned his decision."

"And you mean to let him go, without trying to prevent it, Mrs. Sedgwick?"

"I do, indeed, intend to let him do what he feels to be his duty, in regard to serving his country."

"Serving his fiddlestick," interrupted Bessie; "now I am more vexed than ever, for I had hoped you would have befriended me in this great trial; but I see that I shall not have your sympathy, if I am wretched."

Julia smiled, but did not reply. Bessie paused a moment, and then inquired if Julia had counted the cost of having her husband leave her to be exposed to the horrors of war.

"I think I have looked at the subject in every light in which I am capable of viewing it."

"Then you have reflected that he may be wounded and crippled for life; that he may possibly lose an eye, or be disfigured terribly in some other way?"

"Yes, I have weighed all his liabilities; yet, while I shudder at the thought of what may befall him, I dare not put an obstacle in the way of his enlisting."

"How will you feel, think you, if you have a maimed companion to walk the journey of life with, instead of your handsome Frederic?"

"Sad, at the thought of the suffering of my husband; but he will be my dear, handsome Frederic, always. His noble soul will be reflected in his countenance, even should it be scarred by wounds."

"Would not your pride be wounded to have him return to you disfigured by wounds received in battle?"

"You are not in earnest in asking such a question, Bessie; you cannot be. How could my pride be wounded at such a thing? Impossible! Why, I should be more tempted to be proud of my Frederic than ever. I should be hurt, yes, my heart would bleed, to see my husband return to me wounded in character; to see him morally disfigured. But every physical wound will render him, in my view, more lovely; will make me love him more."

"I don't feel so; I don't want to be married before Raymond goes away, for fear he may lose a leg, or an arm, or in some way be disfigured, and then I should be obliged to be tied up to him during life. He don't like it because I am unwilling to be married; but I can't help that; I will have my way about some things."

Julia did not reply to this last remark of Bessie's, for the reason that she was shocked at hearing such sentiments expressed by one whom she had considered a kind-hearted, though rather a giddy girl. The elder Mrs. Sedgwick did not feel disposed to converse with the young lady, in her present mood, and both ladies experienced a sense of relief when the door was opened by Frederic. A hasty glance at the countenance of his wife led him to think his mother had communicated the intelligence he had wished her to receive; still he queried, for there was something like scorn in her expression, at the moment he entered the room where she sat. Her expression changed, however, the instant she beheld him, and her soul beamed in her eyes as he approached her and sat down by her side. He requested that his entrance might not disturb the conversation, which he concluded was being carried on between the friends ere he came in.

"You did n't interrupt our conversation," said Bessie, as Frederic looked at her as he was speaking; "I was the sole speaker; neither your mother nor your wife thought proper to answer me, so I had the floor entirely to myself."

"We hardly knew how to reply to the sentiments you advanced just now, Bessie. I can truthfully affirm that I did not, at least," replied Julia.

"I was not sure a reply was needed," remarked Mrs. Sedgwick, senior.

"Perhaps there was not any need of answering me," said Bessie, as she arose to go.

Her leave-taking was somewhat abrupt, and the mother, wife, and husband were left by themselves.

CHAPTER II.

"Of all my father's family, I love myself the best."

Event rapidly succeeded event, at the time our story commenced. Great changes took place in family circles, within wonderfully short spaces of time. Every truly patriotic heart glowed with enthusiasm at the thought of helping to sustain our noble Government; and it is true, too, that every lover of his or her country endeavored to do much for its cause, the cause of justice and humanity.

Frederic was rejoiced to find that Julia did not oppose him, in his plan of joining the army, but rather encouraged him to enlist, by her cheerfulness. His mind was thus at once relieved of a great burden. He immediately executed his resolves to take up arms in his country's service, by enrolling his name as a private, in a regiment that was being raised in the town of Oak Dale, where he lived. This was among the first three years' regiments, that were raised for the Union.

Massachusetts was forward in responding to the President's call for troops, and her sons have made gallant soldiers. Among these, Frederic Sedgwick and Raymond Philips were proud to rank themselves; their names stood enrolled together. Raymond Philips was a young man of great promise. He was the eldest son of a family of five children, and having lost his father at an early age, he had been a great comfort and help to his widowed mother, in taking care of her family. By his aid, she had been enabled for several years during his minority, to pursue a business which had been so lucrative as amply to support herself and children, besides allowing her to lay aside something for the future. When Raymond attained his manhood, his mother gave up the business to him entirely, and he had continued to prosper. He was accumulating property steadily, although not as rapidly, as some men make money. He was scrupulously honest in all his dealings, and would rather be defrauded himself, than be the means of defrauding another. His dry-goods store was patronized by the highest class of people in the town; for his polite, cheerful, accommodating spirit and gentlemanly manners, made him a great favorite with the ladies.

A feeling of regret was expressed by his many friends, when it was known that he had enlisted in the army. It did not take long for the news to spread throughout the circle of Raymond's acquaintance.

"What will become of his store?" was a question often asked, but not at once answered. "How foolish," said some, who could not appreciate his motives of action.

"I wouldn't have believed that Raymond Philips would have been such a goose as to leave his fine establishment, and go to war, with a pay of only thirteen dollars a month; it is strange that his mother will consent to such a wild scheme."

The next morning a young lady met Bessie in the street, and asked her if it was true that she was willing to have Raymond go as a private.

"Why ask that question?" interrogated Bessie, somewhat annoyed by it.

"Because, if I were you, I should wish him to have a commission."

"A commission would n't protect him from bullets," replied Bessie, hastily.

"But 't is more honorable to go as Lieutenant."

Bessie did not deign an answer to that remark, and the lady passed on; she hastened to her home, and sought the seclusion of her own room. She had met several of her acquaintances while abroad, and each of them had said something in regard to Raymond's going into the army without a commission. Her pride had been wounded at the idea of his going as a private, if he must go at all. She was unreconciled to his running any risks, by being exposed in battle, even if he was to go as an officer of high rank; but the humiliation of his being ranked as a common soldier, she was still more opposed to; and then to have others remark upon the subject to her, was "the unkindest cut of all." Bessie threw off her outside clothing, and sat down by her bed, where she could rest her head upon the pillows, in which she hid her face. As she sat there absorbed in her own sorrow, she seemed the very semblance of despair.

How long she would have kept herself secluded there is a matter of conjecture; probably as long as she could have lived without food, had not her sighs and sobs led to the discovery of her whereabouts. Her entrance to the house had not been observed by any of her mother's family, and the whole household thought that she was still abroad.

Raymond Philips called towards evening of that day, and inquired for Bessie. When Mrs. Jenkins learned that Raymond had not seen her during that day, she expressed surprise, as Bessie had told her she intended calling on his mother.

"She has not been at our house to-day," said Raymond; "I met a friend of Bessie's this morning, and she informed me that she had just had an interview with her in the street, else I should not have known she had been out."

Raymond accepted the invitation of Mrs. Jenkins, to seat himself in the parlor, and wait the return of her daughter. Hour after hour passed away, and still she came not. Raymond said he would call at the houses of some of her intimate friends, where she might perhaps be waiting for some one to attend her home. Her mother approved of his doing so, and he hastened to go in search of the individual he was more anxious to see at that time than any one else on earth. He called at several places, but learned nothing more than he already knew; then turned and walked again to her mother's, hoping that Bessie had preceded him there. He was disappointed at finding she was still absent, and sympathized in the feeling of alarm which her mother was beginning to experience on her daughter's account.

Bessie had two brothers, — mere youths, — who had retired to rest just before Raymond returned from his fruitless search for their unhappy sister. The chamber which they occupied was separated from Bessie's, by a thin partition. One of the brothers, less inclined to sleep than the other, heard a stifled sob soon after he laid himself down; he spoke to his brother, who had already fallen asleep, asking what the noise could mean.

"Mean what? what is it means anything?" inquired the other, startled, and anything but pleased at being awakened so suddenly. The tone in which the boys uttered these words was subdued, on account of their fears, and no sooner had they pronounced them than another sob, followed by a deep groan, was heard. The eldest of the brothers, whom we will introduce as Willie, jumped out of bed in a fright, and hardly stopping to dress, ran down stairs, followed by his brother Albert. They ran into the parlor, where sat Mrs. Jenkins and Raymond, vainly striving to conjecture the cause of Bessie's absence from home.

"What is the matter, boys?" asked their mother, in surprise, as she noticed the pallor of their conntenances.

"Oh, mother," exclaimed Albert, "we heard such an awful groan, right close to us, up stairs; and such a loud sob, too, that we were so frightened we could n't stay in bed any longer."

"What?" interrogated his mother.

"It is true, mother," affirmed Willie. "Albert fell asleep almost as soon as his head touched his pillow, and as I was lying wide awake, I heard a sob, and as it made me feel afraid, I woke Albert, and afterwards we heard a louder sob, and such a dreadful groan, too, that it made us run as fast as we could. Don't make us go up stairs again to-night, mother, will you?" said Willie, beseechingly.

"Not until we ascertain the source from whence the sounds proceeded that have startled you so much." She arose as she said this, and asked Raymond to accompany her up stairs. He did so, and they proceeded immediately to the chamber the boys had just left. No sooner had they entered it than a loud hysterical sob fell upon their ears, which caused them both to start and look at each other.

"That noise may have proceeded from Bessie's chamber," said Mrs. Jenkins; "it sounded as if it did, certainly," she continued, as she hastened to the apartment. She tried to open the door, and found it was fastened upon the inside. Another stifled sob, with a deep groan, convinced our friends that the room was inhabited, and that, too, by some one in distress.

"Can it be possible," inquired Raymond, "that it is Bessie, who appears to be suffering so deeply?"

"Hardly, I should think, and yet it may be; we know not what may have occurred to trouble her; but she will answer if she is here. Bessie," called the affectionate mother, "Bessie, my dear daughter, open the door, and admit me, your mother."

No answer, however, was given to this loving appeal, save another half-suppressed sob.

"What can this mean?" asked Raymond; "will you force the door?"

"Certainly, if it is not opened at once," at the same time trying it with considerable force. "Bessie," she again called, but with no better success than before. "This is unaccountable, I must confess," exclaimed Mrs. Jenkins, in an agitated tone. "Will you open this door in some way, Raymond?"

The young man was glad to be allowed the privilege, for his anxiety to learn the cause of this mystery was very great. He pressed against the door with all his strength, and, as it was fastened with a button, the fastening gave way under his pressure, in a few minutes, and they entered the room. At first, they did

2*

not perceive Bessie, as she was partly concealed in her crouching position by the bed; yet they were not long in discovering her, and great was their surprise when they approached and spoke to her without her appearing to notice their presence. Raymond put his hand tenderly upon her head, and parted her dishevelled locks; he bent over her in affectionate solicitude, and begged her to reveal the cause of her great suffering to her mother, if not to him.

Her mother had placed the lamp upon the bureau that stood nearly opposite Bessie, as she sat, unmoved by the sympathy that was expressed by her two best earthly friends. One would have thought it impossible for one so young, and so gentle as Bessie had seemed, to resist such kindness as was manifested by her mother and Raymond, as they stood, bending sorrowfully over her. She did resist, however, for a long time, every effort of her friends to gain a knowledge of the cause of her present situation. Wearied by their fruitless endeavors to procure an answer from Bessie, Mrs. Jenkins and Raymond sat down, and gazed at the object of their solicitude, in silence, for some time. Then Raymond went to her side again, and in a kind but firm tone, told her that unless she could speak and acquaint them with her feelings, he should infer that she was physically distressed, and call a physician without delay.

"No, no, no, you shall not," sobbed out Bessie; "let me alone, so that I can die, nobody will care; it is no matter what becomes of me."

"My dear girl," exclaimed Raymond, "why do you talk so; what has happened to distress you so; tell me, do. Do tell us, Bessie, what troubles you, for it pains us to see you so, without being able to comfort you."

"Come," said Raymond, using gentle force, at the instant, to raise her head; "look at me, and see if I don't look as if I cared for you."

Bessie strove to resist him, as he proceeded to lift her in his arms; "come, come," said he, soothingly, "you are to do as I say, just for a little while; it would be cruel in me, to let you stay here alone, in this sad plight. You must go down stairs with your mother and me, and tell us all about your great sorrow, and then you will feel better, for we can share it, by sympathy."

"Just as if you don't know why I feel bad," said this selfish girl, in a sullen tone.

"I am sure I do not know of anything that ought to affect you so," replied Raymond, kindly.

"Neither do I," remarked her mother; "your condition, Bessie, puzzles me and pains me at the same time."

"I am not worth being troubled about," said Bessie, "at least, Raymond thinks my wishes of too little consequence to be regarded, else he would n't oppose me in everything as he does."

"My dear girl," exclaimed Raymond, "do tell me what I have done, to trouble you so very much. Are you really so unwilling to have me go out in defence of our dear, noble old flag? I thought you were patriotic, Bessie."

"There are men enough to go to war, without you," she replied, in a peevish tone. "You are not needed in the army as much as you are needed at home; only think how lonesome I shall be, if you go away; you, who have been always near to go with me wherever I wished to go; and now, to think that you care no more about leaving me than you appear to, makes me really wretched."

Then again tears flowed in torrents down her cheeks, and her sobs again became audible. Her brothers, who were still in the parlor, looked with wonder upon their sister, as they obeyed their mother's command to retire to bed.

"Bother take her," said Albert, "such a fuss got up, to frighten a poor sleepy fellow half out of his wits, it is too bad."

"So it is," muttered Willie; "I wonder if Bessie thinks there is nobody in this world but herself?"

"Like enough," answered his brother; and, as he laid his head upon his pillow once more, his drowsy eyelids closed, and he was floating into dreamland ere the two words had fallen from his lips.

As soon as the two boys had left the room, Mrs. Jenkins expressed her pent-up feelings of sorrowful indignation, caused by the extraordinary manifestation Bessie had given of her opposition to the enlistment of Raymond.

"Before I bid you good night," said the mother, as she arose to follow her sons, "I must say, Bessie, that I feel that your actions to-night, added to your stealthy entrance into the house, which gave us so much trouble, is almost unpardonable. I did not, before this, believe you were so selfish, or could evince so great a disregard of others' feelings. I would advise you, Raymond, to leave her soon to her own reflections, during the remainder of the night, if but little remains of it."

Mrs. Jenkins then bade her and Raymond good night, and retired to her own room. Raymond was sorry to perceive that Bessie did not return the parting salutation of her mother, as he felt that the smallest breach of filial duty was wrong. His own heart was strongly enlisted on her side. He loved her devotedly, and his love aided him in throwing the mantle of charity over the faults he could not hide from his judgment. The selfishness of Bessie he endeavored to excuse by thinking that her nervous system was at fault, and therefore her weakness overcame her. She would feel better after she had had a long fit of weeping, so he would not leave her just then, even though her mother had suggested his doing so. And so sat Raymond, looking at his lady love, as she sat indulging in the luxury of tears, and occasionally of sobs and groans. Poor Raymond! he was one of those men who could not see a woman weep without striving in every possible way to comfort her. But all his efforts now were unavailing. If he took Bessie's hand, she would withdraw it immediately, saying, "O, you don't care anything about me." If he, by gentle words, sought to divert her mind from herself, she would refuse to listen to his pleadings by renewing her loud demonstrations of grief.

At length, weary of expostulating with the wilful girl, whom he would fain believe unselfish, he asked her if she would like to have him withdraw his name from the list of volunteers, and remain at home for her sake.

She did not reply immediately, but her tears soon ceased to flow, and her sobs were no longer heard. At length she raised her head, languidly, and looked at Raymoud, with an expression of mingled suspicion and trust that touched his sensitive heart to the core, as she asked, in a dejected tone, " Raymond, are you in earnest in making that inquiry ? "

" I am, dear Bessie, entirely sincere. I wish you to answer me frankly, too. Yet do not give me your answer to-night ; I wish you to sleep before you think any more upon this subject; afterwards, take time to think upon it calmly, before giving me your decision."

He took her hand while he was speaking, and pressing it affectionately, bade her good night too hastily to allow her time to speak. He did not wish her to say any more upon the subject that had agitated her so much ; he preferred she should consider him abrupt rather than do so. Thus he left her.

CHAPTER III.

"Truth, yet stranger than fiction."

On the following morning, as Raymond was on his way to his place of business, he met a young man with whom he was intimately acquainted.

"Good morning, Ray," said Charles Abbott to Raymond, in a lively tone.

"Good morning, Charlie," said Raymond, returning the salutation in a less animated tone.

"Why, Ray, what is the matter this morning with you? You surely do not regret having enlisted, do you? I hope not," continued the young man, without giving Raymond an opportunity to reply, "for I never felt so proud of anything I have done as I do of enrolling my name on the list of my country's volunteers."

He paused to take breath, and Raymond replied, saying, "I do not regret enlisting, Charlie, but I regret circumstances that exist, which may oblige me to withdraw my name before I am mustered into the United States service."

"For what reason, pray."

"Because my going is likely to result in great evil to one I love."

"Don't your mother consent to your leaving her?"

"Oh, yes; mother says she does not dare to hinder me; but Bessie, the lively, gay-hearted Bessie, is completely overwhelmed with the thought of my joining the army. She seems to have an uncommon dread of the horrors of war."

"Pshaw! now," muttered his friend, in a low tone, making some effort to prevent its being scornful. "I'm sorry," said he, "very sorry, but perhaps she will become reconciled. I'll get Minnie to talk with her; Minnie is a glorious girl, I tell you, Raymond Philips. She strengthens me nobly in my purpose, I assure you."

"All are not constituted alike, Charlie; I suppose Minnie has stronger nerves than Bessie."

"One would n't think so, to see them together. To my certain knowledge, Bessie can endure twice as much physical effort as Minnie can. Why, don't you remember how much she walked and exercised in every way, at the May party the other day, without apparent fatigue, and how she laughed at Minnie because she was forced to sit down and rest while herself was dancing about like a sprite or wood-nymph, as she called herself."

"I know all that, Charlie, but if you had seen Minnie in the state in which I saw Bessie last night, your face would have been as long as mine is this morning."

"Perhaps it would, Ray, but thanks to goodness, Minnie is not a drawback to my usefulness in any sphere. I shall call on Bessie, with Minnie, this very evening."

"Do," said his friend, as they parted.

On that evening, true to his promise to see Bessie, Charlie called upon her, in company with Minnie and Frederic Sedgwick and his wife. They found her alone. She sat in the parlor, expecting Raymond every moment. Bessie welcomed her friends, yet it would be too much to say that she welcomed them cordially and sincerely, although she would undoubtedly have done so had she not felt their presence a rebuke to her weak selfishness. She had heard that both Frederic and Charles had enlisted, with the sanction of those dearest to them, and she dreaded hearing them utter a word in regard to the subject. Charles knew her feelings, and Frederic supposed she was somewhat opposed to Raymond's becoming a soldier, yet did not dream that she could express sentiments in sincerity, such as she had expressed to Julia at the interview with which we are all familiar. Judge then, reader, of his surprise, when, on being asked by Charles if she was not going to consent cheerfully to Raymond's enlisting, she abruptly requested him not to mention the subject of war in her hearing.

Just at the moment she was uttering these chilling words, Raymond entered the room. His entrance was doubly welcome to his friends who were feeling nonplussed at Bessie's mood. Raymond shook hands cordially with each of the visitors, and taking Bessie's, he sat down by her side, and inquired with much tenderness how she was feeling then, and how she had rested the night previous.

"I am well enough, I suppose," said she, "and you have made your inquiries respecting my night's rest late enough, I hope."

"I heard from you, through your brother Willie, quite early in the day, Bessie, else I should have called on you sooner. You see I didn't forget you."

To this pleasant remark Bessie did not deign any

reply. Her mood was too exacting to allow her to be passably polite, even. Raymond's sensitive spirit felt her unkindness, but his loving heart tried to excuse it.

Charles felt unwilling to let pass this opportunity of trying his powers of rhetoric upon Bessie. She had repulsed him at the outset, yet he did not feel quite vanquished; he therefore ventured again to speak upon the forbidden subject of volunteering to serve his country. "Bessie," said he, "I must believe that you will be interested in my going to the war, are n't you, now?"

"I asked you not to speak upon that subject in my presence, again, Mr. Abbott."

"Mr. Abbott, is it, indeed? I have always been Charlie to you, Bessie, until now that I am going to the war, forsooth, I am addressed by my old friend as an almost stranger. What has got hold of you, Bessie? tell me, do," he urged in a supplicating tone.

"You know already," retorted Bessie; "and you had wellnigh succeeded in getting Raymond to join you in going to this nigger war. I don't like it at all."

Charlie laughed heartily at this outbreak of ill-feeling. "Well, now," said he, "that a fellow has something to start upon, he can go to work, and try to prove himself not quite as bad as you think. I had nothing to do with Raymond's enlistment; I can prove that by himself."

"Indeed he can," said Raymond.

"In fact," proceeded Charlie, "he would have been more likely to have asked me to enlist than I him. But now as this subject has been thus unceremoniously brought before us, I would be glad if I could persuade my friend Bessie to view it in a different light."

"It is nothing but a nigger war."

"I don't understand that term, and so I would pass over that remark of yours; for it is in regard to the duty of Raymond, as a citizen of these United States, that I wish you to see differently, Bessie."

"Duty; I hate that word; I detest it as applied to him now."

"Well, say inclination, then, if you like the sound of that word better; for Raymond's inclination would certainly lead him forth in defence of his flag, if no insurmountable object should be placed in his way."

"Surely, Bessie, you will not be the one to hinder Raymond from doing what he considers right," said Minnie; "you have always been braver than I, and I can say to Charlie, go, and God speed you, with all my heart; with all your courage you can say more, can't you?"

"People can say almost anything they choose to; my taste does n't lead me to desire a friend to be maimed and scarred by being in battle, and perhaps a cripple all his days, beside."

"Neither does mine," replied Minnie, "still," continued she, her countenance glowing with a beautiful light as she spoke, "if it should be the fortune of my best loved friend to be mutilated while fighting for the good old stars and stripes, I should love him better for every scar."

"You would, I suppose, love to see him hobble about on crutches."

"No, I should be sorry to see Charlie obliged to go about on crutches; still, if he had been made lame by doing what I feel is right he should do, fight for the land of his birth, I should love him all the better, because he was obliged to 'hobble about,' as you say."

"I have n't any such romantic ideas; I think people had better stay at home, and let the Government take care of itself. As for Raymond, he shall never have my consent to go out South, to be disfigured. You need n't say anything more about it, for, I tell you, it will be the death of me if he goes."

"You will not commit suicide, will you, Bessie?" asked Frederic, who had listened with surprise, not unmixed with disgust, to what she had said. "If you don't conclude to do that, I think your chance for life will be pretty good, even should Frederic leave you."

This was spoken in a playful tone, and Charlie laughingly told Bessie, that he should not be afraid to run the risk of insuring her life. Julia also tried her powers of persuasion with Bessie, but in vain; and the friends were obliged to take leave of her, with very unsatisfied feelings.

"There never was a clearer truth uttered," exclaimed Charlie, as soon as the door of Mrs. Jenkins was closed, after himself and friends had left the house, "than that the present state of our country reveals character. I never was more disappointed in any young lady, than I am in the one we have just left. Where is her patriotism, I wonder?"

"She has n't any, anywhere," answered Frederic; "she is thoroughly selfish. Did n't you notice that she did n't appear to dread suffering for Raymond, as much as she did his risk of being scarred, and losing his good looks?"

"I noticed the other day when she was at our house, that she was the most afraid of that," remarked Julia; "you, Frederic, thought, when I told you what she then said to mother and myself, that she was n't in earnest."

"I know I did ; but I shall not be guilty of judging her so mildly again. The fact is," continued Frederic, " I am astonished at what my ears have heard, and I pity Raymond."

"He is too tender-hearted to deal with so exacting a personage as Bessie," said Charlie; "she will succeed in keeping him at home for a time."

"I hope not," remarked Minnie.

"Well, we shall see," said Frederic, as he had by this time reached his home, where the friends parted.

CHAPTER IV.

"O, woman! thou hast a part to act; look to the end."

"I'M glad they are gone," said Bessie, as soon as the door was closed upon her friends on the evening mentioned in the last chapter.

"Why, my dear girl," said Raymond, "why do you feel so towards these friends? I thought you were much attached to the ladies, at least, and felt some regard for the gentlemen also; they are fine young men, Bessie, I assure you; worthy, well worthy of your best respect."

"You probably think so; I think otherwise, now."

"What has changed your mind or feelings in regard to them, Bessie?"

"Their own acts, of course; don't you see, that they seem to take it for granted that I must think as they do in regard to the war? The design of their visit was to exert an influence, if possible, over my mind, favorable to your enlisting. But they did n't succeed, and so I hope now they'll attend to their own business and let me alone."

Raymond endeavored, though in vain, to vindicate his friends; he was deeply grieved at the feeling Bessie manifested towards them, as well as towards himself. He knew that she would make herself wretched if he went from home, as he wished to. Gladly would he have led Bessie — to whom he had long been engaged — to the altar of Hymen, and left her the loving, trusting wife of a volunteer soldier, had she been willing.

"*I* become a soldier's wife? no never! There are enough poor miserable fellows, that may as well be shot as not; but the man who is to be my husband, shall never run the risk of being hit by bullets with my consent."

So Raymond was obliged, though with great reluctance and mortification, to have his name taken from the enrolment list, and defer going out in the regiment with his friends, though his whole heart was engaged in the cause to which they had devoted themselves.

Frederic did not see Bessie after the evening before mentioned, before he went away with his regiment. He did n't care to, he said, as she was such a hindrance to his friend. It was quite immaterial to him whether she gave him good wishes or not; she was, he thought, such a "selfish nobody."

"I wish she was a nobody," said Charlie, with something like scorn in his tone; "the fact is, Fred, she has too much influence over Raymond, for his good. He does n't like to see her faults, and so he tries not to, and endeavors to excuse her selfishness to himself. I really pity Raymond, and his mother too. She is a real, whole-souled woman, Charlie."

"Indeed she is, and she feels very much tried at the idea some people have of her feelings in regard to her son's going into the army. Bessie is quite willing to have some of her friends suppose that Raymond remains at home for his mother's sake."

"It is n't possible that the girl will allow such an impression to remain upon the mind of any one who receives it?" said Frederic.

"Yes it is, and more than that, she has been heard to affirm that Raymond was glad of an excuse to stay at home. He followed, she said to Minnie, a sudden impulse, in enlisting, and, upon second thought, regretted what he had done."

"Did she tell Minnie that Raymond said so?"

"I did n't understand that she did; she merely made the statement in a careless manner."

"I have been greatly deceived in Bessie Jenkins, I must confess. My wife has been disposed, ever, to be very non-committal towards her, and I have tried to persuade her that she was not charitable enough in her feelings towards the girl; but since the recent developments of her character have been known to me, I feel that Julia has been right."

"Certainly she has; perhaps Bessie is entitled to the pity of her friends in some respects, for she has not been brought up right."

"To what do you allude, Charlie? I thought her mother was a professor of religion."

"So she is; and I won't say that she is not a Christian; but I do say that she is far from coming up to the standard of her duty as a woman, to say nothing of her maternal obligations. I tell you, Fred, just what kind of person she is, judging from her talk, of which I have heard a great deal. She is terribly afraid that a woman should know anything about the condition of the country in which she lives. She may read history, ancient and modern, of every nation on the globe, but she must not feel any interest in what is transpiring in her own land, because that would be meddling with politics. It is a fact that she did not feel sufficient interest in the affairs of the land which gave her birth, to lead her to remember the name of him who filled the office of chief magistrate in our country the four years previous to the inauguration of President Lincoln."

"Charlie, is n't that statement a little fictitious, now? it does n't seem possible that a woman could be so utterly regardless of the condition of things about her as you make Mrs. Jenkins appear to be."

"Well, upon honor, I have told you nothing but truth; I will quote the words of the lady as I heard them fall from her lips. Said she, 'I was a little mortified the other day, on hearing a lady remark that we need not look for a change for the better, under the present administration, to reflect that I did n't even know who was President, and more so, when she appealed to me to say something in defence of her opinion. After the lady, who had called upon me, left my house, I took pains to acquaint myself with the name of our President.'"

"Ha, ha, ha,". laughed Frederic; "that must be wilful ignorance," said he, "in such a land as ours; it is no marvel Bessie takes so little interest in public affairs."

CHAPTER V.

Old friends meet.

It was something new, in the history of the ladies of our country, to know that their friends were at the seat of war;—to feel that they were exposed to danger, far from their homes and loved ones.

At the period of which we are writing, we, who stayed at home, could scarcely realize that all the bustle of preparation for our first soldiers to go forth, was not a troubled dream. It seemed *more* like a dream than a reality, to Julia, when she found herself alone with her little ones, on the evening of the day on which Frederic had left his home.

"How are we to get on without Mr. Sedgwick o' nights?" asked a servant, in a desponding tone.

Julia had just asked herself the same question, as she had never in her life before been so situated as to be without a person under her roof on whom she could rely for protection in case she should need it. Her heart misgave her for a moment, as she thought of her need, but only for a moment, and then courageously she resolved to rely upon God alone, in any emergency; to commit herself to the care of this Almighty Friend, and retire to rest with as little care as she felt when her husband was at home. This feeling she endeavored to infuse into the mind of her whole family; and Bridget's heart was cheered by the evident courage of her young mistress.

The days and weeks seemed long, very long, to the little household over which Julia presided. To her they seemed almost interminable, until a letter came from Frederic. Although it was written amid the bustle and confusion of camp life, the strain of this letter was cheerful, and he expressed much gratitude to his brave little wife for helping him to part with her as she had done.

"Had you wept and clung to me," he wrote, "as I saw some wives cling to their husbands at parting, the trial of leaving home would have been doubly hard. As it is, you have nerved me to effort, and may I prove worthy of such a heroic wife as I am blest with."

Julia did n't feel that she was flattered by the commendation of her husband, yet she was grateful, and felt strengthened to do and to bear for his sake, and for the sake of the cause for which he had gone to fight.

The mother of Frederic had most cordially invited Julia to take her children, and with them become an inmate of her family during the absence of Frederic. Julia felt grateful for this invitation, yet declined it, saying to her mother-in-law, "I must not be so childish as to leave our home because my husband is obliged to be absent; besides, you, mother, have care enough, and a family sufficiently large, without having myself and children added to it; and more than all this, Frederic may be sick or wounded, and come home; then it would be so much better to have his own house to come to, that I can't think of leaving it, or doing anything but living here with the children."

"But it troubles me, daughter, to think that you are here so lonely."

"Perhaps I shall have company; a cousin of mine, Kate Sisson, of whom you heard me speak, has anticipated visiting me for a long time, and I cannot but hope she will come soon, after hearing that Frederic is away."

Julia was not disappointed in her hopes, in regard to her cousin. Kate came on the day following that on which the conversation concerning her had been held. Her arrival was welcomed by Julia and the little ones, as peculiarly opportune.

"I was speaking of you yesterday to Mother Sedgwick," said Julia, "and telling her it was probable that you might come, if you knew that Frederic was away."

"You know the old saying, coz; I was nearing you then, of course. I could n't do otherwise than hasten to you under existing circumstances. Other relatives of mine have left their families to go to the war, but there is n't one of those families that seemed to need me at all; and, moreover, as my patriotic feelings must vent themselves in action, and I am altogether too young for a hospital nurse, I thought that, by coming out and spending a few months with you, I might be enabled to do something for my bleeding, suffering country."

"You are right, Katie dear, and I am delighted at the thought of your making a long stay with me."

"Then you will let me be, in all things, like one of your own home circle, and I shall greatly enjoy my protracted visit with you."

Kate Sisson was one of those frank-hearted, generous natures, who could not fail of being welcome anywhere. She had a faculty of making those around her happy which few possess. To know Kate was to love her. It would be saying too much to say that she never gave offence to any, for she very independently expressed her opinions on all subjects; she was, too, sometimes severe upon those she considered wilfully in the wrong, yet her severity was so mingled with playfulness that it often did good without inflicting a bitter wound. As we are writing a story, a description of our characters will be expected, and we will endeavor to describe Kate, even though we run the risk of having our description called tame by those who recognize her character.

At first sight she was not strikingly beautiful, but her countenance was ever varying in its expression, which was also perfectly open, — a real tell-tale face was hers. Her form was slight and her height about medium. Her eyes were blue, and their expression was of the merriest kind. Her hair was dark brown, and her complexion fair, with a glow upon her cheeks that was ever varying in its tint. Now with all these pleasant features, she did not imagine herself pretty, yet she knew that she possessed the power of pleasing, a gift for which she was grateful to her heavenly Father. She had withal a contented spirit.

She had not been long in the home of Julia ere that friend began to wonder how Kate had lived to be twenty years old without having her heart and hand engaged to some one of the many young gentlemen who had really seemed to admire her. She expressed her surprise to her cousin on the occasion, that she had not entered into any matrimonial engagement, when Kate laughingly replied, "This war has hindered my promising to give my hand and heart to a young gentleman whom I esteem as noble and good."

"Why, Kate, I did n't know that any one dear to you had been killed in this war; how is it that you can be so cheerful, under such trying circumstances?"

"You do not quite understand me, Julia; I did not say that any one had died."

"But you said the war had hindered your being engaged."

"And so it has; I will tell you how. You have often heard of Arthur Bryant, I believe?"

"Yes, Kate; and at one time I understood that he was likely to become your most particular friend."

"Well, all this was true once, and might have been true to-day, had not the sound of the clarion of this terrible war of ours developed traits in his character that lowered him in my esteem so much that I could not possibly love him."

"What new traits did you discover all on a sudden?"

Kate looked at Julia for a moment earnestly, being in doubt as regarding the tone in which she had asked her question, and then asked another by way of reply.

"Do you think me quixotic, Julia?"

"No, dear Kate, but I did n't know but that you might have been governed by impulse in deciding hastily in your zeal for your country, as I have been informed that Arthur did not enlist, in defence of the dear old flag."

"It was not for that reason alone, that I have been led almost to despise him, although I did not feel proud of him, when I heard him assert boldly that he would not go to the war. Had that been all, I might have overlooked his want of patriotism in time; but it was the mercenary motives that governed him, that I despise. Why, what do you think he said to me, the first time I was alone with him after the fall of Sumter?"

"I can hardly imagine, cousin."

"True, you would never imagine a young man like Arthur, to be so utterly selfish as he has proved himself to be. I have escaped a deal of trouble, in discovering his real character as I have done. But I haven't told you what he said. In reply to my inquiry if he was n't going to aid his country in her hour of peril, he sneeringly remarked, that he had no idea of standing up to be shot at, he cared too much for his life to do that; and he said, moreover, that if I cared anything about him, I would be glad he had sense enough to stay at home and make money out of the war. He then told me how present hostilities had opened and would continue to open channels in which wealth would flow in to those who stayed at home and took advantage of opportunities that were continually presenting themselves. He hoped he was shrewd enough to avail himself of such chances."

"I mean," said he, "that this war shall make me a rich man."

"Then you resolve to avail yourself of the woes of our dear land to aggrandize yourself, Arthur, said I."

"Yes, if you so define my expressed intentions; but I do it for your sake, Kate, as well as my own. You have inferred ere this, from my acts, that I wish you to unite your fate with mine."

"There was a pause here, Julia, a rather long pause,

too, for I was so indignant that I was afraid to speak until I reflected a few minutes, and Arthur sat waiting for my reply. At length he asked me if I had understood the import of his words.

"I fear I do only too well," said I.

"Why, dear Kate, you surely cannot object to my making a fortune when I have a chance to do so."

"No, Arthur, if you do so by honorable means; but I do object to your taking advantage of your country's suffering, to further any selfish object."

"I suppose, then," he answered, "you would like best to see me join some regiment, and go to battle as a private, with the scanty pay that the Government allows her soldiers. In your opinion, that, I infer, would be honorable."

"Yes, Arthur, truly honorable. All honor, I say, to the brave volunteers, who have gone forth without stopping to seek for office or emolument of any kind; believe me, I should respect you, as one of their number, however poor, ten thousand times ten thousand more than I should respect you with all the riches you could accumulate in the way you mark out for yourself."

"And I am to take this as your decisive answer to the question I proposed to you, if I rightly understand."

"Yes, Arthur, I am sorry to be obliged to believe you can be governed by such ignoble motives; but it is not possible for me to feel differently in regard to these vastly important subjects."

"'You may repent of the stand you have taken, some day, young lady,' said he, as he arose, with an angry look, to leave me."

"Heaven save me from such degradation," I replied, almost involuntarily, as he bade me a formal good night.

"Is that the last time you have had an opportunity to converse with him upon the subject?" asked Julia.

"Yes, — no; I have tried to influence him when I have met him in company, to think differently, but it is of no use to say anything to him; he will not listen. His mind is made up. I should not have told you all these particulars in regard to this affair, if Arthur had n't told it himself, and given an entirely different coloring to the story. Had he offered me his heart, and I had felt obliged to reject the offer, I would not have mentioned the circumstance, not even to you, Julia; but as there was no heart-work about it, and he has reported that I was in love with a volunteer, I think I may be excused for telling the truth about it."

"I think so, too, Kate; but what is Arthur doing now?"

"Oh, he is engaged in speculations of different kinds; I hear that he hopes to make a great deal of money on cotton."

"He will probably succeed in projects to become rich, then; cotton cloth is one of the must-have articles in our land, therefore people must buy it, if the price should be greatly increased."

"Well, we have talked enough about my affairs. Tell me now, how does Frederic rank as a soldier? Did he go as a private, or did he have a commission?"

"He went in the ranks; he said he did not consider himself qualified to hold an office. If he proved to have soldierly tact, he might be promoted, and if he did not earn promotion, he would remain a private, and serve his country in the ranks."

"I glory in such as he," responded Kate; "they have the good of the Union at heart, and they will do something besides parade in a military dress."

"I hope so," said Julia; "I want every one who goes to the seat of war, to do something towards putting down this inhuman Rebellion."

CHAPTER VI.

"Must we part?"

TIME passed, and nearly five months had gone since Frederic had left his home, when a little daughter was added to the loved circle he had left. Kate was a great comfort and support to Julia at this time. They were both obliged to lay aside, for a time, work which they had commenced for the sick and wounded soldiers, and which they loved to do. Very many garments had been completed by the nimble fingers of Julia and her friend, since Kate had been an inmate of her dwelling; but knitting was now the only work that could be done to advantage, as Kate was busy, much of her time, in filling the place made vacant by the absence of Julia from her family. Her knitting-work, however, was ever at hand, to be taken up, so that whenever she had a leisure moment, she might knit, if but a little. On being asked, on one occasion, by Julia's good-natured nurse, if she could not bear to live without seeing a soldier's stocking, she replied, with a smile, "I might, if I knew all the soldiers could be made comfortable without my help; but while I fear that they cannot be, I love to have my work where I can do something towards its completion, in every spare moment, for in this way I find that many a stocking gets knit, while I hardly realize that I am at work."

Bessie Jenkins came in one day, while Kate sat

with her gray stocking in hand, diligent as usual. She had called at Julia's several times before, since Kate had been there, and having seen her once before, in years gone by, she felt considerably acquainted with her.

"You are partial to grave colors," said Bessie, after she had regarded Kate awhile, as she sat chatting and plying her needles at the same time.

The young lady thus addressed looked up, and finding she was the person spoken to, answered laughingly, "Yes, I like gray, especially when I see red, white, and blue through it."

"Ah, that is what you are looking at while plodding on with those homely old stockings; I thought it strange if the yarn and needles alone possessed power to please and attract you thus."

"I love to knit, even when I do not feel that by being thus employed I am doing good to the soldiers; but now I assure you that my whole heart is in the work. I would like to knit a miniature flag, and sew it upon every stocking I send away, to remind those who wear them of the value I attach to the dear old stars and stripes."

"How patriotic some folks are."

"Yes," said Kate, gayly; "but I have heard of some people that are not at all patriotic; those that are so, you understand, must do more work in order to make up for the sloth of such as do nothing. You have time to do a great deal, Bessie, have you not?"

"No, not for strangers; charity begins at home, you know."

"Yes, I admit that it does; but it is the poorest place in the world for it to end in, unless it takes a large sweep first."

Bessie was silent a few minutes, after Kate had made this remark; when she spoke, it was to say that she supposed she was aware that she did not feel as much interest in public affairs as some did. "I am not willing that those I love should go to the war at all."

"Indeed," said Kate; "well, what good do you expect to accomplish by using your influence to keep them at home?"

"Why, I shall keep them out of harm's way, I hope."

"You cannot be certain that you will do that," replied Kate, gravely; "mishaps may befall them at home. I should be afraid that a friend whom I should dare to hinder from doing his duty, would be arrested by illness, or meet with some disaster. I should not dare withhold my consent, if a friend wished me to approve of his becoming a soldier, at such a time as the present. Look at our Julia, here; I wish all American women were as brave and loyal as she is."

"I am sure," said Julia, earnestly, "that I have done no more than my duty. I should be ashamed of myself if I was n't willing to make sacrifices for my country."

"Perhaps you think I ought to be ashamed," said Bessie, "but there's enough being done without my help."

"That won't be any excuse for you, Bessie," said Kate; "you will be brought to think differently, I trust, ere many months have passed."

"I don't believe that," replied Bessie; "but I must go now; I don't care to stop long with people who don't think very highly of me."

This she said half playfully and half in earnest, and Kate laughingly told her that she was a free agent, and could so conduct that people would esteem her very highly indeed.

"If I should become an abolitionist, I suppose I should find favor here," said Bessie, as she arose and approached the door.

"That alone would n't do," answered Julia; "it is n't so much how people think as how they act, that I look at. Some people have a very fair theory, and a bad practice, while others do a great deal better than they talk. I hope Bessie will be like that servant who said, 'I go not,' but afterwards repented and went."

Bessie shook her head, and bade them a hasty adieu.

Julia soon recovered her wonted strength, and resumed the cares she had laid down for a season with cheerfulness and alacrity. In every possible way she contrived, with Kate's assistance, to do all she could for those who were defending our Government. There was little in her home to vary the monotony of daily life. Not that the sameness of every day's duty was irksome to her; far from it; she felt that she could not be sufficiently grateful for having been spared the pain of startling intelligence from her husband, and, too, that everything thus far had gone so smoothly with her.

"It is true," she often said, "that I feel the want of Frederic's society to be a great deprivation, but what is it when compared with the anguish of heart many experience daily, who are more deserving than myself?"

Would it were our happy privilege to let the reader linger amid the brighter scenes enacted during the fratricidal contest which has thrown a shade of sadness over our once bright land; but we are telling a story of this war, and, in order to be truthful, we must portray some scenes at which our souls revolt.

CHAPTER VII.

Our Kate.

WHEN Julia's babe was nearly two months old, she was sitting in her room by the cradle one morning, engaged, as was her wont, in sewing for the sick and wounded soldiers, when Kate entered and put a letter into her hand, saying, as she did so, " I wonder what this means ; you see this letter is from Oak Dale, and its superscription is in the handwriting of my aunt. Why is it addressed to you instead of being directed to me, as all letters from home have been hitherto ? "

" We will soon know," remarked Julia, as she opened the letter. As she read, Kate watched the expression of her countenance, and the vague fear that had taken possession of her mind, when she first saw the missive, was augmented as she saw the color recede from the face of her friend, ere she perused the first page. With an undefined feeling of dread she interrupted Julia, by asking her if the letter contained bad news. Her cousin did not reply immediately, as she was too much overcome to articulate, and Kate begged her to speak.

" O, tell me, have you tidings of Frederic or of my brother ? for I cannot wait."

" I will tell you, cousin ; it is news from your own loved ones ; your mother and your brother Walter."

" That is why the letter was written to you ; they

feared to communicate sad intelligence to me, abruptly, but I am prepared now to hear anything, so tell me all."

"Your mother is very ill, Kate; she has just received the sad news that Walter is no more."

"Dear, dear mother; I must go to her as soon as I possibly can; and my darling brother; does the writer of the letter say how he died?"

"On the field of battle; your aunt did n't tell where."

"Well," said Kate, "if he must be taken *from earth, I would rather he had died a martyr to the cause of freedom and right than in any other way, but I tremble for my mother. Think of her being obliged to hear such intelligence, when very ill. Walter was her darling; you know he was her youngest child, and O, so dearly loved, not only by his mother but by all of us. So young, too, to lay down his precious life for his country. Noble boy! but nothing but a boy, scarcely seventeen years old."

All this was said by Kate, as the tears flowed in torrents down her cheeks, while she commenced making preparations to start for home that same afternoon. She would be obliged to leave Oak Dale at an early hour in the evening in order to take the express train to New York that night. Very few words were spoken by either Julia or Kate during the hours that intervened between the reception of that woe-bringing missive, and the departure of one who had been a light and solace in the home of her friend. Julia's tears flowed freely in sympathy with the bereaved sister and affectionate daughter. Once she controlled her emotions to say to Kate, that it was sad to think they had been so cheerful, when those so dear to them were suffering so severely.

"Don't let that thought trouble you, dear Julia; I hope we have n't indulged in indecorous levity, and it is certainly a duty to be cheerful; besides, if we had anticipated sorrow and made ourselves prematurely sad, it could not have done our friends any good. I am glad that we have been able to feel cheerful, it has been good for us, and we are at this moment better able to bear up and do our duty under this trial than we could have been had our strength been used in worrying."

"What a girl you are, cousin," ejaculated Julia, while her lips trembled with emotion, "how much fortitude you possess; I do so hate to part with you, you help me so much in bearing up; I fear I shall sink when you are gone, and yet, I would not keep you now if I could."

"I know you would have me hasten to my afflicted mother, Julia; and let my sudden and unexpected departure, strengthen your resolve to look directly up to God, in every moment of need. He will give you 'strength equal to your day.' But for his felt presence, I should sink at this hour." As Kate uttered these words she laid her head upon her cousin's shoulder, and for a few moments they wept together.

"It does me good to weep, Julia," said Kate, as she slowly raised her head from its loved resting-place. "It is not wrong to weep, since our Divine Master wept, if we weep without murmuring; we should not be afflicted, if we could not feel affliction. Think of me, Julia, when it will benefit me most, after I leave you; when you hold communion with Heaven, I mean."

"I understand your meaning, Kate; would I could pray aright for you; I shall try constantly."

This conversation was held just before the moment of parting came to our friends. Kate's journey home was a sad and lonely one; she longed to be with her sorrowing parent, that she might minister to her comfort, yet she shrank from meeting her, knowing how deeply her fond maternal heart was lacerated, by the death of her dear Walter. All along the way, Kate prayed for strength to bear this meeting in such a manner, that her mother, if possible, might be comforted by her arrival. One would have thought at seeing her, when she threw her arms about her mother's neck, as she first entered her sick-room, and spoke words of consolation, that her own grief was well-nigh forgotten.

"To think," said the invalid, "that I shall never hear the loved voice of my dear Walter again; how, O, how can I live and have it so."

"Think of something more consoling, dear mother; think how much cause you have to be grateful that you have been blest with a son so noble, dutiful, and good. What a privilege it is, to feel that we may meet him in heaven; you think he was a Christian, don't you mother?"

"Yes, I do."

"Then think how much happier your lot is to-day, than that of thousands of mothers in our land, at this moment. Is his early, brilliant death a trial, when compared with the sorrow you would have felt, had he been spared to you, and yet been degraded with vice? I have seen one mother, recently, whose grief was overwhelming, and the only consolation she had was to be still, and know that God had afflicted her. Her son had died, not on the field of battle, but a sacrifice to his own sinful lusts. Another, I met, too, in my absence, whose son had fallen a victim to disease that had been increased by his habits of dissipation; he had died in a hospital, far from home and friends, cursing his fate and every one who approached him, until his strength was exhausted."

"How much more I have to comfort me," exclaimed Mrs. Sisson, " and yet my heart has rebelled. I will try to submit to this great trial, although it has come suddenly. I fear I did not count the cost when I laid my boy upon the altar of his country."

There was one thing about which the mother of Walter was extremely anxious; that was, to look once more upon the face of her young son. She had been informed that his remains had been carefully interred by a young friend who had pledged his word to Walter that, if he survived him in battle, he would see that he was buried, and his grave marked, so that it could be found by his friends. Walter had promised to do the same for his friend should he fall first. The weather being cool, it was thought that the remains of the young soldier could easily be conveyed to his home.

Mrs. Sisson's mind was constantly occupied with this subject from the moment she learned the fact that the loved body might be found. Who could go and find the place where Walter lay? Most of the male friends of Mrs. Sisson's family were absent from home, in their country's service; she could think of no one to whom she might apply in this emergency, excepting a stranger, and a person who felt no special interest would not be as likely to take pains to identify the corpse as would a relative. She knew a mother, who had supposed she had received the body of a dear child, who had learned, upon looking at the dead, that the coffin contained the remains of a man who was unknown to her. She could not bear the thought of such a trial as that, for herself, yet how should it be avoided? The mother's anxiety increased her illness.

Kate saw this with pain, and was nerved to effort, for her mother's sake. "Mother," said she, one day, "I can, and I will go, and bring home the body of my brother."

"You, Kate?"

"Yes, mother, I can go; surely if any one can identify him, I can."

"It will be a great undertaking for you, my daughter; a sorrowful one, too."

"I know it, mother, but I think I have counted the cost; this is a day for great undertakings; I must n't shrink from performing my part in the terrible drama which is being acted in our land. I shall be protected and sustained; so, if you say so, I will start to-night, as the sooner we can get dear Walter's body home, the better it will be."

"Go, then, daughter," said the mother, while tears flowed freely, from many and commingled emotions.

CHAPTER VIII.

"Not a heroine, yet heroic."

Two days from that on which the conversation occurred which is recorded in the last chapter, Kate found herself in Washington. A part of the way she had travelled without any company that she knew, but when within a few miles of Baltimore she had met with a lady and gentleman with whom she was somewhat acquainted. She had met them several times at Oak Dale, and it was a relief to her anxious heart to find herself recognized by them, and, moreover, to find that they were going directly to the capital. She soon made these friends, whom we shall designate by the name of Brown, acquainted with her circumstances, and the object of her visit to Washington.

Mr. Brown was a kind-hearted man, and both himself and wife sympathized deeply with our afflicted young traveller. They, too, promised to do all they could to assist her to accomplish the object of her journey. Greatly as Kate felt the need of repose, she would allow herself no time to rest until she had seen the grave of her brother. He had been buried a few miles from the city, that his grave might be easily found if sought for.

At the second battle of Bull Run, Walter had fallen, having been shot by a bullet, in his head. The missile had struck the side of his head, and had destroyed life, without having greatly disfigured the comely countenance of the man. Kate knew how her brother had been wounded, and her fancy portrayed him, as he lay cold in death's embrace. She nerved her heart to the task before her. She must see him; she could not trust to another to do this for her, for she had promised her suffering parent that she would see him herself. As she stood near the spot where one so dear to her heart was sleeping in death, her countenance betrayed the anguish within, and the friends who had accompanied her thus far, begged her to leave the place, and trust strangers to perform the task she had undertaken.

"No, no," said she, in reply to these entreaties, "I must be sure that it is the remains of my brother that I take home with me."

"But," said a gentleman who was standing by, "you know not what a trial is before you, young lady; a strong man is hardly adequate to such a task as you are about to impose upon yourself."

"I know it will be trying to my feelings to look upon the lifeless form of my dear brother, but I must do so, to be sure they are his remains that are to be disinterred. Do not say anything more to dishearten me, but rather try to inspire me with resolution to do what I feel to be my duty."

No more was said against her doing what she journeyed so far to do, yet all who saw her stand waiting for the earth to be removed, which covered her brother from her view, felt an intense interest in regard to the effect a sight of the body that was being exhumed, would have upon the bereaved sister.

There was little doubt existing in regard to the grave that was being opened, as being that of Walter, yet there might possibly be some mistake, and she would not fail of being certain. The cover of the box which was taken from the grave, was taken off. Kate stood a little from it, her eye caught sight of the United States uniform in which the corpse was arrayed; she then approached a few steps nearer, and her friend, Mr. Brown, put her arm within his own, and advanced with her slowly towards the body. Kate bent over the box for a minute or two, and closely scanned the face of the dead; she then stood still, with her eyes raised to the face of the friend upon whom she leaned for support, and exclaimed, "My dear, dear brother Walter; yes, it is he, I am sure."

Mr. Brown then conducted her to a resting-place near by, and she sank apparently lifeless before him; she had fainted quite away. It was sometime ere her overtasked nerves allowed her to recover sufficiently to admit of her returning to the city. Her most severe task had been accomplished, and her strained nerves would not longer be forced to act; they must have rest for a little season, and she lay upon a rustic seat that had been comfortably prepared for her accommodation, in a state of great lassitude. At length, weariness brought one half hour's sleep to soothe her tortured nerves, and she awoke somewhat refreshed.

"I have been a great deal of trouble to you and your kind husband," said Kate, on awakening and seeing Mrs. Brown sitting near her; "I feel that I can never repay your kindness."

"Don't speak of that," said the gentleman just referred to; "I, or we, are glad that it has been in our power to assist you; perhaps some day we may want some such office performed for ourselves; so say no more of what we have done. We must now go to Washington, directly, and see to having things properly and speedily attended to, so that you can start for home as soon as you are able."

"Yes, let us hasten," said Kate; "I shall be able as soon as my mission is performed."

In a few hours from this time Kate looked once more upon the loved features of her darling brother. His appearance, however, was much improved; it was still his lifeless form she saw and wept over, but there was no longer anything to shock her about that form. The expression of his countenance was serene, and every impression that his contact with the earth had left upon him was removed. His hair was arranged by his sister's direction, as he had been wont to wear it when at home, and his clothes, although military, were clean and nice.

"He is fit to be taken to his mother now," said Kate, as she gazed upon him, "I did n't expect to be able to take him home in so good a condition; I am very thankful indeed that I've been able to come here and see to his removal. Now, I must set out for home as soon as I can, possibly."

She did so, for no persuasion could induce her to remain longer to obtain rest, however much it was needed, because she knew that her mother was anxiously looking for her return. Having sent tidings by telegraph when she might be expected with the precious remains she had gone to obtain, she left her newly made friends in and around the capital. She was grateful to them for the kindness they had shown to a sorrowing stranger, and with a hope that she should see them again, began her homeward journey with a lighter heart than she had brought to Washington. She arrived at Oak Dale in safety, without experiencing anything to add to the painfulness of her situation, and felt more than repaid by the melancholy pleasure her mother felt at the result of her undertaking. Kate did not succumb to her feelings of sorrow and fatigue, but bore up and helped sustain her mother all through the mournful days that passed after her return. She saw the body so dear to her placed in its last resting-place, and she saw, too, her mother recover slowly from her trying illness, and then her outraged physical nature would and did have its revenge. The faithful and heroic daughter and sister was laid low by sickness. Only for a few weeks, however, was Kate confined to her room; a naturally good constitution triumphed over disease, and she was again in the dear circle of her friends.

CHAPTER IX.

More of Bessie.

During all the months that had brought so much anguish to thousands, whose friends had taken up arms in their country's cause, Bessie's life had been apparently without trial. She had told her acquaintances she had no sympathy for those who had brought trouble upon themselves, by not being determined that those upon whom they depend for happiness should not leave them to go to war.

"If I had been disposed to remain quiet," said she, "Raymond would have been away now, and I might have been very unhappy, but I knew how to keep him at home, and I have managed to do so thus far."

"How have you managed, Miss Jenkins?" inquired a lady who was in her company one day at the home of our friend Julia, when she had boastfully asserted that she had exerted herself to prevent Raymond from enlisting.

"O, I was very miserable, of course, and wept a great deal, and he couldn't bear to see me suffer, he is so tender-hearted; he wanted to go to the war, but he isn't fit to go; he is altogether too chicken-hearted for that. Think of a man, who is melted at the sight of a weeping woman, going out to battle."

Mrs. Sedgwick, the elder, was present at this time, and had remained a silent listener to the conversation, until the last remark of Bessie, which had been uttered so thoughtlessly, induced her to reply.

"Miss Jenkins," said that lady, somewhat gravely, "you have not arrived at the end of your life's journey yet; you have, perhaps, a long road before you; it may be a thorny one in spite of your managing to have things as you wish. I tremble for you now, as from your own confession you have dared to hinder a patriotic man from serving his country at an hour when she needs all her faithful sons. Chicken-hearted, as you call him, he would, with his strong sympathies, make a better soldier than if he was hard-hearted and stern. One thing I wish you to remember, and that is, that God can as easily protect our friends amid the perils of war, as he can in their homes; and he can, too, bring evil upon those who are near us, and whom we strive too often in vain to shield from danger and harm. You may yet feel, Bessie Jenkins, that all your management cannot save Raymond from dreaded ill."

Soon after, Bessie took leave of the Sedgwick family, feeling that Frederic's mother was severe towards her. "She need n't make such a serious matter of my unwillingness to have those I love shot at," said she, mentally; "I feel provoked at her musty old notions about folks being safe anywhere, if Providence sees fit to protect them; for my part, I like best to see that my friends are in safe places."

With her mind occupied with these and similar thoughts, she entered her mother's house, soon after leaving the friend she deemed so unkind. It was towards the evening of a day in early autumn, and the twilight was fast gathering when she reached her home. "Is it not tea-time, mother?" she asked, as she saw, on entering the dining-room, that the table was not spread.

"I don't know; no, — yes, I suppose so," said Mrs. Jenkins, without seeming conscious of what she was saying, as she stood at a window, with her back towards the door by which Bessie had entered the room.

"Why, what is the matter, mother?" she asked in surprise, as she hastened to her side; "has anything happened? you look troubled; what is it about? do tell me, quick."

Bessie judged rightly; her mother was troubled, more on her daughter's account, however, than her own. She had just learned the fact that Raymond had met with a serious accident. She knew by Bessie's manner that she had n't heard of it, and, with the remembrance of her distress at the thought of his being exposed to injury on the battle-field, she dreaded to inform her of the painful occurrence. As her mother did not reply at once, she urged her to tell her if she was ill.

"No, Bessie, I am not ill; but something sad has occurred this afternoon."

"Since I left home, mother? have you heard anything?"

"Yes, Bessie, and it must be since you went out that the accident to Raymond has occurred."

"Accident to Raymond! what has happened to him? is he hurt?"

"He has been knocked down, and run over, by a frightened horse, and badly hurt."

"In what way is he injured?"

"How, you mean, I suppose, but I do not know. A message was brought to you, from his mother, just before you came in, and a request that you would go to her house as soon as you possibly could."

"Oh, dear," exclaimed Bessie, "what shall I do? I don't want to see him if he is bruised and disfigured, and yet he will think it strange if I don't go now he has sent for me."

"To be sure he will, and you must go, Bessie, right away. I will go with you," responded her mother, and in a shorter time than it has taken us to inform our readers of these facts, they started for the residence of Raymond.

Poor Bessie! we call her poor, because she was one of those unfortunate individuals who has more heart than soul. She would shudder and turn away from a suffering fellow-being at any time, without making the slightest effort to relieve their distress. When they arrived at the door, they were told by the mother of Raymond, who was in the hall, on the way to the chamber of her son, as they rang for admission, that his head was much hurt.

Bessie drew back, involuntarily, saying, "then we had better not go in to disturb him."

"Indeed, you must go in; he is not entirely conscious now, but he will no doubt look anxiously for you, Bessie, at the first lucid interval, and for that reason I sent for you. You will stay here, of course."

"How can I? I shall not know how to do anything for Raymond; and it will be so terrible to see him, with his head injured so much."

"You haven't promised to be his friend only in fair weather, have you?"

"No, oh, no; but I never thought of his being hurt so, here at home."

"Perhaps if he had n't been kept from doing what he thought was his duty, he might have remained unhurt at this moment," said Mrs. Philips, in a tone somewhat reproachful, at the same time beginning to ascend the stairs, saying, "you must excuse me, if you will not go with me, ladies, for I must go to my son."

"Come," said Mrs. Jenkins, taking Bessie by the arm, "we will go with Mrs. Philips."

Bessie moved mechanically, and the trio entered the chamber. Raymond's mother approached the bedside with gentle tread, while Bessie sank into a chair on the opposite side of the room. Mrs. Jenkins moved nearer the sufferer, and asked in a whisper, "how does he seem now?"

"He appears to be sleeping, just now."

It was true, Raymond was dozing, yet his naps were disturbed, and he murmured incoherently. Bessie's name was pronounced several times in a faint tone. At length he spoke louder, and said distinctly, "won't she come to me?"

His mother bent over him; he opened his eyes and looked anxiously in her face a moment, but he could not bear the least degree of light, and he closed them immediately, saying, "I wonder what has happened."

The physician who had been called to him, came in for the third time, since Raymond had been injured, and taking his pulse, gave as his opinion that the young man had held his own for the last two hours. He gave strict orders for the room to be kept perfectly quiet. "Let none be admitted who are not needed to take care of the patient," said the doctor, glancing at Bessie and her mother as he spoke.

"These are friends," said Mrs. Phillips, "who will be useful at this bedside, I trust," introducing them to the physician.

"Then they may remain if they wish," responded he, bowing politely to each of them, "but no common acquaintances must be allowed to intrude, as the life of Mr. Philips depends upon his being kept from anything like excitement."

When the doctor left the chamber, Bessie followed him, and inquired anxiously in regard to his chances for recovery.

"He is young and strong," replied the physician, "and with great care he may possibly get well again; but I think he will carry the marks of his injuries, on his face, to his grave, even if he lives a long life."

Seeing Bessie turn pale, he continued, "the scars, however, will be of little consequence, if his life and reason are spared to him."

Bessie, shuddering, said, "O, dear," as the doctor left her. Her mother came out of the sick-room just as the physician disappeared, and told her daughter that Raymond had asked for her.

"Then I will try and see him," said she, "but I don't wish to."

It was evident to those who saw Bessie approach the sick-bed, that she shrank from the trial. She trembled and turned pale, and Mrs. Philips, fearing she might fall, put her arm around her waist and supported her, while her mother hastened to place a chair beside the bed.

"Bessie," said Raymond, in a faint tone, as he extended his hand to her, "don't feel so badly about me; my injuries are nothing compared with what they might have been."

"O, dear," exclaimed the young lady, interrupting him; "they are very dreadful, I am sure; I can't bear to look at you, and see you so disfigured; what *shall* we do?"

"Be patient, my dear girl, and thankful for the mercies we are experiencing at this moment."

"I don't see any great mercy in your being almost killed, and your head and face cut as it is, I'm sure."

"I feel," said Mrs. Philips, "that the life that is spared is so valuable to me, at least, that it is a cause of great gratitude in my case. The doctor hopes that with good care he will get well, and if he is obliged to carry the marks of his injuries during life, he will not be disgraced by them."

"O, dear," was all the response made by Bessie. Her mother chid her gently for making such a demonstration of saddened feeling in the presence of the sufferer, and intimated that it would be best for her to absent herself from the room until she could better command her feelings.

"She is nervous, poor child," said she to Mrs. Philips, "and unfit, just now, to witness suffering."

The lady addressed did not reply, for a multitude of thoughts came rushing into her mind at this moment, in such a manner as to deprive her of the power of speech. Mrs. Jenkins approached the bed, and bending over Raymond, whispered in his ear expressions of sympathy, trying to excuse her daughter at the same time by telling him that she was so very nervous she could not control her feelings as she ought.

"Will Bessie leave me, and go away now, without

saying any more to me?" asked Raymond, with a look expressive of both regret and surprise.

"I think it will be best for her to go now, and come again when she is in a better condition."

"I fear that will never be," remarked Mrs. Philips, drily, and with a spice of contempt in her manner of expression.

"I am sorry Bessie is so nervous," replied her mother, with a sigh, "but it cannot be helped, I fear."

While this conversation between the mothers was being held, the daughter arose slowly from her chair, and walked towards the door. Her mother followed her and spoke a few words in a low tone, which caused her to stop, and with a shudder turn herself around and approach the bed. Her face was concealed by her handkerchief, until Raymond addressed her, asking if she must go so soon.

"I think I must," she replied in tremulous accents, "but I hope you will hurry and get well, Raymond, so it wont make me feel so bad to look at you."

"But suppose I should n't look much better, would you desert me on that account, Bessie?"

This question was asked with deep feeling. "I should feel very sorry to have it so, — I mean to have your face scarred after you get well."

"Good night, Bessie," was all the reply that Raymond trusted himself to make to this last assertion, and Bessie and her mother withdrew from the room, and from the house also, much to the satisfaction of Mrs. Philips. She knew that the heart of her son had been pained, and on that account she regretted that Bessie had been permitted to see him. However, she forbore any allusion to the visit of the ladies, but exerted herself to do all she could, to relieve the suffering that she might administer to. The heart wound she could not touch, much as she longed to comfort him, who was so dear to her.

The next day, Bessie sent one of her brothers to inquire about Raymond, but did not venture to call herself; her brother said she did n't feel able to do so.

"Is she sick?" asked Mrs. Philips, who met the boy at the door.

"No, ma'am, not sick, but dreadfully fidgetty; mother says she is n't fit to go out."

"She had better stay at home, then," said the lady, "Raymond needs comfort, and it is better that none but cheerful faces should be about him."

Some messenger was sent daily for more than a week to make inquiries respecting Raymond, but Bessie did n't call upon him in that time. Her mother went once, and endeavored to apologize for her daughter's not having been able to go.

"I am glad," said she, "that you are getting better; I don't think that scar upon your forehead will hurt your looks, much; indeed I don't."

"'Handsome is, that handsome does,' Mrs. Jenkins," remarked Raymond's mother with a smile.

"That is true, and yet young girls do feel proud to have a handsome young man to escort them about."

"I regret very much," said the young man, speaking with great earnestness, "that this wound, which is likely to leave its mark upon my brow through all my life, was not received by me while serving my country. I feel now that I have done wrong in not going forth in her defence, when I wished to; however, the past cannot be recalled, much as I regret the part I have acted; but if firm health is once more granted me by indulgent Heaven, I am firmly resolved to become a soldier, and use my strong right arm in defending the dear old stars and stripes."

"That, then, is your determination," said Mrs. Jenkins, in a tone of surprise, "will you go if Bessie grieves about it as she did at the thought of your going some time ago?"

"Yes, Mrs. Jenkins, that will not make me pause and retreat from the very threshold of duty again; I have been chastised for that sin, and shall not, I trust, soon forget the wormwood and the gall of my chastisement."

"You are willing, I suppose that Bessie shall be told what you have just said?"

"O yes, ma'am, very willing."

Mrs. Philips heard this conversation in silence; she was not surprised at the change in the feelings of her son, for she had hoped and prayed that it might take place. She knew that he had been led to reflect much in his late confinement from company, upon the childish conduct of the young woman whom he had imagined so lovely and good, suitable to be the sharer of his joys and sorrows. On reviewing the past, he began to see that he had made a mistake in not endeavoring more earnestly to lead Bessie to set up a higher standard of action for herself, rather than, by indulging her morbidness, lead her to cherish her selfish feelings, as he felt sure he had done, by being moved as he had been by her grief at the idea of his going to the war.

Raymond lay some time absorbed in deep reflection, then spoke in a cheerful tone to his mother, who was sitting by his side, busy at work, asking her if she should object to his going away to join the army. Mrs. Philips raised her head, and looking in his face with an expression of maternal affection upon her own, said, " I think I cannot, I dare not, if you are able to go, but what will you do about Bessie, if she behaves as she did when you talked of going before."

" I cannot help hoping that she will change in some respects ; I have done wrong in encouraging her to act only from impulse. Henceforth I must do my duty, and leave results with the All-Powerful One above. Don't judge Bessie harshly, mother ; I know you think she has acted selfishly towards me since I have been ill ; I will not say she has not, yet others are to blame besides her ; she has been taught in a school that has made her a creature of mere feeling or impulse. I know you will be tempted to treat her coldly if she calls on us again, but I beg you to receive her as kindly as possible."

As his mother did not reply immediately, he asked, " Will you, mother, for my sake ? "

" Yes, Raymond, and for the sake of trying to do the girl good. I am glad you are beginning to look at things through a better medium than your imagination ; it is seldom too late to change for the better."

CHAPTER X.

We know not what a day may bring forth."

RAYMOND had endured a great conflict, from the time he had allowed himself to be governed by Bessie's tears and entreaties in regard to going to the war. It is not possible for a good man to do wrong and not be made more or less unhappy by so doing. A violated conscience will assert its claim too constantly to let the sinner enjoy peace. Raymond had tried to reconcile his conscience to his acts in regard to Bessie, but he could not; he felt less sure that he was doing right every day as the time passed away, yet he had not courage to tell Bessie that he felt he was doing wrong, and that she was the cause of his doing what he felt condemned for, continually. He felt, as soon as consciousness was restored after he was injured, as it were in an instant, and well-nigh fatally, that this casualty was sent as a rebuke to himself, and Bessie also. He pondered the subject long, ere he decided to leave the consequences of doing his duty unconditionally with a higher power, but he did resolve and firmly too, to do right at all hazards. He felt happier then, than he had done during the long season spent in the struggle with duty and inclination. His purpose was high and noble now; in dependence on God, he would go forward in the path of duty, even if he should be opposed by those dearest to him on earth. He recovered rapidly from the effects of the injuries he had received.

Bessie called upon Raymond several times before he was able to leave his room. It grieved him to be obliged to see the horror she evinced, whenever she gazed upon the unfortunate wound in his forehead; he had examined it himself in a mirror, and felt convinced that he would be obliged to carry a deep scar to his grave, yet he was not troubled at the thought at all. His brow of course was less fair, but there was nothing horrifying in the appearance of it in his view, or in his mother's. Why need Bessie be so shocked at the sight of it; did she love him merely because she thought him handsome? He did not like to think it possible; he could not believe his Bessie was so weak-minded; her nervous organization was exceedingly delicate, and would not admit of her looking upon the wound without a shudder, because it reminded her of the pain that wound had caused him.

So love reasoned, if not logically, in such a manner as to convince our friend Raymond that his Bessie was less selfish than others considered her.

Neither Bessie nor Raymond approached the war subject until the latter was able to walk abroad. It was then, on one of his visits to the house of Mrs. Jenkins, that he spoke of his plans to her daughter for the first time in more than a year. Bessie had felt sure that Raymond would never enlist in his country's service, and the matter once so agitating had ceased to trouble her. Her mother, too, had forborne to tell Bessie what Raymond had said to her about joining the army, thinking it not worth her while, as the young man might be under the influence of excitement at the time, which would probably pass away and cause him to change his mind. Bessie's surprise, therefore, was great when she was told by Raymond that he had resolved to go forth to fight for his flag, as soon as his strength should be restored to him.

"You will not go, if I don't consent to your doing so, certainly," said the young lady, regarding him with a look of unfeigned surprise as she spoke.

"Yes, Bessie, I dare not yield to your persuasion again to stay at home, when duty bids me go."

"Duty, that hateful word again," was all the response she deigned, and then sat in sullen silence until Raymond spoke, saying, "Not hateful, my dear girl, when we are willing to do right. It is indeed trying, sometimes, to be obliged to run the risk of bringing upon ourselves consequences that are painful, but even then, duty is not a hateful word. Bessie, I struggled hard and long before I could make up my mind to do right, at all hazards, but I have gained the victory over my weakness. The accident that befell me was sent in mercy as a rebuke to my fearfulness; not fearfulness in regard to meeting the enemies of my native land, but in respect to giving you pain, Bessie. I have been a coward in a moral sense; I am stronger than you, and my strength should be used to assist you. I am firmly resolved now what to do, even if it leads to your breaking your engagement to become mine; I must leave for a season, for my, or our country needs me; I feel that she does."

"You are only one man, besides you are not a military man."

"Not drilled, you mean, Bessie, but, God helping me, this shall not be truthfully said of me long. Where a man's heart is in his work it must, of necessity, prosper; I know I shall make a soldier."

"But think of the vile influences of camp life, how corrupting; you may not be able to withstand it, more than many others; even clergymen have fallen victims to its power."

"I admit all you say, Bessie, to be true. At the same time, I am not afraid to trust myself in the hands of God, even in an irreligious camp, when duty bids me enter one. I cannot keep myself from evil here; I must rely upon the same Power for protection in every place. All we have to do, my dear girl, is to learn which way duty leads, and then walk boldly in its path, trusting results to Omnipotence. Every day duty must be done; we are not to look forward except to think of the rest that remains to us, if we are faithful.

> 'Guide Thou my feet, I would not ask to see
> The future scene, one step's enough for me.'

"Cannot you unite with me, in adopting that sentiment of the poet, Bessie?" asked Raymond.

"I don't know what I can do; I don't know anything or feel anything now; I am almost stunned with what you have been saying to me. It was so entirely unexpected; you have never said a word about your feelings, and I thought you were content to stay at home. I feel distressed, but your mind is made up, and I must do the best I can, I suppose."

"O, my dear Bessie, if you only will do that, we shall both be blest."

"Do what?" interrogated the young lady, in a desponding tone.

"The best you can do; why, that is all I desire, for then you will be enabled to leave me, and every object that interests you, in hands that are sufficiently powerful to take care of all things. Try to be cheerful, Bessie, for my sake. I shall love to think of you when I am gone, as being cheerfully employed in doing what your hands find to do. I want your face to be adorned with an habitual smile, a smile of content."

"But I can't see why it is your duty to go to fighting; you, who have always been a peaceable man, to change so."

"I have n't changed, Bessie; I am still a peaceable man. I hope you don't think that men cannot go out to the battle-field, to save their Government, and all that's dear to every true patriot, from violation, without malice in their hearts."

"All men who go to war, are not patriots; some go for the sake of excitement, and some, I have heard say, went because they might as well fight for a living as do anything else; while others declare that they want to kill the Rebels. I don't think there are many good men in the army, do you, Raymond?"

"As large a majority as can be found, I suppose, in any assemblage of men; there are always Judases in every gathering. Our army is composed of a vast multitude; it is hardly fair to infer that every twelfth man is unprincipled who helps to make it up, and it is true that only eleven among the twelve followers of our Saviour, were sincere. I feel that God-fearing men are needed in our army at this time. The contest in which we are engaged is between right and wrong; it has been termed a war of Jehovah. I want to do my part in striving to free our land of treason and Rebellion, and I feel that woe be to me if I hold back."

This conversation is only one of many, similar in

their features to this, which were held between Bessie and Raymond during the few days that followed. She did not now try to overcome his resolution with sobs and tears, as she did before, for something in Raymond's manner awed her; she did not ask for proof that she was beloved by him, and she felt that his motives must be disinterested and pure in leaving her. He seemed upborne by a Power which she feared to oppose openly, and Raymond went away, feeling that the discipline meted out to his Bessie would be salutary. He did not allow her time to weep a long adieu; he felt it would not be well for either of them, and so put off the disagreeable formality until the latest moment, and then, with a hasty "Good by" and "God bless you," was whirled over the road, that soon separated them, with locomotive speed.

"How soon he loosened his clasp of my hand," thought Bessie, as she stood looking after the departing train, scarcely conscious that she was surrounded by a motley throng, whose hearts were beating in sympathy with hers at that hour. Yet it was even so; many a tear was shed, and many a heart-ache was being endured in silence then, as the swiftly-moving train was bearing away its freight of loved objects. Mothers had seen their sons depart, sisters their brothers, and wives their husbands. This scene was only one of the many, in the dark programme of the war, and it must pass along. Some murmured, and refused to be reconciled; but others felt that a stern necessity demanded the sacrifice, and they accepted this choice of evils.

Bessie did not move from the spot where Raymond left her standing, until her mother reminded her that she was standing too long, and ought to be moving away.

"I will go, mother," said she, pensively, and then began to walk slowly away, when they encountered Mrs. Sedgwick, Frederic's mother. She looked at Bessie, with a feeling of sympathy manifested in her open countenance, shook hands with both mother and daughter, saying: "I did not see you before the cars started, but I saw Raymond, and bade him good by, though I need n't have come to the depot for that, only I wanted to put into his hand a little memento of my regard for him, and my interest in the cause he has espoused."

"I am glad you did come," said Bessie; "but, oh, Mrs. Sedgwick, what shall I do all the long months he is away? I did n't dare to try to persuade him from going, yet his leaving me so seems dreadful; but I promised him I would try and do the best I could."

"You will keep your promise, Bessie?" said her friend, in a kind tone.

"I intend to try, but this trial has come upon me so unexpectedly. I had no thought of such a thing, and my head has done nothing but whirl around, these last few days. It seems to me much as if I had had a disagreeable dream. What will come next, I wonder?"

"Not anything but what you will be enabled to bear, my dear," answered Mrs. Sedgwick; "and now don't pass our house without calling; here we are at the door now, and Julia will sympathize with you with all her heart."

"She knows how, truly," remarked Mrs. Jenkins, as they entered the house. The ladies found Julia ready to mingle her tears with Bessie, yet she could not take time to weep long. A letter had just been brought, informing her that her husband was sick at a hospital, near Washington. He had been slightly wounded, in a skirmish with the foe, and although he could not expect to see her, or any of his friends, it would, he said, gladden his heart to do so. Overexertion had done as much to lay him aside as his wound; that was merely a flesh wound, which would probably heal soon.

"Mother, I want to go and see Frederic; it would do him good to have me go to him."

"But, child, I fear you could not be with him but a short time; perhaps you would be troubled to get a pass to enter the hospital; some have, you know; then you would weary yourself with the journey, to no purpose."

"I cannot think so; even should I not succeed in my attempts to be with him as I wish, he will know that I have done all I could for him, and that will be a comfort."

"There is not one person that you could ask to accompany you, daughter."

"No matter; I can go alone safely, I am not timid when 't is necessary to have courage. Don't discourage me, mother, but say I may go, and you will help me."

"If Kate could go with you I would not object, Julia," was the mother's rejoinder.

"Poor Kate," said Julia; "she will go, I dare say, if she can leave home; I will despatch a letter to her immediately, and ask her to meet me at New York. Let's see; 't is Monday now, I can hurry and mail a letter that will reach her to-morrow night, and she can reach New York and find me at the depot, on Thursday morning."

Julia at once carried her plan of writing into execution ; she could not wait for Kate to reply to her letter, but she did not shrink from going alone, if she should by any means fail of having her cousin's company. Her mother Sedgwick felt some anxiety about the matter, but Julia was hopeful and courageous, and so the good lady left the affair as it was. She saw Julia depart, taking what little comforts she could in haste manage to prepare, to the loved husband and son.

Bessie offered her services to assist the devoted young wife to get ready for her journey, and there seemed so much heart in the offer, that Julia could not decline accepting it, and so Bessie was at her house most of the time after the letter came which has been referred too. She also accompanied Julia to the depot, and saw her borne away in the train. All this time she never paused once in her labor of love, to sit down and indulge in a fit of weeping. After Julia had gone out of her sight, Bessie returned home, thinking how great a change had come suddenly to more than one home, and wondering that she could think of her own trials with so little feeling.

CHAPTER XI.

"There is a faith towards men."

We must leave Julia on her way to the capital, and go back a little in our story. Frederic, it will be remembered, joined the army by enlisting in its ranks; he preferred doing so, for he was not acquainted with military tactics, and without some confidence in his ability to fill an office *well*, he shrank from holding one.

"I can serve my country as 'high private,' very well," he remarked, when rallied upon what some called his queer notions; "If I'm not fit for a private, surely I'm not fit for an officer," he good-naturedly replied; and those who rallied him most were content to respect his straightforward, manly decision, although it was contrary to their judgment. There were few who would not have felt glad if Frederic Sedgwick had received a Lieutenant's commission before he left his home, for he was a young man who had won the respect of most people who knew him.

Many followed his example in enlisting, who would not have been willing to serve their country as a common soldier, had not Frederic Sedgwick done so. On the march, and in the camp, his influence for good was felt. In the hour of imminent peril he was self-possessed and brave, modestly shrinking from anything like presumption or vainglory. He took part, as a private, in the battle of Fair Oaks, and was promoted, for his soldierly bearing, by receiving a commission for second lieutenancy. It was evident that his motive in being at the seat of war was disinterested; he loved his country, and that love he had, as it were, nursed from his mother in his babyhood.

Mrs. Sedgwick was a noble, patriotic woman, and Frederic honored her; he loved to do so. He wrote to his wife and mother, after he had been promoted, giving them an account of the engagement in which he had taken part; afterwards he spoke of his promotion.

"I was not looking for promotion," said he, "but I have been made second lieutenant. I do not object to having a commission, on any account, and for some reasons I am very glad to have it so. I shall have a chance to do more for the men, and it is the privates that we must look to and depend upon to fight our battles. I want to do all I can; I fear that many in our army and navy care too little for anything but their pay. I have seen enough of this mercenary spirit to shock me."

A few months later he was again promoted, and although laid aside from duty at the time he wrote home, of his illness, he was considered a candidate for higher promotion still. He knew this, and was, too, aware that he was liable to be ordered to a department of the army much more remote from his home than any post to which he had been ordered heretofore.

As he lay one day on his couch in the hospital, with closed eyes, thinking of home, and how glad he should be to see his loved ones there, he heard gentle footsteps approaching his bed. He had often heard similar sounds, and thought that some poor fellow was to receive a visit from some female friend, and congratulated him in his heart. As the step was arrested at his bedside, he opened his eyes, and saw standing near by his wife, and her friend Kate Sisson. His surprise scarcely equalled his joy at beholding them.

"You did n't tell me in your letter that you were coming, Julia," said he.

"I thought it better not to, lest something might prevent my coming; and then I feared, too, that if you knew I was on the way, you would feel anxious, and the anxiety would injure you, in your feeble state."

"You were kind and thoughtful, indeed, and Kate is very kind, also, to accompany you."

"Not very, I am sure," said Kate; "it is certainly very pleasant to me to come here with your wife, Captain, as we must call you now. I feel very glad that she gave me an invitation to accompany her. It is not, however, the first time I have been at the capital; I presume Julia has informed you of my coming to these parts, some time since, on a gloomy errand."

"She has; and I can but wish every soldier who falls had a sister like yourself."

"That, surely, is not a bad wish," remarked Julia.

"Provided they could n't have better ones," said Kate, soberly.

Frederic acknowledged himself better; he trusted that now he was comforted with the sight of two such friends, he should recover rapidly.

Julia immediately acquainted her mother-in-law with the fact that she had arrived safely, and that Kate had received her letter, and hastened to meet her at the depot in New Jersey; and that providentially they had met just in time to take the Philadelphia train together. She informed the anxious mother of the exact condition of her son, and also expressed her desire to remain near Frederic, until he should be able to return to duty, saying, "while everything goes right at home, I think you will like to have me stay by my husband until he is able to take the field again. Should any untoward circumstance occur, please inform me immediately."

After mailing this letter, Julia gave herself up to the duties of the hour. As herself and friend daily visited the hospital, they saw, whichever way they turned their gaze, motives for action; and many a sufferer was cheered by their tender ministrations. One day when they were passing noiselessly through one of the wards, they heard some one call, "Miss Sisson, Miss Sisson." Kate started and looked about her, to ascertain from whence the voice proceeded, and was directed by an attendant to the bedside of a young man, whom she instantly recognized as the brother of Arthur Bryant.

"Why, Edwin," exclaimed Kate, in surprise, as she took the hand of the invalid which was extended towards her; "I did n't know you was here, but tell me how you are, and what I can do for you. This lady," she continued, "is Mrs. Sedgwick," looking at Julia, who stood just behind her friend; "it will give her pleasure, as well as myself, to know in what way we can add most to your comfort."

"Yes," said Julia; "I do want to cheer, in some way, every loyal soldier."

"I don't wonder at all at your feeling thus," replied

the sick man with a languid smile, "if you are the wife of Captain Sedgwick."

"You know my husband, then," remarked Julia.

"I do; and I have reason to be grateful to him also."

Julia turned her face away to hide the gathering tears, of which she had no cause to be ashamed. The thought that Frederic was not changed by the evil influences he had been obliged to encounter since he had been absent from his home, filled her heart with emotions of gratitude, that for the moment quite overcame her. She controlled her joyous feelings at once, as she gazed upon the lovely youth before her, and saw, as it were, the pallor of death in his countenance. After obtaining permission of those who had the care of the sick, the ladies administered some little refreshing delicacies, that were grateful to the feverish patient. Julia wet his head with cold water, and combed his hair with a gentleness that brought relief to his fevered brow.

Edwin looked up with a grateful expression and whispered, "one thing more I must ask, and that is, to have the Bible read by one of you; I know your voice will not disturb any one."

"I hope not, said Kate, as she took a pocket Bible from a small carpet-bag, in which she had brought several little luxuries for the sick soldiers. "I have brought a Bible with me; tell me what you wish read."

"O, you know what to read, something for my soul to rest upon, now."

Kate began, repeating the first verse of the 121st Psalm: "I will lift up mine eyes unto the hills, from whence cometh my help." Edwin smiled, saying, "please go on; that is what I need;" and Kate continued, "my help cometh from the Lord, which made heaven and earth."

She then turned to the 23d Psalm, and read in soft accents the fourth verse: "yea, though I walk through the valley of the shadow of death, I will fear no evil, for thou art with me; thy rod and thy staff they comfort me."

"How true are those words; I feel that the rod that has been laid upon me has brought comfort to my heart."

Kate turned over a leaf and read, "The Lord is my light and my salvation; whom shall I fear? the Lord is the strength of my life; of whom shall I be afraid?" She turned to the New Testament, and read those words of solace, "Come unto me, all ye who labor and are heavy laden, and I will give you rest." Then, "I will never leave nor forsake you." Kate here closed her book. "If I may," said she, "I will read more to you another time."

"It must be soon, or never," answered Edwin; "I shall soon be gone."

"As neither Kate nor Julia spoke, after remaining silent a few moments, he said, "I wish you, Miss Sisson, would take my dying message to my brother Arthur."

"I will do so," said Kate, at the same time feeling it would be a hard task for her to perform; however, she did not allow her reluctance to make itself manifest.

"I wish Arthur to be told that I die feeling that, for worlds, I would not exchange conditions with him. I am satisfied with what God does; in my own case, I am more than satisfied. I am happy and grateful. Brother will know that I am not a cripple; life would be as bright for me, could I be spared, as it has ever been, and yet I am not anxious to live. I feel to say, 'God's will be done.' Tell Arthur that my last request to him is, to pause and reflect upon the course he has marked out for himself; tell him, that quicksands lie in his path, which will swallow him up ere he is aware that he is stepping upon them. Oh, I want to say to him, in thunder-tones, it will profit you naught, Arthur, to gain this whole world, and lose your soul."

Here Edwin paused, closed his eyes, and lay silent a few moments, evidently exhausted with the effort he had made to speak. Kate had carefully taken notes of every word, that she might copy them, verbatim, for the brother for whom they were intended. Julia sat silently by, with tearful eyes, fanning the sufferer, as he had been giving this, his last message, to an erring, yet dear relative. Kate hastily put her pencil and memorandum into her pocket, and after a little time spent in looking upon the frail tenement about to be deserted by the deathless spirit it now contained, turned from the bed, with deep emotion, and after being absent a few moments, returned with some refreshments for Edwin. After resting a little, and taking the sustaining cordial offered by Kate, he seemed more comfortable. Julia longed to ask him if he had ever regretted enlisting in the service of his country, and she was glad to hear the question asked by her friend, and delighted with the reply made by the dying young man.

"Regret doing so? No, indeed; I would do the same were I to be again in the same circumstances. All I am sorry for is, that I have done no more in my lifetime to make the land of my birth a better land than it is."

"But you have proved yourself to be a true and noble patriot," said Julia and Kate, both speaking at the same instant.

"In a comparative sense, perhaps; but, oh, the light which a near view of eternity sheds upon the realities of time, showing the relations of the latter to that state that shall never end. None need fear doing too much to spread the light of truth in the earth, and by that means uproot error.

"Had we been thoroughly a Christian nation, we had not known this civil war. May all be faithful to God and to their country. God grant that this may be true of all dear to me."

Although the young man had spoken only at intervals, and in a faint voice, he *would* speak. His heart seemed overflowing with love to all, and a desire that all should tread the path that leads to life. His love for his country, also, was great. On hearing Julia ask her friend, if Edwin had a mother, he opened his eyes languidly, and pointed with his finger to heaven.

"Your mother is, then, in a better world than this," remarked Julia, understanding the motion of the invalid as intended for an answer to the question she had asked Kate.

"Yes," he replied, "God has answered her prayers in behalf of one of her sons already, and he will do so, in his own time and way, in the case of Arthur. Pray for him," said he, looking beseechingly at Kate as he spoke.

The young lady nodded her head in token of assent, for her emotions prevented her speaking. Gladly would she have lingered by the bed of the dying Christian had it been so that she could. But she saw him sink into a doze ere she followed her friend from the spot where her heart had been not only wrung with agony, but made joyous, too, by an exhibition of the power of the gospel of Christ to gild with ineffable brightness the darkest pictures of life, and even the confines of the tomb.

This was the only opportunity our friends ever enjoyed of conversing with Edwin. He lived until the next day, and although he was conscious, and gave the ladies a smile of recognition as they stood by his bedside, the last time he ever opened his eyes upon the world, he was too feeble to speak, and they saw him sink to rest in death as a child falls gently asleep upon the breast of its mother. "So he giveth his beloved sleep," said Kate, as they left the precious remains of the departed to the care of those who had been commissioned by Arthur Bryant to take care of them.

As Captain Sedgwick recovered strength sufficient to enable him to repair to his own quarters, he did so, and his wife enjoyed the privilege of cheering him by her society and kind attentions, until his health was entirely restored.

Kate remained with her friend at the capital, where they devoted most of their time to doing what they could for the comfort of the sick and wounded soldiers. Their ministrations were not confined to Union men, although these received attention, first; but many a

Rebel prisoner was cheered and made more comfortable by their kindness.

Frederic was well able to do without nursing ere his wife thought of leaving him. He was made assistant Adjutant-General and a staff officer of General H, — much to the satisfaction of his many friends, a day or two before his wife and Kate bade him adieu, to return home.

CHAPTER XII.

"You are a kind-hearted and an honorable youth."

"Mother, I have just received a long letter from Raymond." This was said by Bessie Jenkins, as she entered her mother's room one morning, a few months after the departure of the young man spoken of.

"I am glad, daughter, and hope you will hasten to read it, so as to communicate its contents to me," said Mrs. Jenkins.

"I have read it, mother, and I'm anxious to have you explain some things referred to by Raymond."

Bessie then read the letter aloud; she was interrupted more than once, however, by her mother, who was surprised as well as delighted by what she heard.

"Now do please tell me, mother, if you have a sister living at the South. I've never heard you speak of any such relative, I'm sure."

"'Tis true, Bessie, that I have a sister in Virginia, though she has been estranged from me for many years. I have written to her once or twice since your remembrance, yet, as I received no answer to my missives, I could not bear to speak of the fact that I had such a relative, one who felt too proud to acknowledge me, and I have labored to forget her."

"I don't care to see her, if she is such an unkind sister to you, mother, and I hope I never shall."

"You are wrong, my child; if your aunt comes to

this part of the country I shall seek her, and I hope the discipline she has endured has changed her idea of things, so that she will not look with contempt upon her less fashionable sister."

"But only think, how strange that Raymond should have met with her, and found out that she was a relative of ours," said Bessie, musingly.

"It was a kind Providence ordered this event, as Mrs. Sedgwick would say," answered the mother.

It appeared, as Raymond stated in his letter, that Mrs. Murray was not at all in sympathy with her husband, who was a secessionist. He had left his home, not quite twenty miles from Alexandria, to join the Rebel army soon after the commencement of hostilities. Mrs. Murray was suspected, by some, of indulging Union sentiments, but she was very non-committal, and none, save her husband, knew that she was loyal. She had two children, a daughter and son. Very glad did the lady feel at this crisis in our country's history, that her son was too young to bear arms. He was only thirteen at the beginning of our woes.

Her daughter Clara was then sixteen; but we must tell the story of Mrs. Murray. The father of her children had so constantly been occupied with public affairs, that he had been obliged to leave the management of his children almost entirely to their mother. He often cautioned her against instilling into their young minds her plebeian puritanical notion of things, and did what in him lay, whenever he had opportunity to be with them, to elevate their ideas to his standard, as he expressed himself; we should say, lower them.

Mr. Murray loved his family as well as a proud, ambitious man was capable of loving. His wife and children gratified his vanity and his pride, else he had not cared for them at all. He was scarcely if ever at home during three successive days, now that his soul was fired with the unholy ambition of political and military renown. He lent the weight of his purse and the strength of his right arm to destroy the glorious institutions of our land.

"Why try to overthrow the Government?" Mrs. Murray ventured to ask timidly on one occasion, but was silenced by the violent anger of her erring husband. She said no more, but she read, and "thoughts she could not bridle forced their way without the will." Could her sister have seen her as in memory she lived over the days of her childhood and youth, as she thought of the first time she ever met Mr. Murray, and of her mother's gentle caution, whispered in her ear, "All is not gold that glitters, my dear," she would have pitied her. She had found this aphorism true to her sorrow, since then, but at that time; "O, foolish girl that I was," thought the wife of the great man, in her isolation from all that was dear to her except her children, "to listen and turn from all my friends to please him." As she thought of her loving mother, whose heart had been wellnigh broken by her desertion and neglect, she wept long and bitterly. She thought of her sister; she loved her; she had always loved her; how could she have allowed herself to be influenced as she had been to neglect them so cruelly.

The more she reflected, the more wretched she became. The motives by which her husband was governed, and by which he had governed her, were plain to her now. It was pride and love of power that had made him anxious to estrange her from her relatives, and it was these ignoble traits in his character that made him anxious now to destroy the glorious institutions of the United States. She shuddered as she thought of the future, so helpless and hopeless appeared her condition. She thought of her children with trembling. "Would I were in my childhood's home," mused she half aloud; she started at the sound of her own voice, and more, as she felt a gentle touch upon her arm, and looked up to see her daughter standing close by her side.

"Mother," said Clara, "you said something about your childhood's home; where is it? I never knew anything about your relatives; have you any?"

"Your father, my child, never wished me to speak of my former friends, and that is the reason you have not heard about them?"

"Were n't they respectable people, mother?" asked the daughter, in surprise.

"Oh, yes, indeed they were; my mother was a good Christian."

"What was the matter with them, then?"

"They were not wealthy; you know your father thinks a great deal of riches."

"Do you love your mother, mamma?"

"Yes, I do love her, though, for your father's sake, I have never corresponded with her or my sister. I attempted to write to them when I was first married and came here, but my doing so displeased your father, and I gave up the pleasure."

Clara had seated herself on a stool by her mother's feet as she was conversing, and as her mother ceased speaking she covered her face with her hands and laid her head upon her lap. She sat in this posture some time, while there was a silence which was absolutely painful to Mrs. Murray.

"What are you thinking about, Clara?" at length inquired the mother.

"I was wondering, if I should ever have a husband who would require me to forsake you, whether or not I should obey him. But I don't believe I should; I could n't and I would n't. It is not right for you to do so, mother. You never ought to have submitted to such a requirement. I know it was wrong; you are too easy, that's the trouble."

"I have been wrong, my child; I see it now, although during the first years of my married life, I felt that I owed *all* duty to my husband."

"I love my father," said Clara, "because he is my father, and so does brother Edgar; but, mother, we don't think the South are doing right in taking up arms against the Government. We have talked a great deal about the state of affairs, and wondered what you thought about the wicked acts that the 'Confederacy,' as this make-believe government is called, have committed. We dare not say a word in hearing of even our own people, and yet, mother, I know that some of the servants are longing for the Union troops to come, and I don't blame them; do you, mother?"

"I dare not say that I do, Clara; I wish I was at the North, with my friends, now."

"Where at the North did your friends live, mother, when you last heard from them?"

"In the good old State of Massachusetts; that name which has ever been dear to me. The town of

Newdale was my birthplace; it is a small place, but its water privileges give it a high position among the adjoining places."

"Mother, I mean to ask father to let us go North."

"My child, the idea is perfectly insane; you do not know your father's feelings in regard to the North, or you would not think of such a thing."

"Mother, I have thought a great deal of what Hannah says; she will have it that the Lord is able to do anything he pleases to accomplish. I am beginning to believe what she has so many times told me; and more than that, I do feel that God is answering the prayers of our people. I have often heard them pray in their cabins, when they didn't know I was hearing them, and I have often felt that God must be better pleased with them than with us. Hannah has always been a good Christian friend to me, and I love her dearly."

Mrs. Murray seemed awe-stricken; "where did you pick up these notions, Clara?"

"I got them out of the Bible, which I have read to Hannah, and some of the rest of our people, and I think God has heard the prayers that these poor ignorant souls have put up for me; for He has taught me to love my Saviour, and love to pray to Him. I feel, too, that God will hear their prayers for you, dear mother, and then you will not be so afraid ——;" she paused, fearing to pronounce the words her lips had framed.

"Afraid of what, my daughter? Don't hesitate to tell me what you feel."

"Well, then; I was going to say, afraid to do right for yourself."

"My dear child," was all that Mrs. Murray could say. She was silent for some time, and her heart was full, wellnigh to bursting. At length Clara asked her mother if she thought she had been feeling wrong about the things she had spoken of.

"No, no, my child; I do not like our situation. I do not sympathize with these Rebel movements; but what am I to do? alas! I know not."

"Mother, let us ask God to appear for us; He stopped the mouths of lions, in Bible times, and he may help us. He is able, and we can pray to Him."

The heart of this mother was filled to overflowing with gladness, to find that her daughter sympathized with her in her trials. She had for years felt so lonely, she had often thought her burden was too heavy to be borne, ere the Rebellion broke out; but this disastrous event had added bitter drops to her portion. A fearful anticipation of evil oppressed her spirit. She thought now of her friends in the loyal North, and longed for their sympathy.

"Would I could write to my mother and ask her forgiveness," thought she, "for my wicked neglect and desertion; but I cannot know that a letter would reach her. I am wretched, and what can I do?"

We hardly need say that Mrs. Murray was not an energetic woman; her mind was not strong, else she would never have been so completely governed by the absolute will of her husband, as to submit to his authority in becoming estranged from her *plebeian friends,* as he termed her relatives. In her girlhood, she had been dazzled by a view of his elevated position in society. He loved her; she felt that he did, and was easily led by his sophistry, to believe that at marriage her obligations to others ceased; that it was her duty henceforth, to yield to him her every wish, and that, cheerfully. For a short period subsequent to the union of Mr. Murray and his wife, the life that they led was so dissipated, that the latter had little time to think of anything but preparations for the constantly occurring scenes of gayety in which she mingled. Her vanity was gratified by hearing the praises her beauty called forth continually, and she lived in a whirl of excitement from day to day. Yet there had come seasons when her heart had longed for her mother and elder sister.

At the birth of Clara, she would have given much to see her mother; she ventured then to breathe a wish to her husband, that she might write and inform her of the advent of her babe; adding, "mother ought to know it, I think."

"I thought all that nonsense was settled long ago, and that you were contented in the sphere to which I have elevated you. You are to leave everything for me, your husband; and our child is never to be told of the low family to which her mother belonged."

The young mother felt hurt at this unfeeling response of her liege lord; but she had so long yielded to his overbearing will, that it was useless to attempt resistance at this period in their married life. So the years passed on, and Mrs. Murray endured life for the most part cheerfully. Her children were a solace to her as she grew older; she was left more at home by her husband, than in her youthful days; her beauty had faded somewhat, and she felt that he who had once been so proud to have her with him in all public places, was less desirous of her company. She was not grieved at this, farther than it gave her reason to fear that he had been attracted towards her by her loveliness of personal appearance alone. She loved her children.

Mrs. Murray had faithful servants, and until the excitement caused by the nomination of Abraham Lincoln to the Presidential chair, her life had been comparatively comfortable. A sting of conscience, now and then, felt in a moment when she could not silence its assertions that she ought to do right, that she was accountable to a higher power than that of her husband.

During the Presidential campaign of 1860, Mrs. Murray, in the absence of her husband, read many of the various newspapers of the day, and her preferences were all in favor of the Republican candidate. As the time drew near for the great question to be decided, her heart fluttered between fear and hope; and when it was known that the people's candidate was duly elected, she could not be glad, for she had heard too much said in her own home, during the short visits of her children's father thither, to leave her room for doubt as to the course the Southrons would pursue, if they could no longer control affairs at the head of the Nation, as they had done for a long period in the past.

Mrs. Murray heard of the secession of South Carolina with dismay. She learned, too, that Mr. Murray was a leading man in that bogus government. He was scarcely at home during the winter of 1860–61, he had so much public business to attend to. On one account Mrs. Murray was glad this was so, for she was saved the pain of having her children listen to execrations that were constantly heaped upon the North, by the very men whom the mild Government of our once happy land had made prosperous, and who had been made arrogant by the obsequiousness of the people of the Free States, who had for years humored them to keep them quiet.

CHAPTER XIII.

"Great, noble heart."

CLARA now proved a solace and support to her imbecile, hesitating mother. That young lady inherited enough of her father's spirit, blended with some of the gentler traits of her mother's character, to make her truly energetic and noble. As good old Hannah had it, "she han't a bit of her father's ugly, as I see, nor her mother's foolish, scarry feeling; she is n't afraid of nothin' in the world."

"She likes the Yankees, you'd better believe," said Sam, a house servant, to Hannah, one day, just before the Federals advanced to capture Warrenton; "I seed her walking with a young man who belongs to that State Massa hates so bad. I wonder what he'd say or do if he only knowed it."

"I guess he won't know it from me or you, will he, Sam?"

"No; sure's my name's Sam, I won't let him be told on 't if I can help it."

"But, Sam, how come you to know that this young man come from de State of Masschusetts? dat's de place Massa swears 'bout so much, is n't it?"

"Yes, Masschusetts the place, and I b'lieve young Missus got frightened at a runaway horse, or su'thin' like it, and dis young Yankee offered hisself to see her home."

"Maybe you don't know all," said Hannah, with

an air of mystery that puzzled Sam; and Sam did not know all, for even Clara's mother did not even imagine the intense interest her daughter felt in knowing something more of her mother's relatives.

Clara knew that troops from Massachusetts had been quartered near them; that is, within a few miles of their home. "How I wish," said she, mentally, "that brother was the daughter, instead of myself, and yet," checking herself, "that is n't right. I don't feel as I ought; Hannah would say, 'go to God and ask for what you want.' I wish I could be sure that He hears when I pray, always. I think He has sometimes answered me; but then, as Hannah says, it may not be right for me to have what I ask for, so I must trust. I will pray that a way may be opened for mother to hear from her friends; surely it will be right for me to make this request," said she, aloud.

"It is right to ask the bressed Saviour for anything, Miss Clara, if ye 're only willing He should n't think fit to give ye jest what ye ask for."

Clara started, for she had thought herself alone, until she heard the voice of the good old servant. "Dear chile," said the faithful creature, "don't never forget to pray; if anything troubles ye, go ter yer Saviour with it."

"That is what I am resolved to do, Hannah. I have lately been led to believe that my mother has friends now living in the State of Massachusetts, and do so want her to hear from them, and I want, too, to know them myself, that I don't think it can be wrong for me to pray that a way be opened for us to get word to them."

"Wrong? no, indeed, honey; it is right, and the

dear Lord put that thought inter yer young heart, I do b'lieve."

Thus encouraged, Clara went to that God who seeth in secret, and in childlike simplicity and faith, laid her trials before Him. "If it will be for thy glory," she prayed, "restore my dear mother to the love and sympathy of *her* mother. Will it not be right, O Lord, for my father to let her write to her friends? Lord, do thou open a way for this to take place."

Never was a more sincere petition offered to the sovereign Father than this. Mrs. Murray's heart was oppressed with strong and conflicting emotions. Sometimes she was tempted to send a letter through the Federal lines, to her long-deserted friends; she half resolved to do so, and then came the painful thought that they might be dead, or, if living, refuse to answer her; and then, if her husband should know of her having set at naught his authority in this, she feared her life would be made intolerable; he had many times told her that if she should ever *seriously* offend him, he would never forgive her. He might deprive her of the society of her children, to gratify his resentment, and then her life would become a living death.

She was full of apprehension, continually, lest she should be required to take some stand in regard to her sentiments. Every day brought changes to many, within a few miles of her; how could she feel secure? The Rebel flag had floated over her house, and that had protected her, at the time of which we are writing, from Rebel violence, for a time, yet it did not ever; in her inmost soul she detested the sight of the foul thing, and would have raised the "stars and stripes," had she not feared the anger of her husband.

"Was ever woman more troubled," inquired she, mentally, "than I, at this moment?" at the instant a text from which she had heard a sermon preached in her girlhood, came into her mind, causing her acute pain for the time.

"Yes," she murmured sadly, "it is true, 'the way of transgressors is hard,' how hard I never could have imagined. Were it not for my children, I should be tempted to wish I had never been born."

As Mrs. Murray sat in her chamber one day, indulging in such sad, unavailing regrets, she was startled from her morbid reverie by receiving news of the fall of her husband. He had fallen, it was reported, in one of those seven days' engagements in the vicinity of Winchester and Warrenton. Clara had brought a paper containing a notice of the death of Colonel Murray, but there were no particulars given, and the daughter was inclined to doubt the correctness of the statement. She wished to go out and learn if possible something in regard to the truth or falsity of the report, and it was while abroad on this errand, that she was knocked down by a runaway horse, and taken up and cared for by a Union soldier, with whom Sam had subsequently seen her walking.

Clara's prolonged absence had given her mother uneasiness, and she was anxiously watching for her return, from a window, when she was surprised to see her approaching the house slowly, leaning upon the arm of a gentleman dressed in the United States uniform. Unable to command her feelings of interest and curiosity, she hastened to the hall, and as the door was opened by a waiter, stepped forward to ask if anything had happened to Clara.

"Nothing serious, madam," replied the young man, who was none other than Raymond Philips; "she has been knocked down and sadly frightened, but I am happy to say that she is nearly recovered from the effects of both."

"O, mother," exclaimed Clara, forgetting in her zeal, that she was transgressing the rules of propriety in neglecting to invite her protector into the house; "this gentleman is from Massachusetts, and he is acquainted with a lady whose name is Jenkins, who lives in Oak Dale; maybe she is your sister."

Mrs. Murray cordially invited Raymond to enter, saying, "I should love to converse with you about the old Bay State."

He politely declined her invitation, however, informing her that his duties forbade him the pleasure, then, but he would be glad at some future time to give her any information in regard to Massachusetts which she might desire. Then, bowing politely, he began to descend the steps.

"Stop one moment," exclaimed Mrs. Murray, "you must give me an opportunity to express my gratitude to you for your kindness to my daughter; I am sure, I thank you most sincerely."

"I should have been less than a man had I done otherwise, under the circumstances, madam; I do not merit thanks."

"I think otherwise," and then she returned his good by, reluctantly, as he walked away at a rapid pace towards the Union camp

CHAPTER XIV.

*"This above all—to thine own life be true,
And it must follow, as the night the day,
Thou canst not then be false to any man."*

CLARA had not been able to get any information in regard to her father; the fact was, that meeting with the accident, and so soon afterwards with the soldier from the very State her mother so wished to hear from, had, for the time being, caused her to forget an item of news she did not believe. On being asked by her mother, she was obliged to confess that she had been guilty of forgetting her father, in her anxiety for *her* to have, if possible, some communication once more with her friends.

"Why, mother, I don't believe father is dead; we certainly should have been informed of the event in a different way, if he had been killed in battle."

"We ought to hear from him if he is living, for a letter has been due some days already; you know we have looked some time for an answer to our last."

"I know that, but something may have happened to prevent his writing."

"It may be," said Clara, "that he is a prisoner."

News from the father and husband came that very hour, that was thought reliable; he had been captured, and was a paroled prisoner at Washington.

"This is good news compared with the other, is n't it, mother?" said Clara.

"Yes, my dear. I don't believe your father will suffer anything as a prisoner, more than the mortification of temporary defeat, and that cannot be much."

"I should say it was just nothing at all; and I am not sorry that he is sure to be away for a little time, because I do so want to learn something more from that young man about your sister. He told me that he wrote home often, and would make inquiries of some of Mrs. Jenkins's family, respecting her relatives."

"I don't suppose the man will ever give you, or the subject that interests you so deeply, another thought. I would cease to think about those things, daughter, if I was you; it only troubles you, and it makes you grow old too fast, to worry so much."

"Don't you care to know if this Mrs. Jenkins, spoken of, is your sister?"

"Yes, I care a great deal; but there is so little probability of my ever knowing anything satisfactory about my friends, that I try to forget my own situation."

"But, mother, are you content to sit down and see the Government you love overthrown, without saying that you do not sympathize with traitors, even?"

"No, Clara, I am not happy; but I don't know what to do."

This conversation was held one afternoon, in the chamber of the mother; the daughter could not sit down quietly, so she paced the floor with an uneasy tread, the while.

"I cannot set myself about anything, mother; I never was so restless in my life. I am lonesome, too; I don't see anybody, hardly, but those who talk so fiercely about Southern independence, that they provoke and disgust me, and I feel shut out from every good we might have."

"Don't be ungrateful," said Mrs. Murray, "but look at some who have suffered for opinion's sake, while you are not disturbed, although there is as much reason you should be, as some who have been martyred for their loyalty."

"One may as well be turned out of house and home, as live as we do."

Just then there was a ring at the hall door. "I hope that is something or somebody to bring some change," said Clara.

A few moments later a servant came into the room, and told Mrs. Murray that a young Yankee officer was in the parlor, and wished to see herself and daughter. Clara clapped her hands in delight. "It must be that same young man."

"It is, Miss Clara," said the servant.

The young lady waited to hear no more, but hastened to descend the stairs. She bethought herself, however, ere she reached the bottom, and waited for her mother to lead the way into the parlor. The young lieutenant arose with a graceful bow, at their entrance, and both Mrs. Murray and Clara recognized him as the companion of Clara's walk homewards, on the day of the accident.

"Have you heard from your friends?" asked Clara, impatiently.

"I have, and have had an answer to a letter in which I made the inquiries I promised to."

"Oh," said Clara; but checking herself, she quietly asked, "is the Mrs. Jenkins, with whom you are acquainted, my mother's sister?"

"She is, and I have a letter which she enclosed in a packet to myself. Here it is," said Raymond, at the same time taking from his pocket a missive, and handing it to Mrs. Murray. The stay of the young officer was brief, but Clara told him, ere he left, that she wished the "stars and stripes" had been placed over their heads, as it would represent their feelings.

"I'm not secesh," said she, and I want to go somewhere, where I can speak as I think. You'll hear of us at the North, sometime, I am certain."

Mrs. Murray felt an interest in the Yankee soldier; she felt that a friend had gone when he took leave of them, for he kindly offered to enclose a letter in a packet with his own letters home, if she wished to reply to her sister's letter.

"I presume its contents will not be contraband," said he with a smile.

"Not to the United States Government," said the lady, as he bowed and withdrew, after handing Mrs. Murray his address.

It was with mingled emotions that Mrs. Murray broke the seal of the letter she had held with trembling hands since it was given her.

"Mother, why are you so long about opening that missive? why, I am quite impatient to know its contents," said the daughter.

"Hope and fear alternately taking each other's places in my heart, affects me so much that I am hardly in possession of my reason; I am very nervous."

"What do you fear, mother, from your friends, when they have addressed you without waiting for you to write first?"

"O, Clara! you cannot imagine my feelings. But you may read this letter aloud, and then I shall know the worst at once," said Mrs. Murray, as she handed the important missive to her daughter.

Clara took from its envelope a small sheet of note paper, and read with eagerness the following:—

"I cannot, my dear sister, deny myself the privilege of communicating a few thoughts to you, as I have an opportunity to send a letter, although I have some reason to fear that it may not be acceptable. A young friend has written to my daughter an account of a little adventure he had with a young lady, who, I am persuaded, is your daughter. This friend spoke of the anxiety expressed by this dear girl, to know something about her mother's relatives. I hope her mother is not feeling indifferent still, in regard to the mother who bore her, and whose heart has bled for years at the thought of the unnatural estrangement of a much-loved child. My heart goes out in tenderness towards your daughter, while it yearns to clasp a sister who can *love* me, to my heart. Would you could come to your Northern friends now, if you have not ceased to love us. I hardly dare hope for an answer to this, and yet, what your daughter said to Mr. Philips, or the manner in which she spoke of her mother's friends, bids me hope your neglect has not been wholly voluntary on your part. The bearer of this to you, will, with pleasure, forward a letter from yourself to your affectionate sister,
"B. JENKINS.

"OAK DALE, *August*, 1862."

Mrs. Murray wept, even sobbed convulsively, as she listened to the tender words addressed to her, by this long-neglected relative. As soon as she became sufficiently composed to write, she penned an answer.

"My ever dear, though sinfully neglected sister: I thank you for your letter; how grateful I *do* feel, you cannot know. I have acted an unnatural part, my dear Bessie, I confess. I have not wished to be estranged from yourself, mother, or my other friends at the North, yet I have been unable to do as I have wished. I long to see our mother and yourself very much. Does mother still love me? My daughter is very anxious to know you. I hope I shall be permitted to see you once more on earth. I do not like to live in this region now; I have not a particle of sympathy with this wicked Rebellion. My husband does not view things as I do at this crisis, and I don't know what to do. Your kind letter is indeed a God-send at this time, to my faint heart. My children, too, are a comfort, without which, I feel that I should die. My dear sister, write to me again, and love and pity your afflicted sister,

"CLARA MURRAY.

"*August* 30, 1862."

When Mrs. Murray had written the preceding letter, she leaned back in her chair, and covering her face with her hands, gave herself up for the time, to perplexing thoughts.

Clara entered the room, and perceiving the letter and position of her mother, requested permission to add a postscript to her aunt. Her mother readily consented, and she sat down and wrote the following: —

"MY DEAR AUNT: —

"Although I have never seen you, and but recently heard that I had such a relative, I feel it a privilege to be allowed to address you. I want much to see you, and so does my brother Edgar. I have no sister, and only this brother, who, with our mother and the servants, at present compose our family.

Perhaps I feel more interest in you because you belong to the North; for since I have been old enough to understand right from wrong on the agitating subjects discussed in our country, my sympathies have ever been with the people of New England. I have known some very good and very intelligent people who came from the land of the Puritans, and it has made me love that part of the country very much; and since I have learned that mother has friends there, I feel as if I could fly to reach the place. Do write to mother again as soon as you can. I don't want to be an undutiful child, dear aunt, still, I do not and can not think it right for my mother to be kept from her friends, just to gratify my father's pride. What if our relatives are not as wealthy as father is, they are good; they are worth as much as if they were rich. I think mother ought to visit her Northern friends, and brother and myself never mean to cease urging her to do so, until she goes to her girlhood's home once more. I am very, very glad that I have seen Mr. Philips; I hope his regiment will not be ordered away for a long time to come, for I love to have the Union soldiers so near us. We hear that father is a prisoner, but we don't believe that he will be shut up in any *loathsome* prison. I cannot tell you how sorry I am that he is not a friend to the good old Union; and I cannot tell you either how troubled I am at the state of affairs here in the South. I am determined not to stay here if I can get mother and Edgar away with me. Give my love to grandmother, who I am glad to learn is still living and well; and ask her to pray that we may be able to leave this now, to me, hateful place. Pray too, yourself, dear aunt, for your unseen niece,

"CLARA MURRAY.

"*August* 30, 1862."

What have you written, my daughter?" inquired her mother, as Clara laid down her pen.

"You can read my long postscript, mother."

"Will you read it to me, my dear?"

Clara willingly complied with this request, and her mother was surprised at the rapidity with which her daughter had written, for she had been busy with her pen but a few moments.

"Why, Clara, how much you have written," exclaimed she, as her daughter finished reading her letter. "I wish I could write as fast, and I wish I was gifted as a writer, so that I could earn a livelihood, if anything should make it necessary for me to take care of myself and family."

"Isn't it strange, my dear mother, that I have wished the same thing for myself? It seems to me, that something is likely to take place that will make a change in our situation."

"The times threaten evil, certainly," replied Mrs. Murray, "and I would like to be prepared for the worst that may come upon us."

Just then a heavy step was heard in the passage; the door of the room was opened, and Col. Murray stood before them. The wife arose and advanced to meet her husband, while Clara took the letter which was lying unfolded upon her mother's writing-desk, and laid it in a drawer of a bureau which stood near her. Her father had perceived the letter as he entered the room, and ever jealous lest his wife should hold communication with her friends, he at once resolved to know its contents. After greeting his wife and daughter, and learning that affairs at home were in much the same condition in which he had left them, he turned to Clara, and remarked, with some appearance of carelessness—

"I should suppose you had amused yourself at times by using your pen, in your hours of loneliness."

"I have written a little, father, for I love to write, you know," was the daughter's quiet reply.

"What have you written on the sheet I saw you put by, daughter? I feel interested, and would love to see your manuscript."

"I don't feel that it would be worth the trouble of a perusal, father."

"I think I must be the judge in regard to that."

"But, father, you will not insist that I shall expose any girlish sentiments I may have penned to another, to you; you are too generous to do so."

"What have you been writing, a love-letter?"

"No, I have not; my missive is addressed to a female friend."

"What is the name of this friend, Clara?" asked Col. Murray, studying the countenance of his daughter in the mean time.

Clara did not reply at once; she would not utter a falsehood, and she dreaded the storm which she feared would burst upon her mother's head if she mentioned the name of her aunt. For herself she feared little; hers was not a timid nature, and her courage was strengthened by the unhappy circumstances in which her mother was placed. "I can bear anything myself," thought she, as she sat considering what she ought to do, "but my poor timid, sensitive mother; and then, if father should place Edgar away from us or from her it would be terrible."

"I am waiting for your reply, Clara," said her father, thus abruptly intruding upon her reflections, in no very gentle mood. "I insist upon knowing the name of your correspondent, at once."

Swiftly came to the mind of the trembling girl those precious words of sacred truth, "What time I am afraid, I will trust in thee." Her heart responded to them, and leaving results with God, she answered in a mild, yet firm tone, "I have been writing to my aunt Jenkins."

"Your aunt Jenkins," repeated her father, in a scornful tone; "and who, pray, authorized you to write to that plebeian woman? or, I should ask first, who told you that you had such a relative?"

"I was not told to address her by any one; I wrote to her because I wished to; and providentially, I learned that I had such a relative, although,——" here Clara hesitated, and sat silent a minute.

"Go on," said her father, angrily. "Go on; although what?. I would hear all you have to say."

"You seem angry, father, but I would not offend you," said Clara, rising and approaching him.

"Sit down, and tell me what it was you hesitated to say."

"It was, that I have wondered, ever since I was old enough to think, that my mother had not relatives as well as yourself, father; and I have asked mother, but she has always evaded my questions upon the subject, so that I had come to the conclusion that there was some horrible mystery hanging over her birth. Had mother told me her friends were all dead, I should have rested content; but her desire always to evade my questionings, led me to think, and to think a great deal. Edgar, too, has sympathized with me in these feelings, and because we could n't talk with others about our anxieties, we have talked with each other. You need not blame my mother," said the heroic girl, seeing her father glance angrily at his wife; "if there is any blame, I deserve to have it laid upon me."

"Give me the letter you have penned, Clara," said her father.

The young lady arose and walked leisurely to the bureau, opened the drawer, and handed the unfolded sheet to her father, whose face, as he perused it, grew black with passion. When he had finished reading it, he tore it to atoms, then arose, and stamping furiously at his wife, asked her how she dared to disobey him thus. Terrified beyond measure, she could scarcely articulate, but at length she spoke mildly, saying, "It surely is not a crime for me to wish to hear from my own dear mother and sister."

"It is a crime for you to disobey your husband. You will pay dearly for this, madam."

The timid woman was about to reply, but ere she could speak, Clara confronted her angry father.

"You, my father, have forgotten," said she, looking earnestly into his excited countenance, "that the Bible says wives and children are only to obey their husbands and parents, in the Lord. They are not to disobey God, to please any one. Mother owes her relatives duties, as well as you."

"And you dare stand here and say that to me," said the angry man.

"Yes, father, I dare, even if you knock me down for saying it, because it is sacred truth; I would not be impertinent, but I must say that my mother has been wronged, is still wronged, by you; my dear father, don't wrong her any more, but vent all your anger upon me; I am strong, and can bear it. It was

I who desired and urged mother to try and communicate with her relatives, and I will never give up my efforts until I am acquainted with them myself."

Clara paused, and still keeping her eyes upon her father's face, waited for him to speak. He regarded her a moment in silence ; it was plain he felt that he had not one like her mother to deal with, in his daughter. When he spoke, it was in a husky tone. He said, " and this from you, a girl scarcely eighteen years old. Remember, miss, you may be disinherited for your disregard of my authority, if you don't repent of your folly."

"I do not defy your rightful authority, but I do know that we must obey God rather than man."

"The Bible says a wife is to forsake father, mother, and every friend for her husband ; and I'll make you all feel that my authority is not to be treated lightly, with impunity ; and I command you, Mrs. Murray, and you, Clara, to stay within the enclosure of this yard until I give you permission to go beyond it."

The chivalrous gentleman did not wait for an answer, but walked from the room with stately step, and entered his library.

CHAPTER XV.

"God has put the veil of secrecy before the soul, for its preservation."

"WHAT if Lieutenant Philips should call here while father is in such a mood," thought Clara; "he must not;" and she mentally resolved to prevent his calling. She took her pen and wrote a few hasty lines, informing him that, for reasons she could not then explain, she feared to have him come to the house at present; and thanking him for his kind and polite attention to her family, she committed to his care a hastily written note to her aunt. It was as follows:—

"DEAR AUNT:—
"My mother wrote a loving answer to your kind letter, and I added a long postscript, by her permission; but the letter fell into hands that destroyed it. We will write to you again as soon as we can. Pray for us, dear aunt; we need the prayers of those who love to pray. I don't know what will befall us in these dark times. Good by.
"Your troubled niece,
"CLARA MURRAY."

Clara didn't know how to reach Raymond herself, but she knew that she could trust faithful Hannah to invent a plan by which to get her note to him; so as that servant entered her room soon after she had finished her little missive, she told her in a low tone that it was very desirable that the note should in some way be taken to Lieut. Philips, without delay.

"Can you get it to him, Hannah?" asked Clara, with some agitation of manner.

"Bress your heart, honey, ye can trust me for dat; I knows all 'bout it, I specs; don't worry your young heart, only look ter de Lord, and 't 'll all come straight in good time." So saying Hannah concealed the note about her person, and pretended to be busy in the room near the library for a few minutes, then hastened away to do her errand.

Clara's heart beat anxiously. Her mother sat in the same position in which her husband had left her, with her head bowed low upon her hands, that rested upon a table near which she sat. She had been too much absorbed to notice what Clara had done, and her daughter did not think it best to disturb her with the anxiety she knew a knowledge of it would cause her.

"She has enough to bear already," reflected Clara, "O, is it not true that one's foes shall be of their own household? I wonder if these are the terrible days predicted by our Lord? In any case, however, all I need be anxious about is to know my duty, and do it fearlessly. I must try to comfort mother; how I wish she was a Christian."

With these thoughts filling her mind, she took a seat upon a low ottoman standing by her mother's feet. "Mother," said the dutiful girl, as she leaned her head lovingly upon the arm of her afflicted parent, "don't give up all as lost; cheer up, we shall find a way out of this; I am sure we shall, only keep up good courage."

"My dear, dear child," exclaimed Mrs. Murray,

wringing her hands in a despairing manner, "but for you and your brother I should wish now to die; I am not prepared I know, but what can I do?"

"Don't feel so sadly, mother; I wish you were a Christian; you would be so much stronger if you could only lean upon God."

"Would I were a Christian, Clara."

"You may be, my dear mother; God is waiting for you to make Him your portion."

"My dear daughter," was all the mother could say, while she kissed the cheek of her noble child, with a feeling that she was not utterly desolate while she possessed such a blessing.

Edgar at this moment entered the apartment. He approached very near his mother and sister, and asked in a whisper what had made his father so angry. "Why," said he, "he has been stamping his feet upon the floor, and walking the room with rapid strides for ever so long. I have n't spoken with him since he came home, for I did n't dare go into the library where he is."

"He is offended with me," said Clara, "because I wrote to Aunt Jenkins. He came in unexpectedly, saw my letter, read and destroyed it, and I don't know what he will do next."

"I fear, Edgar," said the mother, "that you will be sent away from us."

"Don't worry about that, mother," replied the boy, "I can take care of myself; and even if father takes me into the army, I can manage to get away, and you may depend that in case he sends me anywhere from you, I shall find a way, if my life is spared, to get to your relatives at the North, where I hope I shall see you, before a great while. So don't be unhappy, will you, dear mother?"

His mother folded him in her arms. "Hush," said she; "hush, don't breathe a thought of what you intend, to any one."

"Let me alone for keeping my own counsel," replied the boy, in a soft whisper. "I wonder folks don't stop to consider how they teach children and servants to be artful, by being too exacting in their demands," said Clara. "I have been practising in scheming ever since this war began, and even longer," she continued, "though I don't love to do so at all."

Mrs. Murray sighed deeply, but made no other response, for the thought came like a dagger to her heart, that she, by her foolish vanity and love of display, had placed those dearest to her in the unhappy condition they then were. The ringing of the bell for tea, at the usual time, smote upon the ears of Mrs. Murray and her children that evening. The summons came all too soon; they did not feel the need of refreshment; they could not eat, so they remarked to each other.

"But we must go down," said the mother; and she arose and led the way, followed by her children. The husband and father entered the supper-room as they descended the stairs, and they all sat down to the table together. The party was silent; this could not be termed a social board. Little was eaten, except by Mr. Murray. Edgar made a show of eating, but most of the food to which he had been helped, remained upon his plate. As for Mrs. Murray and Clara, they pretended to eat nothing; they tried to swallow, but found they could not.

When Mr. Murray had finished his meal, he leaned back in his chair and regarded his family a few moments, without speaking. Then, pushing his chair back from the table, he said, he felt himself a much-abused man.

"Even my wife is arrayed against me; my daughter, too; but I shall take care this accursed influence reaches no farther. You, madam," said he, addressing his wife in a stern tone, "shall not practise your wiles upon my son."

"I have never said aught to influence the minds of my children contrary to your orders," replied his wife.

"That is so, father," said Clara. "I did not get my ideas of things from hearing my mother's sentiments, for she has never, until within a few days, spoken her thoughts at all."

"Yet she has looked them for years. You, Clara, dare not say you have not read in your mother's countenance, disapprobation of my course."

Clara did not reply for a moment.

"Speak, you minion, and tell me the truth."

"It is true, father, that since I have been able to reason, I have felt as I do, in regard to the Government. It is also true that I have studied my mother's countenance for years, hoping to read sympathy with my own feelings in its expression. Of late, I have felt that, although she labored hard to keep her feelings concealed, I have been able to read them."

"Have you no sympathy for me, ungrateful girl?"

"Not in your feelings towards the dear old stars and stripes, father."

"Don't speak again in that way of that accursed symbol of tyranny, in my hearing," said the deluded man.

"Mr. Murray," said his wife, in a meek tone, "you reverence our patriotic forefathers, do you not?"

"I do; but what of that? it has nothing to do with the point in question."

"I was thinking how very noble your grandfather was to bear patiently, not only the heavy burden laid upon him for his country, but also the want of his wife's sympathy. He tried to persuade her to think as he did, yet he did not coerce her, and he left her in charge of a large family of children, that were as dear to him as they were to their mother."

"Well, what is that worth? because old Colonel Clifford acted in this respect like a fool, it does n't follow that I must."

"Yet he acted nobly toward his family, you will admit."

"Nonsense. A man is head of his own household. I contend that a wife forfeits her claim to her husband's regard and protection, too, when she dares utter sentiments at variance with those he cherishes."

"No, husband; not if her opinions and sentiments are in accordance with the word of God; for we are commanded to obey God rather than man."

"Do you claim, madam, that the Bible sanctions your admitting beneath my roof a plebeian Yankee, whom I despise?"

"I feel justified, under the circumstances, certainly. I know I have not done you a wrong; I would not wrong you; I never have, excepting in one way, and I pray I may never be guilty of doing as I have done, again, in that respect."

Mrs. Murray was aroused; she spoke with warmth, not angrily, but earnestly, and with a strength she had never before felt. Her husband was surprised at the vigor she evinced; for she had been so long in the habit of yielding silently to his control, that he thought she could not do otherwise. He could not but respect the womanhood that he saw developed in her, yet felt chagrined at the evidence that she was beginning to act as a free moral agent, accountable to a higher power than his own. She had confessed that she had wronged him; he must know in what way. In an authoritative tone, he bade her tell him. She hesitated, not wishing to provoke him.

"Tell me," he vociferated in thunder tones; "I have a right to know your every thought."

"If you will not be angry, I will cheerfully tell you, my husband."

"Do so, then."

"Well, if I must, I can in a few words. I have long and often violated my conscience to please you, my husband. I have incurred the curse of my heavenly Father, for my undutifulness to one of the best of mothers, and I pray that I may be kept from this great sin in the future."

She paused. Clara looked upon her mother with a feeling of admiration she had never felt before.

"I did n't know what was in mother until now," thought this dear girl, while a feeling of gratitude glowed in her young heart. Her father was nonplussed for the moment, yet his anger was kindled to a fiercer flame than ever. He stamped and raved like a madman.

"What," said he, shaking his chivalric fist in the faces of both wife and daughter, as he walked the floor furiously. "A wife and daughter set up a standard of right, independent of their husband and father! I'll make you feel that I am not to be disobeyed with impunity. You shall both suffer for your temerity."

Thinking to execute his unprincipled threat, he ordered a servant to have the wardrobe of his son ready to take from home in a day or two, when he himself should leave.

"How large a trunk shall I pack for him, massa?" inquired Hannah, with a sorrowful expression of countenance; and her face was a true index to her heart, which was sad indeed. Having heard most of the conversation that had been held in the house since the return of Colonel Murray, she was prepared by her previous knowledge of his terrible temper, to expect the worst. She had secretly resolved to do all in her power to get her mistress away from her home, away from the wrath of that infatuated man.

"He's crazy, sure 'nough," thought she.

While Hannah was thinking these thoughts, which her master "*could not bridle,*" he was walking with furious step, backward and forward across the room. As he approached her in his walk, he paused a moment and gave orders to have a moderate-sized carpet-bag made ready for Edgar. One that would hold two or three changes of apparel; and that must be made to do, he said. "See," said he, "that my orders are obeyed."

"Yes, massa," said the servant, as she left the room.

She did obey her master's orders to the letter; she made ready the carpet-bag as she had been told.

"I hope I'll be forgiven, if I am doing what aint right," said Hannah, mentally, as she hurriedly packed the wardrobe of Edgar. "I aint doing this for him to go with his 'stracted father, an' I pray my heavenly Father to send the poor boy far away from these terrible things. I'd die e'ena'most, if I thought the poor, dear boy would have to go 'mong them Rebels. I hope Sam wont be found out in his journey; if he don't, we 'll git 'long, but if he does, he 'll be killed sure, for massa's blood is up, bilin' hot, I do bleve."

Mrs. Murray's heart bled, as she reflected upon her situation, and that of her children. "I could easily bring fair weather to my home again, if I could only tell my husband that I sympathize with him, now, but I dare not. I feel that he is wrong, all wrong. I dare not, for the sake of pleasing him, pretend to what I do not feel. O, my offended Saviour," cried the wretched woman, as she threw herself upon her face upon the floor of her chamber, "I am sinful and lost; O, save me, for thy mercies' sake."

This prayer, as it came from the heart of this sufferer, was heard in heaven. Mrs. Murray soon arose from the hopeless attitude she had taken, with a feeling of trust in God, her Saviour, to which she had hitherto been a stranger.

CHAPTER XVI.

"Calamities come not as a curse;
—— struggle, thou art better for the strife,
And the very energy shall hearten thee."   TUPPER.

WHEN Clara left the supper-room, she went directly to her own chamber. Her heart was deeply burdened, and she felt that she must seek relief in prayer before she could talk with her mother. With the simplicity of a trusting child, she went to her heavenly Father, in her extremity; she asked that her mother might be sustained and brought to an experimental knowledge of the love and mercy of God; that her father might be turned from his sinful course, and that she might be assisted in her attempts to save her mother from greater suffering. She felt strengthened, as she sought her mother after an hour had passed, while she had been alone with her heavenly Father.

The first glimpse Clara had of her mother's countenance told of unwonted resolution, and when that loved relative expressed her determination to abide by the decision she had made in regard to her Northern friends, Clara was delighted. Mrs. Murray wondered at her daughter's joy, and told her it seemed strange to her that she could feel pleasure at such a time of trying uncertainty.

"I cannot help it, my dear mother," she replied; "it is true that, in our present circumstances, there is much that is depressing, still, I am pleased with your resolution to go on as you have begun, in regard to your duty to your relatives. Why, I don't know but I shall want to thank Mr. Jefferson Davis & Co. for bringing about this war, since it has opened your eyes to behold the wrong you were doing under cover of duty."

"O, that is what pleases you so much then, my daughter; the idea that you are to know your relatives."

"That is not all, mother; it is true I want to see my grandmother, aunt, cousins, and the place where you were born; it will be delightful to me; but the thought that you are aroused to a sense of the slavish, miserable condition in which you have lived, in order to keep peace, so many years, is the one great source of pleasure to me now."

"We shall be obliged to suffer, Clara, and I fear for you and Edgar."

"Don't worry about us; only be firm and determined to abide by the right, and a way will be opened."

"You are young to be a heroine, daughter; you don't know anything about the difficulties that may meet you in the way you have marked out for yourself."

"Mother, God says our strength shall be equal to our day. His word is sure."

"I wish I could feel that it is, continually," said Mrs. Murray, "I will pray that I may."

Little opportunity was afforded this mother and daughter to solace each other during the days that followed that on which Colonel Murray surprised his family by his unlooked-for return. The day appointed by this unkind husband and father to separate his family dawned, as he thought, auspiciously, to aid him. The breakfast-bell rang, and the family assembled and seated themselves at the table where was spread the morning repast. Colonel Murray scarcely noticed his wife or daughter until he had finished his own breakfast; then, without seeming aware that very few mouthfuls had been tasted by any one excepting himself, he moved his chair a few feet from the table, and announced his determination to those whom he styled unworthy to be called his wife and daughter.

"I am determined, madam," said he, addressing himself to Mrs. Murray, "to separate you from Edgar, from this time. He shall be influenced to regard you with the contempt you merit from him, as well as myself."

As these words were uttered by him who had been regarded by his wife with a feeling bordering on idolatry, the susceptible and unhappy woman fainted. A scene of confusion ensued which interrupted the Colonel for a time. He sat with lowering brow in unnatural silence, unmoved by the distress of her whom he had so deeply wronged. What was her suffering to him? She had it brought upon herself by daring to think and act according to the dictates of her own conscience. This, he contended, she had no right to do. Suffering might bring her to think as he wished her to; at any rate, she should be punished for her temerity, and so should Clara.

He was too much occupied to notice the egress of Edgar, which took place at the moment his mother was sinking to the floor, under the terrible blow his father had inflicted upon her peace of mind. The noble boy was spared a knowledge of this, for his haste took him immediately beyond the bounds of his father's estate, large though it was.

As soon as Mrs. Murray recovered partially from her swoon, and was able to look about her, she missed Edgar; yet she spoke not of his absence, but listened to the threats of her husband with less terror than ever before. There was something in the expression of her daughter's countenance that inspired courage, and led her to think of a power that was higher than that of her husband. When he told her she was to be a prisoner in her own house, she was unmoved by the threat, and he supposed she was sinking in the gloominess of despair, for her eyes were fixed upon the floor, as if she heard not. Yet she did hear, but her hope was becoming fixed upon the Rock of Ages.

Clara, too, was not dismayed at her father's threats, although she well knew the power of his anger. When he said to her, "I have arranged matters so that your detestable Yankee paramour will be shot if he ventures to pollute my premises again with his presence," she did not reply, neither did she faint. Her cheek paled, as she thought it was her father who addressed her thus, and she offered a silent petition to Heaven that his obdurate heart might be softened by divine grace. When her father told her she was to be put under the espionage of a neighbor, whom she had great reason to despise and dread, she offered no remonstrance, but her plans were formed, and she committed them and herself to God.

It was not until Colonel Murray was about to depart, that he missed his son; he supposed even then that he was somewhere about the place, taking leave of the people; and no wonder he thought so; for Edgar was a thoughtful, affectionate boy, and could not have been induced, under ordinary circumstances, to leave his home without kindly bidding each servant good by.

Upon inquiry, his father was told that he was nowhere to be found.

"Nonsense, you niggers," said he; "go and call him this minute, or I'll have you all whipped."

"De good Lord knows, massa, that we's looked an' called," said Sam, deprecatingly, "but we can't find him, sartin."

The Colonel went himself to every place about the house where he was likely to find his truant boy, but no boy was visible. Returning to the dining-room, which was still occupied by his trembling wife and exultant daughter, he demanded his son of them.

"I know not where he is," said the mother, alarmed at the rage manifested in her husband's manner.

"Neither do I know, father," said Clara.

"You lie," exclaimed the Colonel; "you've hid him somewhere; I don't believe a word you say, you vixen."

"Then I will say no more," replied Clara, mildly.

Her father approached her with his arm upraised, and his fist tightly clenched; she raised her eyes to his face, without flinching or speaking, yet something in the expression of her countenance caused the muscles of the arm uplifted against her, to relax, and the threatened blow was not given.

"Who has Edgar gone away with?" inquired Colonel Murray, drawing near his wife, and pausing for a reply.

"I don't know any more about it than you."

"If this is true, how do you know but he may be drowned, or killed by some accident?"

"I don't know."

"And yet I notice that you do not seem greatly distressed about the matter, madam."

"It is true I feel as if he is even now no more; but the trial to me is a choice of two great evils. It would grieve me more to have him taken from me by his father in anger, and placed amid the influences of traitors, than it would to have him removed by death as he now is, uncontaminated by the foul touch of treason, the blackest of crimes."

"And you dare speak this to me?"

"If I speak at all, I must speak the truth. You know I have never sympathized with you in your hostility to the United States Government; I have sacrificed my own feelings on every point to please you, because I blindly believed I owed you submission in everything, until my eyes were opened by your expecting me to subscribe to your opinions in regard to overthrowing our dear, good Government, to take a stand against the home of my childhood and youth, and my own relatives, also. With shame I confess I have neglected my mother, to please you, and wrongfully estranged myself from my own family. But I can do so no more; I must obey God rather than you. I wish you would allow me by your acts to obey you, too."

"Then, by all that is good, I swear you shall be turned out of my house. You are no wife to me, and you shall see that I will make this home too hot for your ladyship's comfort."

Mrs. Murray was not at all moved by this last vehement threat. Her home had been anything but comfortable, since the last presidential campaign. She felt that it was probable her husband might refuse her a home, for his pride would not, in these times, prevent his doing so. As she had confessed herself an enemy to the "Confederacy," he should not be disgraced among the chivalry, if he did turn her from his door. She would rather he should turn her homeless into the street, than place her under the espionage of the neighbor referred to, who was a relative, and one, too, who was somewhat dependent upon the patronage of Colonel Murray. This gentleman deferred his journey a few hours, in order to give more particular directions to those at home, and to have an interview with Mr. Smith, the individual before alluded to. He then left, without acquainting his wife or daughter of his designs. He had generally left money with his wife when he left home, but he did not at this time, although he did not know but she was in need of it.

After the departure of the Colonel, several hours passed quietly in the house of our friends; the calm was merely external, for Mrs. Murray was greatly troubled, lest the young Federal officer should attempt to call.

Clara was hopeful in regard to this, for she felt sure that her little note had been carried to him, although she had not been able to talk with the servant to whom she had entrusted it. She had perfect confidence in Hannah, and could not believe that money would bribe her to betray the trust committed to her. She was not so sure in regard to the other servants, who were not governed by religious principles, as was her good old nurse.

Sam loved his mistress, and Clara and her brother, too; but his master he did not love, and never had. He had been in the family from a boy, notwithstanding Colonel Murray has, as often as once every year, for a long period, threatened to sell "the scamp, be-

cause he could not understand his nigger nature."
When the Colonel left, Sam exhibited much regret
that he must leave without being able to take his son
with him; and he essayed to console the boy's father
with the thought that he would soon turn up.

"Ye sees, massa, I can't help being sangin, in 'gard
to his turnin' up all right, 'cause I don't see where
he'd go about here to stay; he dunno anybody any-
whar else, so if he aint dead, he sure to come."

"You don't know anything at all about it," was
the surly reply of Colonel Murray.

"Not's ye knows on," said Sam to himself, chuck-
ling. "Ye may sarch and sarch, but if I don't know
sartain, I specks he's where ye don't dare show your
face, old feller."

And he returned to the house, after seeing his master fairly on his way. There was great consternation
felt by the servants when it was ascertained that Edgar had disappeared. At first, they were fearful that
he was drowned; but as every place had been
searched carefully where such an event could have
occurred, they wondered greatly what could have become of him.

CHAPTER XVII.

' Away distrust ; —
My God hath promised : He is just."

How Clara wished for a strong-minded, sympathetic friend, to aid her mother and herself in this hour of need. Poor Mrs. Murray was greatly shocked at the idea that the father of her children could seem so estranged from his daughter and herself. She did not love to reflect that Edgar was learning to despise his father. She wished her children would separate the acts that were despicable from himself, and not forget that he was their father. She could not bear to have him estranged from herself; she felt lonely; how lonely, she realized that few could imagine ; and it is true that no being on this earth is so desolate as an ill-treated wife. A widow has the sympathy of the world to sustain her spirit ; yet the woman who is widowed in a sense far more deplorable than the one from whom death has taken a loving companion, is scoffed at, and left with a lacerated, bleeding heart, by the multitude, who practically say to her, as they pass by, "Keep away, for I am holier than thou." Mrs. Murray had often felt that the greatest trial that could come upon her, would be a separation from her husband.

Mrs. Murray had often thought, when she had known of a wife's leaving the home of the companion she had chosen for life, that her conduct was inexcusable. "Why did she not bear the trial," she asked, "and not expose herself to the censure of an ill-judging world? I will die before I will ever be separated from my husband." Poor Mrs. Murray had been very sincere in thinking thus, and she had too often reflected with pleasure that she had borne a great deal from her husband, whom she was forced, much against her feelings, to believe a despot in will; "and I shall bear to the end," she had often said to herself; "I have promised to be faithful as a wife, and I owe my husband my first duty."

Had Mrs. Murray remembered that only in the Lord had she promised to be faithful to her husband, and had she told him that she could not neglect the mother that gave her birth, and guided her to womanhood, without displeasing her God, and that, much as she loved him, she loved her Saviour more, God would have sustained her, and carried her, perhaps, through life, without having obliged her to feel the rod laid upon her in the form of taunts and jeers, from a world who were not fitted for judging her, because they did not, and could not, understand the circumstances in which she had been placed. How her poor heart ached, as she found her husband had executed his threat in regard to making her a prisoner. Shame wellnigh sunk her to the earth. Suspicions might have been entertained by some before that all was not just right in her home, but now it was known to be a fact. How could she bear the withering consequences of the disclosures that the past day had made?

"My punishment is greater than I can bear," she exclaimed in an agony of feeling, as a full sense of her situation was felt by her. She walked her room in anguish of spirit, for a time; then her eye rested upon a Bible; she stopped in her walk, took it up, and opened it. She read the expression of a soul, uttered when borne down by sorrow, and her soul caught the inspiration, and with one of old she exclaimed, "I will bear the indignation of the Lord, because I have sinned against Him." "Yes," said she, mentally, "I will bear this chastisement, and God will help me;" and as she unfastened the door of her room, and emerged from its solitude, she felt that she was overcoming, and could plead the promise made to those who have conflict with sin, and are enabled to overcome through the blood of the Lamb. She could bear to think now of leaving her elegant home, better than before; still, the thought of the wickedness that made it necessary that she should do so, was dreadful to her. Yet this spot so dear to her, was not the first lovely place that sin has defiled and polluted with its loathsome presence. It dared enter Eden in the guise of a serpent, and why should it not lift its hateful head in the beautiful mansions of the South?

"Could I only have the privilege of thinking as I wish, and see and hear from my relatives, how beautiful this place would seem," remarked Mrs. Murray to her daughter, whom she met in the hall soon after she left her room.

"It would, certainly," replied Clara; "but as we are situated now, it is only a very genteel prison."

"I know it," answered her mother with a sigh, "yet how are we to get away?"

"We must wait and be patient awhile, and if father does not come again to make any change, we will allow Mr. Smith to watch us for awhile, and I will watch him at the same time. He will relax his vigilance after awhile, for I heard him say to an acquaintance only this morning, that neither you nor I had pluck enough to do anything. We will let him glory in this opinion for a time, for it will facilitate our escape."

"But, oh, where can Edgar be? If I might only hear from him, I should be stronger to act, I think."

"My dear mother, let us believe that God will take care of him, and answer our prayers by guiding him to some friendly influence, by means of which your heart may yet be made glad. Let us trust him with God."

Mrs. Murray remained silent a short time, and then said firmly, "I can do nothing but leave him with God; where else can I look but to Him, or to whom else can I go in this hour of distress? This terrible waiting in suspense, and dreading untold evil. But we will wait and trust."

CHAPTER XVIII.

"Love, hope, and patience, these must be thy graces,
And in thine own heart let them first keep school."

"It may be thou art entered into a cloud, which will bring a gentle shower to refresh thy sorrows."

As Raymond Philips was standing in his tent door on the evening that Clara entrusted her note to Hannah, he saw a form approaching him, and looked long ere he determined that he was not experiencing an optical delusion. So singular did this figure appear, that when it drew near he was uncertain whether it was a man or woman. He gazed steadily until the spectral figure halted before him, and spoke, "Can you tell me, massa, where I can find Captain Philips?" asked the decrepit person in a strange voice.

"Are you sure it is Captain Philips you want," asked Raymond, kindly; may it not be Lieutenant Philips?"

"I want a young Yankee gentleman, what helped a young lady, when a hoss knocked her down one day," was the reply given.

"I assisted a young lady, not long ago, who was knocked down by a horse, and my name is Philips."

"Did you ever call at de Colonel's?"

"Colonel Murray's you mean, I suppose; if so, I have called there."

The head of the figure nodded as if in approbation of what the young officer had uttered.

"But," Raymond interrogated, "who are you?"

"I's a friend to de dear young lady, Miss Clara, I's no enemy."

These last words were spoken in the lowest tone possible.

"Have you a message, or anything for me, that your young mistress has sent?"

"Will ye tell me what State ye come from?"

"To be sure I will. I belong to Massachusetts."

"Then I reckon ye're the one I want, so here's a letter for ye from my missus."

Raymond took the note handed him by the faithful woman, and she disappeared, but not as she had come. There was no longer any doubt existing in his mind in regard to her sex, or relation to the family in which he had become so deeply interested; still, he marvelled how she had managed to pass the guard, for he could not know that she had won upon the feelings of one who had authority to pass her in and out. This Hannah had done by means of her own contriving; she had taken some pies along with her, which she requested or rather got permission to sell to the soldiers in camp. She had sold them all for a mere trifle, too, ere she found the tent of the young officer she sought. Before she left the camp, Hannah remembered that she ought to have cautioned the Lieutenant about speaking of her having been there, so she returned to Raymond's tent just as he had read Clara's note. He saw her at the door, and requested her to stop there a few moments. He put the note addressed to Mrs. Jenkins, with the one that accompanied it, into his pocket, and then asked Hannah to go with him a few yards from any tent so that he might speak to her without risk of being overheard.

"Tell your mistress, that I will not call at her house again," said he, "and tell her, too, to send to me if she wants me to do anything for her."

"I will, tank ye, massa," replied Hannah, "and I want ye to 'member, and not tell anybody that I come here."

"I won't tell," said Raymond, "you need not feel afraid of that, only be faithful to your young mistress."

"Dat I will, honey, sure, for massa is dun gone off stark mad, 'cause missus and my young lady don't like such doins'."

Previous to hearing the unsophisticated remarks of this honest servant, Raymond had suspected that Mrs. Murray and her daughter knew something of the trials to which many people who were constant in their attachment to the dear old flag had endured. He was greatly interested in the welfare of Clara, and when he wrote to Bessie, he gave a glowing picture of her womanly loveliness in his letter. He also enclosed the tiny note to her aunt, which had been handed him by the faithful Hannah.

"How pleased Bessie will be," thought Raymond, "with my description of her unknown cousin. How glad I am, that Providence directed my footsteps where I can be a medium of communication between these sisters, who have been so long estranged from each other. And then, this cousin of Bessie's, it seems, is becoming something of a heroine. I would be glad to take this note in person to Mrs. Jenkins, and see her and Bessie when they read it."

Thus thought Raymond, and he was judging Bessie by his own feelings. He thought he judged her rightly; he thought he understood Bessie thoroughly, and he longed for a reply to his missive, feeling that he should enjoy, in sympathy, the pleasure Bessie would experience in reading the account he had given of her Southern friends. Days passed beyond the usual time that he was wont to receive an answer to his letters, and still no answer came. He was not much occupied with business at this time, so the days passed wearily in expectation. He waited more than a week, after he had a right to look for a letter, and as none came he determined to write again, thinking his missive had miscarried. He again wrote a very affectionate letter, repeating much that he had written before, and mentioned the fact that he had enclosed a note from Mrs. Murray's daughter to Mrs. Jenkins, which he hoped had reached her, although he feared it had not, as Bessie had not written a reply to his.

He stated also that he was convinced that Mrs. Murray and daughter were suffering for indulging Union sentiments, and for that reason, alone, he felt they had a claim upon his kindest regards; but they were relatives of Bessie beside, and he felt a lively interest in the welfare of both mother and daughter. He entreated Bessie to write without any delay when she should receive his letter.

CHAPTER XIX.

"The wicked work their woe, by looking upon love and hating it."

Raymond's letter containing the note of Mrs. Murray had been duly received by Bessie, and the note it contained was read and re-read by her mother, with feelings of joy. Bessie's pleasure was qualified; she read the description Raymond had given of her unseen cousin, and his expressions of interest in that young lady without a particle of unalloyed joy. Her countenance betrayed her feelings.

"Why, Bessie!" exclaimed her mother, "what has Raymond written to you to make you look so dolorous? I should think you would be delighted to hear from your cousin, you have been so anxious to know her."

"But," said Bessie, with an expression of dissatisfaction upon her countenance, "I did n't expect Raymond to go into ecstasies about her."

"Why, my daughter; are you not glad that he is pleased with her?"

"He might be pleased with her, and yet not think her so very lovely."

"How can he help it, if she is as he describes her?"

"He need n't have sent home a glowing description of her charms to me. I am not pleased; I don't care to hear of her loveliness through him."

"Bessie, read Raymond's letter to me, will you?"

"I suppose I can;" and Bessie proved that this supposition was right, by reading it to her mother. When she had finished reading, she burst into tears.

"What ails you, daughter?" tenderly inquired Mrs. Jenkins. I see nothing in that missive to bring tears. I think it is very affectionate, and I love Raymond more than ever before, for the nobleness of feeling he has manifested towards our almost stranger relatives."

"If Raymond loved me as he ought to, he could not think as much of any other woman, as he seems to think of my cousin. You know he was attracted towards her when he did not know but she was an enemy."

"True; but suppose she had proved to be an enemy and needed help, would you have respected Raymond if he had not run to her assistance?"

Bessie did not answer this question, and her mother went on. "I should have thought much less of him than I now do, and so would people in general."

"I don't care what people would think; I don't want Raymond to care for any woman, so much as he appears to for Clara."

"I am sorry you feel so, Bessie; you are jealous, and it is very unreasonable in you to feel so about your cousin. I am sure she is entitled to our warmest sympathy. I think, from what Clara says in this hastily written note, that her mother and herself must be very unpleasantly situated. I don't know what I can do for them, as they are so far away, unless, through Raymond, I could send means to bring them to our home."

"I don't want Clara to be here with Raymond

when he comes home, now that I know that he likes her so well."

"Nonsense! how do you know that she is not already engaged to some young man at the South, who will love her well enough to come here for her sake."

"She does n't sympathize with secession at all, Raymond says, so she won't be likely to leave her heart at the South."

"I don't suppose all the young men at the South sympathize with secession. Very many of them, I dare say, have hardly given it a thought, unless in relation to the draft, which they dread. The young men, South, have good tastes and warm hearts; at least, many of them; and it is n't to be supposed that your brilliant cousin has passed unnoticed in the circle to which she belongs, until now."

"O, dear!" exclaimed Bessie, with a sigh, "I wish Raymond had n't written so much about her, that's all."

"I hope it will be all," said the mother, "and that you will not continue to dwell upon Raymond's courtesy to a stranger in such a way as you have done; but answer his letter kindly and without delay."

But that day passed, and Bessie neglected to write to Raymond; and so did the next, as well as several succeeding days. Mrs. Jenkins penned a kind letter to her sister, and her mother, who came to spend a few days with her at this time, added a loving postscript to the daughter who had been so long estranged from her. Mrs. Jenkins wished to inclose her missive in a package with Bessie's letter, when hers was ready to send; but upon inquiry, she learned that her daughter had not written, or even commenced a letter. Both her mother and grandmother remonstrated with Bessie for her neglect, and endeavored to persuade her to write. For some days they were unsuccessful in their efforts, and Bessie contrived to let the time slip away without even taking up her pen.

"Don't you intend to answer Raymond's kind letter, my grand-daughter?" asked her grandmother, after waiting impatiently, day after day, to have her note on the way to Mrs. Murray.

"There is n't any hurry; he will be able to prize it more, if he expects it some time before it reaches him."

"You may cause him to expect it too long for your own happiness, my dear girl," said the old lady; "take the advice of one who has had experience, and don't pervert that which would be otherwise a comfort, to a sorrow."

"Your experience could never have been just like mine, grandmother; I think I know how to manage with Raymond Philips better than any one can advise me."

"Well, my dear Bessie, be careful and not manage too much; if you scorn this advice now, the day may come when you will wish you had heeded it."

Neither her grandmother nor mother could influence her to write; she cared not that her friends wished to inclose missives that would carry comfort to her afflicted aunt. Raymond had hurt her self-love, and she would show him that she felt hurt at his daring to write in a "strain of admiration" of another, when she ought to be all in all to *him*.

Mrs. Jenkins was obliged to send the letter she had written to her sister, to Raymond, and she penned a little note to accompany it, in which she tried to apologize for Bessie's not writing; but after many fruitless endeavors to think of something to say that would excuse her erring daughter, she could do no better than inform Raymond that Bessie felt indisposed to writing, although she hoped he would soon receive an answer to his last kind letter to her.

"Will you let me send this, without any word from you, to Raymond, Bessie?" asked Mrs. Jenkins.

"I've no message for him," was the unkind reply of the daughter, and the letter was mailed, and reached the young man, who read a portion of it with wonder and pain.

"Bessie not feel like writing to me," he mentally ejaculated; "what can it mean? I am sure I have never written a syllable that could offend her. I will sit down at once and acknowledge the receipt of Mrs. Jenkins's note, and entreat Bessie to tell me what has induced her to feel thus. Would she were less a creature of impulse; but, poor girl, I will try my best to comfort her."

Raymond did so, and wrote long and tenderly, too. He strove to convince Bessie that she was distrusting his love for her, when she concealed from him any cause of sorrow, and he besought her, in touching strains, to write to him without delay, and tell him all her heart.

"You may be assured, my dear girl," said he in closing, "that I cannot be happy when I know you are enduring disquietude."

This letter was despatched, and Raymond waited anxiously for an answer.

CHAPTER XX.

"It is a pang known only to the best, to be injured, well-deserving."

BESSIE was little moved by the earnest appeals of Raymond; she had become so much absorbed in her own selfish feelings, and dwelt so constantly upon her fancied wrongs, that she was poorly prepared to write a reply to his missive. The foolish girl wished it had been less affectionate, so that she might have an excuse for the indulgence of her wrathful, jealous feelings. As it was, she contrived to construe some sentences of the letter, so as to adapt them to her case.

"Why," thought Bessie, "does he seem so earnest to aid my relatives? He does n't know as I care much about them, and he need n't trouble himself so much for my sake; he knows this, or ought to guess it, at least. No, he does n't care so much to please me, as he does to exert his gallantry in behalf of my handsome cousin. I 'll write to him, perhaps, sometime, but it will be when I please. I am not so particular to please one who cares so much for others, at the risk of displeasing me."

Thus the poor child strove to think she had reason to ill-treat one of the best of friends. This last letter of Raymond's she decidedly refused to show to any one, or even to read portions of it aloud, in hearing of her mother or grandmother. Mrs. Jenkins was astonished and indignant at the perversity of her daughter.

"I ought, Bessie, to know whether it contains anything of interest to me," said Mrs. Jenkins, when her daughter had refused to tell any of the contents of the missive. "Tell me, does Raymond think he can convey my letter by any means to your aunt?"

"He says he will endeavor to, and there is no danger but what he will try hard enough, while there is a pretty girl to meet with, if he succeeds."

"Fie, my daughter, how childish you make yourself appear; I would rise above such littleness, and overcome these miserable feelings, if I were you," said Mrs. Clement, Bessie's grandmother.

"If I were you, I might," responded the granddaughter, in a surly tone; "perhaps you would think it a trifle to feel that some one beside yourself enjoyed the kind regards of a person who has promised to love you better than all the world beside."

"I should not feel that this was so, without a more substantial cause than you have at present."

"Every heart knows its own bitterness," said Bessie, sullenly.

"True, but some hearts create their own bitterness, and turn the sweets of life to gall. I fear that you are doing this now, and because I love you I tell you the truth, my dear girl."

"I don't feel as if it is the truth you have spoken to me, grandmother," said Bessie, "at least it is not true that I have not cause for unhappiness."

It was useless to talk with Bessie upon this subject, and her friends soon desisted from their persuasions. She had resolved to feel aggrieved, and she took great pains to carry her resolve into execution. It grieved her mother that she neglected Raymond, yet that lady knew not what to do, in order to influence her daughter's mind aright. She had tried persuasion without avail ; then ridicule, but to no better purpose. Severity was merited by the obstinate girl, she well knew, and she was half tempted to write to Raymond, and ask *him* to try the effect of it upon her.

Mrs. Jenkins was tried severely by the stand her daughter had taken, in more than one way, for it cut her off from free intercourse with the only one whom she could rely upon to communicate with her far distant sister. "I must write to Raymond, much as I feel ashamed to let him know the reason I am obliged to resort to such a measure," said Mrs. Jenkins to her mother, in presence of Bessie, when a week had elapsed since the second letter of the young man had been received.

"You need n't do any such thing, mother," said the daughter, "I am going to write myself, but Raymond wont be any too glad to get my letter, that is certain."

"Why, Bessie dear," remarked Mrs. Clement, "you would not surely be guilty of writing an unpleasant letter to a common acquaintance situated as our young friend is at present. Only think, he is away from home and most of the comforts of life, perilling his own noble life, to support the blessed institutions of our country. You cannot certainly be guilty of sending a missive to him that will not cheer his heart."

"He had no need to leave his home, and those he loved ; 'tis his own fault if he has made his condition uncomfortable. I shall write as I feel."

Such was the answer irreverently given by Bessie to her excellent grandparent. We must remark here, that we have endeavored to weave our story so as not to have particular characters recognized, yet it will not be our fault if some of our readers think we have brought them before the public.

The grandmother made no reply, save by heaving a deep sigh that would not be restrained. Mrs. Jenkins was silent until a few moments had past, at the end of which Bessie retired to her own room. When Mrs. Jenkins found herself alone with her mother, she gave vent to her long-restrained feelings in a flood of tears.

"I feel that as I have sowed, so I am now reaping," said she, as soon as she could control her emotions so as to articulate. "I have done wrong by my daughter, for I have indulged her to her hurt, and made her selfish and exacting. I have never realized that this was the case until recently. O, may I be forgiven," continued this unhappy mother, "and Bessie brought to see herself as she is, before she shall have estranged from her one of the noblest hearts that ever beat."

"Amen, I repeat, amen to that," responded Mrs. Clement.

"But, mother," said Mrs. Jenkins, "I must perform my duty to my misguided child, if I can but ascertain what that duty is."

"I do not see that you can do anything to benefit Bessie, besides making her case a subject of prayer, and evincing your disapprobation of her course; then you must leave her with God, who can subdue even the most perverse will."

While her friends were conversing thus, Bessie was busy in writing a letter to Raymond. She had slept quite a number of nights over the letters she had received from this friend, that had aroused her anger, and yet it cooled not. Heedless of the admonitions of those who loved her, she wrote in an angry, injured, jealous strain, to Raymond, in reply to his affectionate letter; then, without allowing her mother to see what she had written, or asking for any message from her, she hastily enveloped, sealed, and directed it; then, throwing on her shawl and bonnet, she hurried to the Post Office, and having deposited her letter, called upon an acquaintance and remained until evening. She did not see her mother until the following day, and that friend did not suspect what her daughter had done. Great, therefore, was the surprise of Mrs. Jenkins when, in a little more than a week from this time, she received a letter written by Raymond, in which was inclosed a note for Bessie, also one from Mrs. Murray.

Raymond very respectfully addressed Mrs. Jenkins, and stated that he could but feel thankful that he had been made a minister of comfort to her afflicted relatives, even if his acts should be misconstrued, and that result in the destruction of his fondest earthly hopes. One thought sustained him, although his heart was saddened by the thought that he had been misunderstood by one he loved, and had entrusted with his earthly happiness, and that thought alone gave him courage; it was, that he had acted from principle. He had endeavored to obey the golden rule.

Mrs. Jenkins did not ask to see, or hear read, the contents of the note her daughter had received. She watched Bessie closely, and she could easily discern the truth.

"Raymond, I think, has resented the neglect of Bessie," said she to her mother, the day after the note had been given her.

"I shouldn't be at all surprised if he has," answered Mrs. Clement, "for she seems really troubled now; it may be she will write at this time, and answer three missives at once."

Mrs. Jenkins replied to her letter, and again asked her daughter if she would send a note with her letter.

"I shall not write again to Raymond; he doesn't wish me to."

"How do you know that, Bessie?"

"Because he says it will be better that our engagement be suspended awhile, so that I can learn to view things in a different light."

"How could he learn anything about the light in which you see things; has any one written to him, think you?"

"I told him myself in a letter, last week; but I didn't think he would be so serious over it."

"Oh, Bessie, what have you done?" exclaimed her mother.

The daughter answered not, but hastened from the room. The perusal of the letter that Bessie so madly penned, was like a poisoned arrow to the heart of Raymond. It struck deep, very deep, because he felt it was so entirely undeserved. His reply to it was very brief, for he felt that

———"words were idle;
Words from him were vainer still,"

and he wrote only a short note, in which he kindly told Bessie that she wronged him, but that it would be well for their interests to be separated, at least for a time. Should she ever understand his motives of action, the case would be different; until that time, she might be sure of his friendship; communication with each other was useless, and had better end. Bessie felt, when she read the note, that she had risked too much when she sent him that letter, so full of reproach. In her heart, she wished she had been influenced by her friends, yet pride forbade the acknowledgment of these feelings. Gladly would she have replied to the last note, could she believe that Raymond would care to receive a missive from her under existing circumstances. She felt that he was angry with her, from principle, yet she was too proud to confess this truth, even to herself.

Raymond, too, suffered greatly. He blamed himself for having helped to strengthen Bessie in her exacting feelings. He reviewed the past with pain on account of his having been an accomplice with one in wrong doing, whom he was under sacred obligations to influence aright. Bitter was the thought that Bessie and himself were to be as common acquaintances to each other; still, he determined that it should be so, for it would be unkind in him to pass over without reproof, the manifestations of evil temper which Bessie had repeatedly given him.

He thought of a future for this girl whom he devotedly loved, darkened by the indulgence of base passion, and shuddered at the idea of what it might be. "I must help her to govern herself, if I can; if she is really attached to me, a little decision on my part will benefit her." And, although a pang shot through his heart as he thus reasoned, he continued firm in his resolve to cease indulging Bessie to her hurt.

CHAPTER XXI.

"Be ye long-suffering and courageous; abide the will of Heaven. God is on your side; all things are tenderly remembered."

GLOOMY days dawned and closed upon Mrs. Murray, while she remained a prisoner in her own home. Her husband did not remain long away, before he returned to seek Edgar, anew. He did not, however, deign to speak to either his wife or daughter, although they sat at the table with him, and he saw them frequently on various occasions. Clara ventured to address her father when he first returned home, but was repulsed by his stern silence, and did not attempt to do so again. Mrs. Murray wished to speak to him, yet dared not. His stay was not long, and he seemed perplexed in regard to the absence of his son. His wife pitied him from her inmost soul; how she longed to see him humanized, so that she could rush to his arms and weep upon his bosom. The affection of her children was a solace to her bleeding heart; yet her nature yearned for a stronger love, a love to protect her, as well as soothe her sorrow. But such a blessing was not allowed her.

The departure of Colonel Murray from his home was a relief to his wife and daughter, notwithstanding he had tightened the bars of their prison ere he left. He had questioned every servant, and he was sure that he could find out all the truth by some of them; of others, he was less sure. He was afraid to trust implicitly in Hannah or Sam; he therefore set others to watch them. He could not find out by Sam, whether the Yankee officer had called at his house in his absence, or not; for that servant delighted to tease his master, and, therefore, gave very evasive replies to all questions concerning that point.

"I asked you, you black dog, if that d—d Yankee has been here since I went away?"

"Wall, I telled, massa."

"What did you tell me, you rascal?"

"I telled ye as I could n't say he had, massa."

"Well, has n't he been here?"

"'Pears like he haint been about these parts lately. Specs he 's afeared to come; mebbe he 's hearn the crack of massa's pistol; golly! don't wonder he stay 'way."

Hannah, when questioned, replied frankly that she had not seen him. The other servants protested that nobody had been there but Mr. Smith and a man who came with him; and as Mr. Smith declared that all had gone on right, the Colonel was easy on that point. Yet there was something in the expression of Hannah's countenance that boded evil to his jealous mind; and for that reason he set a watch upon *her* actions, and a double guard about his wife and daughter.

"How long, O, how long shall we be obliged to live in this way?" exclaimed Mrs. Murray, as she wrung her hands in agony, one morning, a short time subsequent to the second departure of her husband. This poor woman felt herself cast out, and forsaken of all. The habitual insolence of Smith she could have borne, for she did not expect anything better of such a tool, as he was degraded to; but there were those who had treated her with seeming respect heretofore, who, since the stand her husband had taken in regard to her, jeered at her whenever they saw her at a window or door, as they passed her house.

Clara was the subject of like treatment; yet her spirit was naturally too elastic to be easily crushed.

"Don't despond," said she to her mother, in answer to the question she, in her distress, had almost unconsciously asked. "I am waiting patiently for the next violent thunder shower we are to have in the night."

"What do you expect to do then?" inquired the mother, interrupting her.

"Get so far within the Union lines, that it will not be easy for secession friends to reach us. We must be very brave, mother; I know it will seem terrible to expose ourselves to the warring elements, but 'the lightning's flash and the thunder's roar, will, on some night, surely be welcome to me, because I know there is not a servant about the premises but will fear to go abroad during a tempest."

Mrs. Murray shuddered; she had always been exceedingly timid during a thunder-shower, and the thought of going abroad at such a time, with only her daughter, without a servant, appalled her greatly. Clara saw her mother's distress, and strove to inspire her heart with courage.

"Don't feel so troubled about it, mother; we shall not be the first persons who have been out in a storm. I am not afraid for myself, at all; if you will only be courageous, we shall do nicely."

"I will try to be brave, my daughter, but I am the veriest coward in the world, I know."

"We shall have the cowardice all washed out of us

before we reach Washington, mother. I have planned everything, so we can get away well enough, if a heavy storm of thunder and lightning only comes at the right time. It is very fortunate that Hannah got a pass for us before father came home, for she would find it difficult to get away now, to go to the camp. I hope we shall be able to keep ourselves out of sight of any but Federals, until we can find Lieutenant Philips; then I am sure we need not fear."

"But, Clara, it may be that we have not funds enough to take us through to our friends."

"Don't be concerned about that, my dear mother; I have laid aside money for some time, for I have been looking for something 'to happen,' as Hannah says sometimes, and I knew that if we should ever need to go from home, as so many people have been obliged to, that money would be needful to help us along."

"You are a thoughtful girl, my daughter, and a great comfort to your mother in her grief."

Clara was greatly moved at this affectionate assurance of her mother, that she was gilding the dark cloud that enveloped that loved parent. She wept in silence for some minutes, and then affectionately entwining her arms about her mother's neck, she kissed her; then, rising and wiping the tears from her face, said with animation—

"I am so glad, my dear mother, that we can comfort each other."

"So am I," was the rejoinder, uttered with a voice choked by strong emotion.

"Do you suppose Hannah will be willing to go out during a tempest, Clara?" asked Mrs. Murray.

"I think she would go if you wished her to, but I

do not see that she will be needed, or at least, how we can afford to take her along with us."

"I shall hate to leave the good soul behind, very much indeed, although I suppose we could do without her. I waited upon myself before my marriage, I can do so again. But I love Hannah as a friend, as well as a faithful servant. Her piety entitles her to my warm affection."

"I love my dear old nurse too well to be separated from her willingly, yet I fear I shall be obliged to leave her," said Clara, speaking in a sad tone.

"Can't we contrive, through our young friend, to have Hannah sent on after us?" asked Mrs. Murray.

"What a bright thought, my dear mother; I will try my best to have this accomplished, for I know Hannah is desirous to go with us."

Hannah was indeed so anxious to go with her mistress and her 'dear young lady,' as she termed Clara when speaking of her to Lieutenant Philips, that she had sought that young gentleman in his quarters, and begged him to help her go after Mrs. Murray and her daughter, if they should ever be obliged to go away and leave her behind. Raymond had promised the affectionate woman to do all in his power to assist her, should it ever be necessary for her to need such assistance. Clara had informed Raymond that, owing to adverse circumstances, her mother and herself would be obliged to ask his protection as far as Washington, if he could meet them by the roadside, near his camp, on the first stormy night, for it must be on such an occasion that they would be obliged to leave their home.

Raymond would have felt some surprise at the

statements made by Clara in her note, had he not been prepared for anything that might occur, by the disclosures made by Edgar's appearing before him one morning, a few weeks previous, and begging to be sheltered from pursuit, and sent North to his aunt or grandmother, whose names he had learned of his mother.

"Then you are Mrs. Murray's son," said Raymond.

"I am, sir."

"Do you feel willing to tell me why you wish to leave your mother and sister, and go away?"

"I don't wish to be separated from them, sir, and that is the reason why I have come to you to make this request. I know that my mother will reward you, if you will only help me."

"I wish not a reward, my dear boy, but you will be separating yourself from your mother and sister if you go to the North."

"True, sir; but only for a time. Had I not taken French leave of my home this morning, I was to have been separated from them, perhaps forever; and worse, too. I was to have been carried to the headquarters of the Southern army, and that would have killed my mother, for she does·n't love to have any one take up arms against the good old stars and stripes."

"I hope you will never be left to do that, my boy," said Raymond, who was greatly interested in Edgar, and resolved to seek an opportunity as soon as possible, to send him, under the care of some reliable person, to Oak Dale. Edgar had concealed some necessary articles of clothing about him when he left home, and he had money, with which he bought a comfortable change of linen. His new friend placed him in the home of a good friend of his own, who gladly consented to keep him until he could go to his friends. An opportunity presented, soon after Raymond had mailed his last letter to Mrs. Jenkins. He informed her in the missive, that it was probable a lad, a son of her sister, might visit her erelong, though he could not tell her at what time she might expect him, as he was waiting for company.

Mrs. Jenkins marvelled at these tidings; it seemed to her so strange that a child like him should come without his mother, to relatives who were entire strangers to him.

Mrs. Clement thought it spoke volumes in disclosing the trials of her long-absent daughter. Bessie was indifferent upon the subject of her Southern friends visiting her home, and said little about them. Mrs. Clement was rejoiced at the thought of seeing any of her daughter's family, and longed to see her dear grandchild. Mrs. Jenkins also expected Edgar with some impatience.

CHAPTER XXII.

"The furnace of affliction may be fierce, but if it refineth thy soul, the good of each meek thought shall outweigh years of torment."

Had Mrs. Murray known how comfortably Edgar had been disposed of, for the time, it would have saved her many a sad hour. She heard, as soon as word could be sent by Hannah, that all was right in regard to his reaching Lieutenant Philips. More she could not know at that time; it was very difficult for her to have communication with Raymond, without exciting suspicion in the minds of those about her. Her whole soul revolted at the idea of acting a falsehood, and sometimes this feeling so oppressed her, that she faltered in her purpose of leaving her home privately, and half resolved to go boldly, in broad daylight. But Clara set before her the trouble it might cause herself, besides the amount of sin it would be a means of others committing, by the free use of profane language, if no outrage should be committed against them; and she consented to be guided by her daughter, and yield to her wishes, until this terrible ordeal should have passed.

Life, at this period in the life of Mrs. Murray and her daughter, was a state of peculiar suspense. All their hopes of future comfort hung upon the most trying uncertainty. Should not a storm come at a time favorable to their plans, they scarcely knew what they could do. Hannah seemed possessed with the thought that something was going to happen; she expressed this fear several times, as she was busy near her mistress, and at length Mrs. Murray was constrained to ask her why she thought so. On this occasion she seemed oppressed with sadness, which was not usual with her, for her temper was one of the sunniest kind.

In reply to the interrogation of her mistress, she said, "I's 'bleeged to think so, missus; I's heered strange talk when I's been gone out 'round, and so has Sam. 'Pears like, missus, Clary, is n't safe here. I wish ye's off somewhar."

"What have you heard, Hannah? tell me all you know; but first tell me if you would like to go to the North. If I should go there, would you follow me if you could?"

'Deed I would, missus; and it'll kill me if anything happens to you and Miss Clary, 'fore ye gits away. Can't ye go to-night, some 'ow? I's feered for ye all the time."

Well the poor creature might fear for those she so dearly loved, for she had witnessed great wrongs that had been inflicted and endured for opinion's sake; and she had heard the name of her mistress spoken by coarse, profane lips, and threats of violence uttered by such, as in days of moral sunshine at the South, had never polluted her home with their brutish presence.

Mrs. Murray endeavored to calm the mind of the faithful nurse, by promising to get to her friends in Massachusetts as soon as she possibly could. Yet her own fears refused to be quieted; she feared the worst, and it was with a feeling of gratitude and pleasure, that late in the afternoon of that day, she heard the sound of distant thunder. The atmosphere had been sultry all day. As the curtain of night fell over her dwelling, and the lightning's fitful flashes gleamed more and more brightly, Mrs. Murray trembled. Conflicting emotions filled her breast. The thought of exposing herself to the fury of the elements abroad, sent pallor to her cheek, and filled her heart with fear; yet a more dreadful uncertainty hung over her future, if she remained at home. She felt sure that Hannah had not told her all she knew, and the thought of being obliged to endure what some of her Union friends had endured, was agonizing to her soul.

Mrs. Murray sat alone for a time while Clara was attending to many little matters of importance, that were connected with their anticipated journey. The storm gradually increased in violence; the sky grew darker, and the lightning quivered across the blackness, presenting a scene of awful sublimity to the eye of such as love to watch the clouds when the grand artillery of heaven is sounding through the air. But Mrs. Murray was unmindful of all the grandeur of such a scene. A choice of evils was set before her, and she chose the least. Like king David, she preferred to fall directly into the hands of God, in her calamity, rather than receive chastening through the instrumentality of her fellow-beings. Mrs. Murray looked from her window, not as in by-gone days she had done many times, to see if the cloud containing electricity was not passing over, but to see if all was still about her premises. She knew that Mr. Smith had been at her house early in the evening, and that he had left at an early hour, for his own residence. She did not fear his return on any account, because she was aware that he was one of the few men who are so greatly terrified by lightning, as to be made sick by a storm such as was then raging.

All was quiet about the house, too, and the unfortunate lady was glad, as she turned from the window, to see her daughter enter the room with two India rubber blankets in her hand.

"Mother," said Clara, with an expression of concern upon her countenance, which she strove in vain to hide, "we may well bless God for this tempest, terrible as it is, and we must hasten to avail ourselves of the protection it will give us from something more trying, than going out at such a time. But for this rain we should at this hour have been suffering at the hands of a lawless mob, composed of some of the basest of men. But I must n't tell you now, we must be gone."

"Suppose that young man cannot meet us?"

"Don't suppose any such thing," said the daughter, distressed at the bare possibility of such a misfortune, "but let us go forward and hope all will be well."

While this conversation was being held, these two adventurous females had prepared, in the greatest haste, to leave a home blighted by the foul reptile, treason.

"Take your overshoes, mother, I will assist you to put them on. Hannah wished to help us, but I was afraid she would give way to her feelings, and make a noise that would disturb and arouse the rest of the household. Let me throw this rubber cloth over your shoulders, mother; there, now, let us go out softly. Only hear that peal of thunder, how tremendous; and sent just in time to prevent our being heard, if any one had been listening. Thank Heaven, we are on our way."

"Amen," replied Mrs. Murray, in a voice made tremulous by excitement. The pair reached the highway, and walked toward the Union Camp, as rapidly as it was possible for Mrs. Murray to walk, and faster than she had supposed she could travel. They went on in silence. O, what a walk was that, for two delicate women to take alone.

Don't let any secession sympathizer throw aside this book, as his eye rests upon this description of suffering inflicted upon innocent women for their love to the dear old Government established by our fathers. It is but a part of the sad truth we might tell you, for it is true, that crimes too horrible to describe have been committed out of hatred to the flag of our country by those who have been long protected and blessed under that signal so dear to loyal hearts. We write not in malice; we love our Southern brethren, but we will not keep back the truth, to please such as sympathize with the dark brutal acts sanctioned by their bogus government. Neither do we feel moved when we hear the friends of traitors say of facts laid before them which they do not wish to believe, "that is falsehood." We tell the truth, yet not the whole truth, in regard to the ill treatment of Union people at the South; and we challenge the whole host of secession sympathizers, to prove that we have sought out extreme cases.

Yes, what a walk for that mother and daughter to

take alone. The rain had poured in torrents for some time, and the road had been made exceedingly muddy, ere they set out on their desperate adventure.

"Daughter, I've been thinking we asked a great deal of that young man, when we requested him to watch for us, on such a night as this."

"I know we did, mother, but if I have judged that young Yankee aright, he is not a stranger to self-sacrifice. He may be prevented by circumstances he cannot control, still, I believe he will meet us if he can."

These few words were spoken in a low tone of voice as the troubled pair went on, wading at times in mud so adhesive in its nature, that they found it difficult to lift their tired feet out of it; and as the darkness prevented them from discerning the many little rivulets created by the pouring rain, they often found their feet and ankles submerged in water. Occasionally, a gleam of lightning would reveal some object in their pathway, the sight of which would fill their souls with dread, and then they would welcome, as a guardian angel, the black darkness of their way. They spoke seldom, for the hearts of both were too full for utterance.

Once Clara stepped into a hole and plunged headlong. Her mother was wellnigh paralyzed with fright, when she knew that she had fallen; see her she could not, but in a few moments the loving daughter was upon her feet again, and, extending the hand that was not covered with mud to her parent, said, in a cheerful tone, "I am glad it was not you that fell, dear mother."

"Dear child," was all the reply Mrs. Murray could make.

"Don't get discouraged, mother, mine," said Clara, "we have come over the worst of the way now, and we shall be able to rest before long."

A deep sigh was heaved by the mother, in answer to this cheering assertion. Yet, in a moment, she recollected herself, and felt that her daughter's heart ought not to be saddened by her. "You're a noble girl, Clara, and I ought to be grateful that I have your sympathy and assistance, but I have little fortitude; I will pray for strength to endure all that shall be laid upon me, without murmuring."

"We shall be carried through every trial as Hannah says, if we look to the right source, for strength and consolation; so let us be cheerful, for then, mother, we shall not be half as weary with our hardships, as we shall be, if our spirits are depressed. You know Solomon says, 'the spirit of a man can bear his infirmity,' then why not the spirit of a woman. Let us look on the bright side of our troubles, and we shall feel better. Only think, we can hope soon to see your friends, and to sleep, too, where we shall feel safe from enemies."

"That is a pleasant thought, daughter; I will not dwell upon my trials; how near are we to the Federal camp, Clara, do you know?"

"I do, pretty nearly; and I think we are within sight of it, if we could discern objects."

"How can I be sufficiently thankful, O my God," ejaculated Mrs. Murray. "It really refreshes me, to feel that we are so near friends."

This poor midnight wanderer was even nearer the goal of her hopes than she imagined. The camp lay just before them.

CHAPTER XXIII.

"On, on, on; to the breach, to the breach;
Life, like a dome of many-colored glass,
Stains the clear radiance of eternity,
Until death shiver it to atoms."

THE mother and daughter would have passed the place where they wished to stop, had not their footsteps been arrested by a pleasant voice, calling, "Who goes there?" They could not recognize it as Raymond's, having heard his voice so little; yet, there was something in the tone that inspired confidence. They stood still for a minute or more, and both mother and daughter were considering what to say in reply, when the voice called again; and this time it seemed approaching them, as the words, "If it is any one needing help, fear not to speak," sounded like music, to the ears of our forlorn travellers. They then felt almost sure that it was Raymond who addressed them, and they answered his welcome salutation, by asking if it was Lieutenant Philips whom they were addressing.

"My name is Philips," replied he, "and I think I have the pleasure of conversing with Mrs. Murray and her daughter, although the darkness prevents my seeing you."

"You are right in your conjecture; the unfortunate women you expected, are here to tax your kindness," said the elder lady.

"Do not, I entreat you, feel that it is a trouble to me to do what I can for your comfort. The fact alone, that you felt it necessary to leave your elegant home, and come here, on such a night as this, is reason enough why I should wish to aid you. But the night is far spent, and I will take you to a place of refuge at once."

The ladies were obliged to walk a short distance farther, in order to reach a house, where Raymond knew they would be kindly cared for. He was sorry it was not in his power to provide a carriage to transport them thither; but when he told them his regret on this account, they were surprised that he should have even thought of such a thing, as they had not. They were very grateful for his kind protection, and they were ready now to see the tempest abate without terror. The lightning gleamed less brightly now, the thunder sounded from a distance, and the rain descended gently. The sky was less black, yet there was nothing visible before them, as they went on. Never did a shipwrecked mariner feel more delight at beholding a friendly sail approaching, than our midnight wanderers experienced, when they saw that they were nearing a dwelling-house, which was made visible to them by its lighted windows; and they were told by Raymond that for a season, they would find a haven beneath its roof.

As they stood upon the steps at Bloomdale Place, Raymond had not time to ring for admittance, before a middle-aged man, with a benevolent expression, opened the door, exclaiming as he did so, "What a night for females to be abroad; please enter, without stopping to think of your wet garments," added the gentleman, as the ladies hesitated on account of their dripping clothes: "my wife has a good fire in the sitting-room to dry you, so don't mind tracking the floor a little; we don't mind trifles in these dark times."

Thus encouraged, Mrs. Murray walked into the house, followed by Clara, and was met, ere she had gone the length of the hall, by the mistress of that quiet, hospitable abode. They were quickly conducted to a room, made cheerful by a blazing fire, and relieved of their outside garments. The rubber cloth had kept their shoulders dry, but the skirts of their dresses were exceedingly wet. Clara had worn two pockets that she had filled with such small articles as might be carried thus. She had foreseen that a change of stockings would be necessary, and had provided against that emergency; but for a change of dress she was obliged to depend upon the kindness of others.

The hostess of our friends, was one of those women one cannot see without being attracted towards them, by the kindly, loving expression of their countenance. Mrs. Adams, for that was the name of the lady who opened her door so readily to our distressed friends, was not one whom the world would call handsome; still, her face was usually bright with a smile of cheerfulness. Sad indeed must be the case of wretchedness that discouraged her efforts to make it better. No outcast that applied to her for shelter and protection was ever left to pass on without experiencing her kindness. Her heart was large enough to embrace the whole world, and her strong sympathy was ready to share the sorrows of all mankind.

An occasion like that presented by the necessities of Mrs. Murray and her daughter was suited to call forth her tenderest sympathies. Scarcely had Raymond mentioned the case of his friends, before Mrs. Adams proffered her assistance, and assured him of her willingness to take them to her home, and lighten their cares and sorrows by every demonstration of kindness and sympathy in her power; and now that they were beneath her roof, she cheerfully sacrificed rest and personal comfort to minister to them. "How glad I am that you have arrived here in safety," said she, as with nimble hands she removed the wet clothing of her guests, and assisted them to array themselves in garments brought from her own wardrobe.

"You can never know how glad and thankful we are to be welcomed so kindly to your house," said Mrs. Murray; "I feel that I can never repay your kindness."

"Don't speak of what I do; it is nothing more than I ought to. But how you tremble; how cold you are; your mother is sinking into a fainting fit, my dear," said she hastily to Clara, and that young lady turned and looked at her mother just as she sank, faint and exhausted, upon the sofa. The overtaxed nerves of the poor lady were beginning to have their revenge.

Mrs. Murray recovered partially from the swoon, but was not able to leave the bed, to which she was borne, in the arms of her kind attendants, for some weeks. Clara's youth and elasticity of spirit buoyed up her slender frame. She suffered greatly from weariness and exhaustion, yet she was not prostrated by it, even for a day. She watched by her mother almost constantly, but she was not permitted to have the entire care of her, for good Mrs. Adams was jealous of her right as hostess, because she well knew that Clara needed rest.

"You must rest, my child, for your mother's sake as well as your own," said she, when the daughter was one day remonstrating against being anticipated in so many things that she was intending to do for her mother, to prevent her being too heavy a burden to the kind-hearted lady.

"Don't talk of my being burdened; who knows but I shall need the same offices performed for me, some day? This unnatural war is not over yet; remember, you may have the opportunity, before long, of doing more for me than I am now doing for you."

"I don't see how it would, in any circumstances, be possible for us to do more," responded Clara, with a grateful smile; then, heaving a sigh, she remarked that she hoped Mrs. Adams would be spared the trials they had been called to endure.

"I know you must have felt a dread of something terrible, to have chosen such a night on which to leave your home; such a home, too, as Lieutenant Philips had described yours to be."

"We were driven, by adverse circumstances, first to choose a tempest of thunder and lightning to escape from home in; and we were held to our choice by learning that the coming on of the storm, on that dismal night, saved us from the power of a wicked mob. Perhaps our courage would have failed us, had it not been for this."

"Is your mother a Christian?"

"I trust so," was Clara's reply.

"Then she will be sustained; otherwise, she would sink in despondency, under such a weight of sorrow."

"That is just the way I feel about her; it seems to me that the worst is over now, both in regard to my mother's illness and our own misfortunes. It will take some time for one like mamma to rally from such an illness, I know; but the kind, patient feeling you evince towards her, in respect to the lingering nature of her sickness, will aid her recovery very much. She feels this, herself; could I know that Edgar, my brother, was now safe with our relatives, I should be almost happy."

"Hope for the best, my dear girl," said Mrs. Adams, soothingly.

"I trust young Philips will be able to call again soon. I have wondered that he has not been here since the day after he left us in your care; but perhaps I ought not to have expected him."

"You should not have looked for him, Miss Murray, for he cannot go where he pleases always, if he is an officer; but the mention of your brother's name has excited my curiosity and interest greatly, and I must be excused for asking his age."

"Certainly, my friend, you have a right to ask such a question. He is not far from fifteen; and now I must be indulged in questioning you; I would have you tell me why you so much desired to learn the age of my brother."

Mrs. Adams at once gratified Clara's wish. But we will leave her explanation for the next chapter.

CHAPTER XXIV.

> " Since he doth lack
> Of going back;
> Little whose will
> Doth urge him to run wrong, or to stand still."
> BEN JONSON.

> " The one remains; the many change and pass;
> Heaven's light forever shines; earth's shadows flee."

MRS. ADAMS had often heard "little" Edgar Murray spoken of by a nephew of hers. She knew, also, that this young man, whose father was a secessionist, was devotedly attached to the sister of this lad, and had felt anxious, ever after she first saw Clara, to know if she was this same young lady, but had from time to time resisted the temptation she felt, to make the inquiry, which, when she could not longer forbear making, had brought to light a fact that made Clara thrice welcome to her home and heart.

George Ashley, the young man referred to, was very dear to Clara, and although no decided engagement of marriage had been entered into by them, they both understood that it was the will of the other to cherish such an affection as might, and probably would, result in their forming a conjugal relation with each other at some future day. George had never attempted to conceal his attachment for Clara, and she had never denied her preference for him. She hardly ventured to think of obstacles that might prevent the consummation of her youthful wishes. She was not obliged at present to think of anything so unpleasant, she said to herself, and so she had lived on, for more than

15*

two years, making bright fancy sketches, every day, of her future life, when she should become the wife of her noble George.

The knowledge of the fact that her new friend, Mrs. Adams, loved this dear object of her affection and present solicitude, made her seem very dear to Clara.

"What a kind providence it was that led that young officer to bring us to your house," said Clara one day to her hostess; "or I should say, how many little events, that were providential, concurred to bring us here."

"Very true," replied the lady addressed, "and I love to adopt the sentiment of that poet, who says —

> 'In each event of life how clear
> Thy ruling hand I see;
> Each blessing to my soul most dear,
> Because conferred by thee.'

"I feel that God has a purpose of love and mercy to fulfil, in everything that occurs. I don't love to hear people talk of things happening, because I feel that the same power that clothes the lily, and 'feeds the ravens when they cry,' controls the smallest events of our lives in such a manner that each helps to

> 'Fulfil some deep design'

of our wonder-working Father."

"How dear you are becoming to me, Mrs. Adams, I can't tell you; it seems as if I had known you always."

"And I, too, my dear, feel that our sympathies have created a strong bond of friendship between your mother, yourself, and me, which it would have required years, under ordinary circumstances, to create. I only wish George could come here now, poor boy."

Mrs. Adams sighed deeply, as she pronounced these last words, and Clara looked anxiously into her face.

"Why do you call him poor, Mrs. Adams," asked Clara.

"Don't you know his situation?" interrogated her friend.

"I *know* nothing; I have suspected he might be in circumstances that were not pleasant, because I believe he sympathizes with me in my strong attachment to the United States."

"How long since you have seen George, Clara?"

"Not since the Spring of 1861, or a few weeks after the war commenced. Have you seen or heard from him since?" asked Clara.

"Yes, several times, stealthily; I have helped him out of trouble more than once, by concealing him from those who were in pursuit of him, who would have him take up arms against the dear old stars and stripes."

"Then he has never been forced to fight?"

"No, he has not, because he would not, and has managed to keep out of the way, else he would have been compelled to join the Confederate army, or suffer for not doing so."

"What a life he is obliged to lead, poor young man," exclaimed Clara; "how much misery and woe a few ambitious politicians have brought upon our land."

"It is even as you say; yet 't is a comfort to reflect that infinite wisdom is at the head of these seeming tumultuous affairs, and will guide the helm of the universe aright. 'He will make even the wrath of man to praise him,' reluctant as the wicked are that this shall be so."

"Thoughts of this bring comfort to my heart when I feel sad," responded Clara. "But I am desirous to know if this New England friend of ours has ever seen George."

"Don't ask the Lieutenant that question, and don't expect me to answer it to your satisfaction. I would not betray confidence, or make known anything that would mortify, in ever so small a degree, either of these noble young men."

"I admire that decision of yours, Mrs. Adams, and will wait until George shall tell me his own history, to know what I wish to; but you may be willing to tell me how long it is since he was here."

"It is only a few weeks. He came in disguise, to visit a friend in the Union camp, and contrived to make us a night visit. I do not know where he is now, but should not be surprised to learn, by and by, that he has gone to New England. I pity him most of all, because he has not been taught to rely upon himself. He does n't know how to get along without considerable money, and he is poor now, for his father has withdrawn his support from him, and swears that this son shall be an outcast from his home, and a beggar, until he will comply with his wishes, and join the Southern army. This, George says, he cannot perjure his soul to do, so he is entirely thrown upon his own resources."

"If he could only get to some city in the North, and procure a situation in some business establishment as clerk, to write, and attend to branches of business that are not hard, he might get along, until this war is over; don't you think so, Mrs. Adams?"

"I fear, Clara, he will have to support himself, after the war shall have ceased, even should it continue many years. His father will never forgive him because he has outraged his pride so terribly, in refusing to do all in his power to distinguish himself as a Southern soldier. At the commencement of the war, Mr. Ashley flattered himself that both his sons would fight for secession; and he confessed that he gloried in having two such noble boys, to help assert the rights of the "Confederacy." Then, to be so disappointed, was a great mortification to his proud heart. We are proud of him, because he will not fight against the old flag; because he would rather give up his birthright than do so."

"Yes, and well we may be proud of him; he has not been bribed to be true to our Government, to serve it for a large bounty, but he has sworn to be true to it, always; and if his feelings revolt at the idea of meeting his father or brother in deadly conflict upon the battle-field, he is ready to serve the Union in any way in which he can, without taking up arms. Even that he will not shrink from, should circumstances render it necessary for him to assist in defending his country."

"Is George's mother a Union woman, Mrs. Adams?"

"No, my dear; I cannot say she is, much as I should like to be able to tell you so. She is one of the infatuated ones, and as her temperament is ardent, she takes a strong stand on the wrong side, and has used her powers of persuasion to endeavor to bring her son to a right state of feeling, as she expresses herself in regard to the subject. She has also tried to convince me that I am wrong in cherishing these old-fashioned puritanical notions, as she calls adherence to the good old Government, until she despairs of changing my views; and I begin to think that she will disown me as her sister."

"How many families will be broken up by this unholy conflict," said Clara, partly to herself and almost unconsciously.

"Yes, Clara," said Mrs. Murray, who was now awake, and had been listening to the conversation of her two loving attendants. "Darkness hovers over our land now, but since I have been so mercifully brought out of the house of moral bondage, and my lot has fallen in this pleasant spot, I feel that I can trust God with everything, always. The cloud that has obscured my sky has a silver lining, which is now visible to me."

Mrs. Murray recovered her strength slowly; yet, as the weeks glided by, it was plain that she improved some during each week. Raymond called, when she had been with her new friends about three weeks, and gladdened her heart by bringing a letter from Mrs. Jenkins, and also one from Edgar, penned at the home of his aunt, where he said he should be happy, if he might have his mother and sister with him. He mentioned his nurse, Hannah, with affectionate interest, and spoke, too, of Sam, who, he said, was a good friend to him; still, he felt sorry that he should act so deceitful a part towards his master.

"I told Sam that morning, that I did not wish him to know that I was going to take a walk; that I wished him to go into the house and stay until father might want him. But he would n't do as I wished him to; he took me up while I was urging him to let me alone, and jumped upon Lion, that fastest of all fast horses, and galloped off. It seemed to me not more than two minutes before we were out of sight of the place. I then leaped to the ground, and he ran the horse back, at least until he was out of my sight. He told me, if father saw him, he should tell him he was looking for 'young massa.' O, Sam," said I, " why need you go with me, when you expect to be obliged to tell what is n't true, if you do?"

"'Don't fret,' said he; 'I knows how to get along with massa,' and away he went. Poor fellow! I hope he will not get into trouble on account of his devotion to me."

This letter was like cordial to the heart of her to whom it was addressed. A postscript was added, addressed to Clara, written in a playful, hopeful strain; he spoke in high terms of his grandmother, aunt, and cousins.

"One of them I don't admire very much, though," said he; "to be candid, I must say I don't know what to think of my eldest cousin, Bessie. Sometimes I am almost ready to love her a little; but she will drive all my lovable thoughts away before they get really settled upon her. Perhaps Clara will see her through different spectacles, and will discern traits in her which are invisible to me."

Mrs. Jenkins had been informed of her sister's whereabouts and condition, by Raymond, and her letter was full of expressions of sympathy and affection. It contained also a fifty dollar United States bank note, and an apology for the appearance of said note, which had been enclosed with trembling lest it should offend. Still, Mrs. Jenkins thought it might possibly be needed, and if it was not, her sister could bring it back to her, when she should visit her. But all Mrs. Jenkins's apologies were needless, for her kindness was appreciated by her sister.

CHAPTER XXV.

"Cease, fond caviller at wisdom, to be satisfied that everything is wrong,
Be sure there is good necessity even for the flourishing of evil."
TUPPER.

MRS. MURRAY wept over the letter of her sister; tears of joy flowed freely, as she thought of her own demerits and the kindness expressed towards herself by her neglected friends. Her sister's letter contained loving messages from her mother, that were like water to a thirsty soul to the heart of the long-absent daughter. Both Mrs. Murray and Clara looked forward with pleasure to the time when they should be with their Northern friends; still, they enjoyed the society of Mrs. Adams very much, and were as happy under her kind protection as they could be, under the trying circumstances that had procured for them the friendship of this lady, "this real sister of mercy."

During the hour that passed while Raymond was at Bloomdale Place, Clara heard the name of George spoken in low tones more than once by her hostess and her New England friend, and she conjectured that it was George Ashley who was the subject of remark, yet she refrained from asking questions. The pulsations of her heart were quickened, however, although she did not anticipate evil from what little information she had gathered by the incidental remarks that had been made in her hearing. But O, how much she longed to ask Raymond to befriend the young Southerner, if he should ever meet with him, when he should have an opportunity to do so. She did not realize how needless was this request.

Had Clara seen this Union officer when he had had the care of some of his Southern brethren, who had been taken prisoners by the Federals, she would have seen the needlessness of her anxiety. A kinder feeling never glowed in the breast of man than that which was cherished by Raymond Philips towards enemies as well as friends. No vindictive feeling ever found lodgment in his heart a moment. He acted from principle, and all his derelictions from the pathway of right, were on the side of mercy; for, strange as seems the statement, to one class of people in the world, the exercise of benevolence is sometimes a fault. No unkind wish was ever known to fall from the lips of Raymond upon the foes of his country. Violent as was the language that had reached his ears sometimes, when he had involuntarily been a listener to conversations held by those who loved to see our old flag trampled in the dust, he thought it beneath his notice, although from his inmost soul he pitied those whose hearts were so hard, and whose judgment was so perverted, as to allow them to use these diabolical epithets on any occasion. And well might he pity these erring ones, both North and South; and how appropriate for Christians to offer, for all such, the prayer breathed by our Saviour when upon the cross. He exclaimed, "Father forgive them, for they not what they do."

On taking leave of his friends at Bloomdale, Raymond told Mrs. Murray and her daughter, that he thought it doubtful whether he should be able to see them again before they would start for the North.

"It is possible, however," said he, "for we have had marching orders more than once that have been countermanded in a few hours after we have received them."

"I hope it will be so the next time you are ordered to the field," said Clara; "for I wish you to remain where we can sometimes see you while we stay at Bloomdale."

"Is that on the whole a good wish, Miss Murray?" asked Raymond, with a slight attempt at smiling, while he spoke.

"Perhaps it is too selfish," answered Clara, "for I was only thinking of the comfort of our little circle here when I spoke, and yet, while you are here, your friends at home may feel easy about you."

Alas! this affectionate girl knew not that the thought that Raymond was where he could visit Bloomdale, was "wormword and gall" to the heart of her whom Raymond loved more than any other object upon earth. Still, it was even so; the bitterest drop in the cup of trial, now tasted by Bessie, was the thought that he could now see and converse with her unknown cousin, whom she considered her rival.

In answer to this last remark made by Clara, Raymond said, "I feel that you are mistaken, Miss Murray, in thinking that my friends have any more cause for uneasiness respecting me at one time than at another. It is not to circumstances we are to look for preservation, but to God. My life is as safe upon the battle-field as at home by the fireside of my mother; until my life's work shall have been accomplished, no missile of destruction can take me from earth."

"That is true, my friend; but you may be wounded, perhaps maimed, and become a cripple for life," said Clara.

"Yes, very true, I may; but can I avoid this evil by remaining in a state of comparative safety? I think not. I know a young man who lost an arm by the accidental discharge of his own rifle, when he was, as he thought, secure from all harm. You have heard, perhaps, of the sudden death of a young man of great promise, who belonged to the self-denying New York Seventh, as I love to call that regiment of brave men. Then, the dear little "Drummer Boy" was summoned from earth by the accidental discharge of a weapon, when his position was considered entirely safe. I could mention very many more such incidents to prove that

> "Fate steals along with silent tread,
> Found oftenest in what least we dread;
> Frowns in the storm with angry brow,
> But in the sunshine strikes the blow."

And fate is not just the word I would have had the poet use in speaking of the power of Omnipotence, executed in doing what "He will with his own." That word fate seems to imply a sort of despotism on the part of the Disposer of events, which is foreign to his character as a

> "Sovereign Father, good and kind,"

which his acts to the children of men have ever proved him to be, since the world began."

"You are right," answered Clara; "but I often find myself forgetting the important truth, that we need only concern ourselves to learn and do our duty;

I am ever feeling the necessity there is of the 'line upon line, and precept upon precept' teaching of the Bible, in my own case."

"You are like the rest of mankind, Miss Murray. It seems to me that I need more teaching and stern discipline than any one I know. But I am stopping too long. I will hope to meet your mother and yourself sometime, in Oak Dale."

Raymond then bade the new friends adieu, and returned immediately to the camp of his regiment, where preparations were being made to march at the earliest notice.

16*

CHAPTER XXVI.

" But one must begin to love somewhere, and to do good somewhere: and I think it is as natural to love one's own family, and to do good in one's own neighborhood, as to anybody else. Charity does not end where it begins, my friend."

WHILE Raymond had been occupied with the various little matters to be looked after for the comfort of the two ladies, who, he felt, were thrown by a direct Providence upon his care, he had been kept from sad reflections upon his peculiar trials. He felt that a heart possessed of strong sympathies was a blessing to its possessor, since it keeps one from that worst of all calamities, being buried alive in one's own grief. Never had he realized that this was true, as he had done while forgetting in a sense his own affliction, in administering to the necessities of Mrs. Murray and her daughter.

Sometimes a pang would cross his breast when he thought of Bessie's jealousy of his attentions to her cousin; yet he did not for one moment falter in his purpose to do all for the unfortunate girl and her mother that he would like another to do for those dear to him, should such ever be placed in circumstances to require similar attentions.

"Bessie must appreciate my motives in befriending her relative; surely, she would not have me do less for any unprotected strangers than I have done for her aunt and cousins," thought the young man; "but if it is otherwise, I must do my duty and leave results."

Thus his manly soul was strengthened for the moral conflict before him, and he passed on, outriding the heavy surges that were encountered by him in the sea of passion.

Bessie, during all these weeks, had been drifting along the tide of morbid feeling, borne by the current of impulse, until she found herself driven upon the shoals of discontent and fretfulness. She was indeed really unhappy herself, and it seemed as if she wished others to be as miserable as she was.

"Bessie, dear, what ails you?" tenderly inquired her grandmother, one evening, while the family were expecting Edgar's arrival. "Can I do anything to make you happy?" continued this kind relative, as Bessie did not answer the first question.

"I don't care for anything," was Bessie's reply, uttered in a sullen tone. "I wish I had never been born," she continued; "everything goes wrong, that I have any interest in; it's no use for me to care for anybody, or anything, and I don't mean to."

Mrs. Jenkins had heard this last remark as she was entering the room where sat her mother and daughter. "Bessie, it really distresses me to see you in this unhappy mood. I hope you will exert yourself to be cheerful, when your cousin Edgar comes to make one of our family, for he will need cheering. Instead of unhappy, gloomy face, she ought to have bright countenances to gaze upon, in this home so new to him, and where each person is a stranger."

Mrs. Jenkins paused, but her daughter did not answer her kind suggestions, but sat in moody silence. How long she would have remained thus is uncertain, had not her revery been interrupted by the ringing of the door-bell. On hearing this summons for admittance, she hastily arose and hurried from the room. A moment or two later, a lad was ushered into the room Bessie had left, who introduced himself as Edgar Murray. "My own dear grandson," exclaimed Mrs. Clement, clasping the youth in her arms; "thank heaven, I have lived to see your face."

"My dear grandmamma," responded Edgar, "I feel that you love me already."

"And I, too, welcome you with much love, my dear nephew," said the boy's aunt, with deep feeling.

"My dear aunt, you cannot know how glad I am, to find myself safe under your roof."

"We are very glad also that you are here, and we long to have an opportunity to welcome your mother and sister to our home," replied Mrs. Jenkins.

Bessie's brothers came in soon after, and were delighted at the sight of their cousin. His aunt, rightly judging that the lad was very weary, soon set refreshments before him, and having eaten a light supper, he soon after expressed a wish to retire for the night.

"To-morrow," said he, as he arose to go to his room, attended by one of his cousins, "I shall have much to say; I am too sleepy now; so good night, my dear friends."

Bessie was in her own room, and she could not help hearing the "good night" of Edgar, or his voice, as he ascended the stairs, talking cheerfully with his attendant. If she had not known before that it was him who had been announced soon after her hasty retreat from the sitting-room, she could be ignorant no longer; yet she was in no mood to welcome the youthful guest. Clara was associated in her mind with this brother, and she was determined to vent her ill-will towards the unoffending Clara upon Edgar. "I don't care to see him," said she, mentally, when she had heard him ask her brother if his sister was absent from home, as he passed her door on his way to his chamber. Bessie did not join the family again that evening, but her mother went to her room, and, with all the powers of persuasion with which she was gifted, strove to bring her to a better state of feeling towards the new comer.

"Don't, my daughter, mortify us all, by appearing in such an ungenerous mood before your cousin. It will be trying enough for him to feel that he is surrounded by strange faces, if they all look pleasant; but for him to meet you with such a lugubrious countenance as you have recently carried about, will be terrible."

Bessie could not restrain a smile at her mother's earnestness of manner, and that lady hailed it as an omen of good. Therefore she was not surprised when next morning Bessie met her cousin with something like an attempt at cheerfulness, which was even more successful than her mother had dared to hope. But Bessie's pleasant impulse was transient; her moods varied during the day, and towards night her feelings again took the shade of sadness, and she sat silent and unhappy. This state of things continued for some time with Bessie, while Edgar regarded her with a puzzled feeling, and this was why he mentioned her in his letter to his mother, as the only one of his aunt's family with whom he was not entirely satisfied.

For one reason, Edgar felt grieved that Bessie was not more congenial to his taste; he had hoped she would make a pleasant companion for Clara, but he thought she seemed the least companionable of any young lady he had ever met with.

"How do you like my sister, Edgar?" asked Albert, when his cousin had been in the family a few days.

"I would like her if she would only give me a chance; but something, it appears to me, must be the matter with her; if it was my sister who seemed so strange, I should be afraid she was going crazy."

Albert laughed outright at his cousin's confession, and Willie joined in his mirth.

"Why do you laugh?" asked Edgar, soberly.

"Because we can't help it," said Willie, "to think you should be so innocent in not blaming Bessie for her ugliness, when 't is nothing but temper that makes her seem so awful-like; I don't know what to call it."

"But she is pleasant sometimes, and very sociable with me," said Edgar; "and I'm very sorry that she is not so all the time, for she is a pretty girl."

But Edgar was obliged to regret Bessie's unsocial conduct for many a long day, and sometimes he felt that her brothers were not far from right in rendering the verdict of "ugly" upon her actions. She mystified him very much, and he could not but feel that she was a strange girl.

CHAPTER XXVII.

"Such a stress does the established order of nature teach us to lay upon little things."

"Education, fashion, and habit, have a vast influence on our intellectual operations, and exercise a powerful sway over our moral judgments."

THE marching orders which had been received by the regiment to which Raymond belonged, were not, on that occasion, countermanded. The regiment moved forward in high spirits, the movement was such a pleasant contrast to the dull monotony of camp life. Raymond felt glad that this order to move had not been given before he had seen Mrs. Murray and Clara in a place of safety, and with friends whom he was sure would do all that could be done to assist them in reaching Oak Dale.

The passionate, unfeeling course which Bessie had pursued caused him pain. She should have cheered him by her kindly letters, such as she had written to him until recently. Would she ever feel kindly towards him again? he hoped so, and he trusted that she would be led to, and at no very remote period, too. Comforting himself with this last reflection, his spirits rose with the inspiring thought that he was now to be permitted to do something towards putting an end to the cruel Rebellion that was bringing untold calamity to the whole of our dear land. Raymond's mind was not fettered by sectional prejudices; he loved his whole country. He had none of that narrow-mindedness which causes one to despise a people because they have faults, and because they may be led to commit great wrongs by confiding in leading men who are unworthy to be trusted.

He felt that the United States Government would be recognized, at the judgment-seat of Christ, as the power that should have swayed this nation both North and South, and that the individual who it was found there had acted a disloyal part, would be proved, before an assembled universe, guilty of one of the vilest offenses, — treason. With convictions like these forced upon him, he could not feel himself justified in withholding the strength of his right arm, even though he should be obliged to raise it against his erring brethren.

"Why should the South force us to shed the blood of their young men when it is so unnecessary?" said Raymond, while, on this march, a sense of the wickedness of this conflict came with renewed force to his mind, as he was conversing with a comrade.

"The South itself could not tell you why," replied the person addressed. "Even the political aspirants could not make this subject clear to others if they understand it themselves. The truth is, the head men at the South did not count the cost of this Rebellion. They could not imagine that the blow given at Fort Sumter would be felt all over the North, as it has been, ever since those first shots were fired, else they had not discharged a single gun."

"Misguided men," responded Raymond. "Having commenced rolling this traitorous ball, pride compels them to keep it moving until it can be stopped without branding them with cowardice. But it is hard for us to be obliged to fight even strangers; harder still to go to battle against our brethren; and yet we have no alternative, unless it be the overthrow of our Government, and should we allow that to be wrested from us, without a hard struggle, we should receive punishment from heaven, undoubtedly. This war is our choice of calamities."

"Yes, and we must accept it cheerfully; don't feel too tender-hearted toward these Rebels, Philips; you won't fight well unless you get your mad up."

"I differ from you, Dean; I think we ought to be in a temper of mind that will fit us to pray for our enemies all the time. How can you think of going into the presence of a Holy God with your breast glowing with rage."

"I don't think of such a catastrophe as that, Phil. I expect to come out of this battle, unhurt; there is nothing like hoping against hope, you know"

"I feel that there is something worth more to one's soul than the hope that we shall escape physical harm; something too, that has a firmer foundation than all your present hopes of escaping injury."

"I know what you would say farther, Phil; but I am no Christian, you know."

"Then, how did you dare come where you are so exposed to the missiles of death, almost continually?"

"Because I hoped to be spared through all the danger, and return home. I don't expect to be killed, or even wounded."

"It would be better to trust ourselves with God, my friend," was Raymond's earnest reply.

This march was a tiresome one; the roads were in a bad condition; the air was extremely chilling to our brave boys as they pursued their way. Night came on early, for the days were shortening very fast. The regiment halted but seldom, for it was important that they should be near Fredericksburg as soon as possible; and they did reach their destined position, and take part in that sad slaughter, before that fortified city of secession, as it stood before the "Army of the Potomac," in the autumn of 1862.

Raymond was near the front during that engagement, the result of which produced intense excitement throughout the North, and gave rise to many unpleasant speculations and grievous criticisms. This was the most severe conflict in which Raymond had borne a part. His horse was shot under him, but he passed through the whole struggle without injury. After the firing had ceased, he stood upon the battle-field and wept, as he beheld the carnage around him. Familiar faces lay all around, whose features were still in death. How ghastly this spectacle! How horrible this evidence that war is a fearful scourge to humanity! Raymond could not spare time for contemplation, surrounded as he was by men who were writhing in anguish. Some were dying, while others were suffering, perchance, more than pangs which ofttimes cause the dissolution of the frail casket that contains that precious gem, the human soul.

Raymond did all in his power for both friend and foe. He looked anxiously for his comrade, Dean, yet he was nowhere to be seen. Through all that cold night after the battle, Raymond labored with all his might for those who needed assistance; and many a life, precious beyond description to a dear circle at home, was saved by his timely efforts. He noticed the body of a young man as he was passing over the field, in whom life seemed extinct. He passed by it, letting fall a tear over its youth and loveliness, when a sudden impulse caused him to turn his head and look again upon the mortal part of one who appeared to have left a home of refinement, for that field of strife.

Raymond retraced his steps, and bent over the inanimate form before him; and as his ear was close to the face so comely in its stillness, he caught a sound that made him start, for it came from what he had thought a corpse. How his bosom thrilled with pleasure at the thought that possibly he might be instrumental in prolonging the life of this young man, whose countenance had interested him so deeply. Placing his ear near the lips he had thought would never more emit sound, he was sure he heard a sigh, then a stifled groan sounded on his ear. He had water in his own canteen, and he bathed the face of the sufferer with it, and strove to assist him to swallow some of the refreshing beverage, after staunching the blood that was flowing from his wound.

In a short time the youth languidly opened his eyes and said, in a whisper, "Don't kill me, don't, for my mother's sake."

"I will do you good, if I can," replied Raymond, tenderly; "you need fear nothing from me."

He now noticed that the young man wore a secesh uniform, but the kind impulse to do all he could for him in his helpless state, was as strong as before. "Poor fellow," said he mentally, "although he has been arrayed against me on the field of battle, he has a claim to my compassion, and shall not be passed by." So Raymond called to a man near by to assist him in raising and bearing the youthful Rebel to the nearest shelter. This proved to be a house occupied by a family who were opposed to the Union; but they opened their doors gladly to admit the bleeding youth, as he was carried upon a litter constructed for the occasion, of pieces of board, which was carefully covered with a blanket. He was wounded in his thigh, and his wound had bled profusely. It is probable his life would have flowed entirely away, had not the steps of Raymond been directed to the spot where this wounded soldier lay.

Raymond did not leave the young man entirely to the care of those under whose roof he was sheltered, for he wished to know more about him. The idea that he felt a strong regard for his mother, caused his own heart to yearn towards him. His extreme youth, too, won upon the feelings of our friend. "Such an experience," thought Raymond, "for a mere boy; how hard it seems," and his preserver longed to know his history, and determined, if possible, to draw it from him. But circumstances did not favor this object, and Raymond was obliged to leave the neighborhood without learning anything farther than the young man's name, and the fact that he did not volunteer to join the Confederate service. He appeared very grateful to all who ministered to his necessities, and expressed unbounded gratitude towards the Yankee Lieutenant, who, he was conscious, had saved his life.

"I hope I shall see you again," said he, as he pressed the hand of Raymond warmly, at parting. "I shall never forget it was a Northern soldier who has been the means of rescuing me from the grave. The surgeon says 'tis only a flesh wound, but my life's current had wellnigh oozed out, ere I became unconscious; you must have found me very soon after."

"I think I did," answered Raymond with emotion; "but it was a Higher Power that swayed the human instrument that brought you back to life. I passed you, but was impelled to turn back, and my turning to look again, at what I supposed was your corpse, resulted in your restoration. You must thank a higher Being than I, that you live at this hour."

"I will try to; but O, I must see you again, sometime."

"I hope we shall meet again, when the olive branch of peace shall wave over our whole country. But now, adieu."

Raymond went away with a feeling of disappointment at his heart; the history of the youthful stranger was still unknown to him.

CHAPTER XXVIII.

" Here lies a man! not the one I have been seeking, but still, it is one who needs my aid, because he is my fellow-man."

SERGEANT DEAN had been invisible to Raymond for sometime previous to the termination of the battle he had anticipated with so much hope in respect to himself. His comrade had vainly sought him, but no one had seen him, whom the Lieutenant met with. He thought he must be among the fallen; but where, amid so many, was he to be found!

"O, war, war!" said our young friend, as he gazed upon the ghastly faces that were presented to his sight, as he strolled over the battle-field in search of his brother soldier, "O war, horrible, fratricidal war has done all this. How much wretchedness has a few hours' conflict occasioned. How needless and how sad!"

It is even so, and how many hearts respond to these sentiments, all over our land. But to return from our digression.

Raymond was obliged to renounce the hope of finding Dean, anywhere. His duty called him in another direction, and with a pang at his heart, as he thought of the uncertain fate of his friend, he gave up the idea. Sometime before the engagement had closed, Sergeant Dean had been wounded; a shot entered his left shoulder. It had been aimed so as to strike him aslant his body, pass through his arm, and emerge on the outside of it. He did not fall when he was wounded, but left the ranks immediately, and hastened to find a resting-place upon the ground beyond the range of the enemy's guns. His wound bled so profusely, that he felt his strength diminishing rapidly, ere he had reached a place of safety. As soon as he dared to, he threw himself upon the ground, and never was mother earth, more valued as a resting-place, than at that moment it was by him. Dean lay quietly for a few minutes, but the effusion of blood continued, and he feared that he had laid him down to die alone.

Ah! how rapidly his thoughts flew back to the home of affection and plenty he had left. In fancy, his mother was before him, grieving at the news that would soon reach her from her youngest, and now her only son. His brother she had mourned for many months; he, too, had been a soldier, and had fallen a sacrifice to rebellious ambition. And now must this remaining one perish upon the same altar upon which his brother had been slain. "Heaven forbid!" exclaimed he; and Heaven did forbid this last sacrifice.

When Dean had lain some little time unable to staunch the crimson gore that oozed continually from his wound, and despairing almost of ever seeing the sun rise again, as he saw it sink behind the western horizon on that memorable night, his attention was arrested by the sound of approaching footsteps. He turned his head and saw a Union soldier near. The man perceived his situation, and stopped when he came to the spot where he lay.

"Can I help you?" asked he, in a feeling tone.

"Oh, I need n't have asked that question;" he continued, as he saw the blood flowing from the arm of the prostrate soldier, and hastened to do what he could to stop it. "You must n't lie here any longer; I'll try and get you to yonder house, where your wound can be properly dressed and cared for."

So saying, he raised Dean upon his feet, and supported, or rather bore him in his strong arms, to a neighboring house, where the wounded man was kindly received. The stranger stayed by him till his wound was dressed and the crimson life-tide ceased to flow. Then he prepared to go.

"To what part of the land do you belong?" asked Dean.

"To Massachusetts. I belong to a regiment that came out from that State, early in the summer of 1861. I have a brother that was in the battle to-day, and I was looking for him when I came upon you."

"And you gave up looking for your own brother to take care of me?"

"To be sure; what else could I have done, when you lay before me with your life running away, rapidly? I could not pass on and leave you: and I can hope that some one has been led to aid my brother, if he has needed assistance, as I have helped you."

"I shall never forget your kindness in saving my life," answered Dean, with emotion.

"It is a comfort to me to know that I have been of service to you," remarked the other. "I never could have been happy again, for one moment, had I left you without knowing that you had been cared for."

"Our homes are far apart, I may never see you

again, even if we both survive this war; yet I shall hope to meet you again, although not even your name is known to me; but you must tell me to whom I am so deeply indebted before we part."

"My name is Andrew; still, I am not related to our Governor," said the soldier, with a smile.

"I thank you," replied Dean. "Andrew is the name of the Governor of Massachusetts; but I had forgotten it, until you spoke as you did about the name; however, it isn't a bad name anywhere, that I know, and I am very sure it will always sound musical in my ears, associated as it will ever be with your kindness towards me. I shall look with interest to every source from which I may be likely to learn if anything befalls you."

"Then you must know that my first name is Joseph, and I have a middle name that commences with W. But I must hasten away, so good by."

These two acquaintances of a few hours shook hands heartily, and parted with a feeling of mutual regret.

"Joseph W. Andrew," said Sergeant Dean, mentally, after his preserver had left the house. "I need make no effort to remember that name, much as I am prone to forget the names of most of the people I meet with. My own existence is an ever-present memento of this man. I wish all the world was like him, for I know he must be a good citizen, because he seems to act from principle. I hope he will live a long life, for it seems hard to have good men taken away, when there are so few of them."

Yes, Dean, it does look dark when the good are removed from earth at any time, but especially at a time like this, when the land mourns for reason of the wickedness of many. Yet some have been taken from our army whom we felt we could not spare; but we must remember that we see only in part, now; yet, 'what we know not now we shall know hereafter.'

Dean was not long confined with his wound, but was soon able to return to his old quarters with his regiment, and when he again saw Raymond, he related, with moistened eyes, the incidents we have already given our readers.

"Philips," said he, after stating what had befallen him, "you know that conversation we had while on our way to the field, after I was shot. I had always been such a lucky dog, that I did n't believe those thundering bullets would strike me. But when I laid bleeding to death, as I feared, I wished I was a Christian. I confess a man does need something more than I have, to support his soul when he sees death approaching."

"Accept, then, the support of the gospel, my friend. It is yours, if you will only give it your acceptance. Have you a Bible?"

"Yes, one that my sister gave me, years ago."

"Read it, then, Sergeant; it will show you the way to happiness.

CHAPTER XXIX.

"It is more blessed to give than to receive."
"One man has one way of talking, and another man has another."
"I reckon this always, that a man is never undone till he be hanged."

We will now follow the fortunes of some of our other friends for a time, as doubtless the reader will like to know what has befallen Frederic Sedgwick and his little interesting family during the months that have passed since he left the capital and went again forth to battle. It was in the winter of 1863; great changes had been made in our army since the time when it was first called to assemble for the defence of our capital, not two years before. Many officers had been called to leave the men to whom they had become attached, and lead those to whom they were strangers in person, in military duties.

Frederic Sedgwick had been ordered to a division of the Western army, quartered not far from Holly Springs. He was acting as Provost Marshal, when he was laid upon a bed of sickness. He had been attacked with a fever, which raged with violence for a fortnight; at the end of that time, the enemy attacked Holly Springs. It will be remembered by those familiar with the history of this war, that the Union forces felt obliged to surrender to the Southrons at that point, and soon the trying intelligence reached Frederic that himself, with the regiment to which he belonged, was in the hands of the Rebels. He soon was apprised of the fact that he was expected to go before the Rebel commander to be paroled.

"How can I mount a horse?" said he to one of his own men.

"O, we will help you, Colonel."

They did help him; and by the aid of two kind friends, he was enabled to get upon his horse's back, feeling very faint, yet kept from sinking by the excitement attending his situation. Having passed through what, to him, was a most severe ordeal, he was, with all of his regiment who were not killed, sent to the parole quarters, a few miles distant from Holly Springs. Upon arriving at the place, he found that he was to be quartered in a mansion house, the appearance of which was rather imposing. His official position procured for him some consideration, for he had been promoted to the office of Colonel, sometime previous to his being ordered to the post he had recently occupied.

A lady was looking out of the window as Frederic rode up to the door. "What a death-like countenance that man has," exclaimed she to some person near by, and then she hastened to meet Frederic, as he was assisted to enter the hall.

"You are very sick," said she to Frederic. "Assist him to lie down upon this lounge," continued the lady, addressing those who were supporting him. Her orders were obeyed, and she quickly ordered a reviving cordial to be administered to the patient, and stood by, until Frederic had swallowed it, and seemed somewhat refreshed by its influence. She then told one of the officers who had the care of these prisoners, that they had acted without any show of mercy in bringing that suffering man from his sick-bed.

"But he's a Yankee prisoner, madam, and must accept whatever falls to his lot, in the chances of war."

"But has humanity no claims upon men who are engaged in war?"

"Yes, madam, we mean to treat our prisoners as well as we can; we have not been unkind to this captured officer. It is no fault of ours, that we found him on a sick-bed."

"But it was wrong to make him mount a horse and ride from Holly Springs. I imagine you would n't any of you like to be treated as you have treated him."

"All the Southern ladies don't feel so much for Yankee prisoners as you do for this one, madam."

"If they don't they ought to. I feel towards the enemy's men who are captured, as I wish to have them feel towards our boys when they fall into their power. I have always felt so, and I am determined to treat our prisoners of war as I should like to have my son treated, were he to become a prisoner."

"That may be a good rule, madam, yet I can't see how we can make it work, as we are situated."

"It ought to be made to work, as you say; for it is the golden rule, given us by our Saviour."

"Indeed!" said the man addressed. "I had about forgotten that it was in the Bible, though I have read it no doubt, but not lately."

If the lady of this Southern mansion was surprised that this Rebel officer was not familiar with the Scriptures, we are not. This lady, whom we shall designate as Mrs. Palmer, strictly observed the letter of the golden rule, in her conduct towards Frederic. She had him placed in a bed, and saw that he was attended faithfully by her servants. These, however, needed no second bidding to move them to wait upon the Yankee Colonel. They were glad to do anything for him, and some were emulous of the right and privilege of ministering to his necessities.

"How pale that Yankee looks," said an inmate of the house, a day or two after Frederic arrived, to Mrs. Palmer. It would n't be strange if he should die here. Do you know who his friends are, and where they live?"

"I have n't asked him yet," responded the other; "but I should like to know, so that in case he should die, I might write to his wife or mother, sometime. A brother officer would probably write and inform them of his fate; but if anything should ever happen to my son under like circumstances, I should feel that a woman could tell me particulars, that a man would overlook or forget."

Mrs. Palmer went, immediately after this conversation had taken place, to the room of her patient. His attendant informed her that he was sleeping, so she approached his bed with noiseless footsteps, and stood gazing upon him for some time. How like the sleep that knows no waking, did the slumber of Frederic appear. His face was very pallid, and the long, black eyelashes that rested upon it, contrasted strangely with its whiteness, while his thick locks of jet black, silken hair, hung carelessly around his marble forehead. His features and form were attenuated, so that he reminded one of a skeleton; and his hands seemed to Mrs. Palmer as she looked at them, a fit representation of the claws of some large bird.

"Poor man," said the kind lady, mentally, "how I pity him;" and while she looked and pitied, her patient opened his eyes. He seemed some surprised to see his good hostess standing so near his couch; but the lady told him at once how she happened to be there, and he thanked her for the friendly interest she manifested in him.

"I have thought that if I should die beneath your roof, I should like to have my friends hear the particulars, that would interest them so deeply, from *your* pen. Yet I have felt it too great a favor to ask of you. Yourself and my dear mother are widely separated as regards your sentiments respecting our country, still, you agree in respect to your principles of action; for you, like my loved parent, seem to wish to do as you would be done by, at least, in your conduct towards me."

"I do mean to do by you as I would wish your mother to do by my son, should she ever have such an opportunity to minister to his comfort as has been afforded me to care for you; but you are talking too much, I fear, and you have not yet given me your mother's or your wife's address."

Frederic then gave the lady the address of both these loved ones, and mentioned also, some little circumstances, with which the reader is already acquainted. "If you should ever visit the North, I should love to think that you would go to the place where my wife and mother reside. As I understood you to say on one occasion that you had never been south of Philadelphia, I wish you could visit New

England for your own sake. 'I think you would regard the people of those States very differently, if you knew them well, from what you do probably at present."

"I might; yet I don't expect ever to go North; still, should I ever be led there by any circumstances, I hope I shall see your mother, Colonel Sedgwick. But you don't belong to or command a Massachusetts regiment, I am told."

"I enlisted in the 'Old Bay State,' but was promoted, and then sent to this part of the country."

"It appears from that, that you have been pretty active in fighting your Southern brethren."

"It isn't in me to do things by the halves; if, in my opinion, anything is worth doing at all, it ought to be done thoroughly."

"I shall know what to expect from you, then, when you are exchanged," said Mrs. Palmer, as she left the room; then, after reaching the hall, she turned, and bade her guest 'good day.'

Frederic did not know but he had offended his hostess; still, he was conscious of being innocent of doing so, intentionally. He felt grateful to her, for her kind interference in his behalf, and he also admired her ladylike deportment. He had felt surprised at her kindness to himself, exerted just at that juncture when the famous proclamation of Jefferson Davis, had been issued, which threatened the commissioned officers of the United States with assassination, if they should fall into the power of the Confederacy. Therefore, this unexpected good treatment was appreciated more highly by Frederic, and he felt that the good hand of the Lord was to be acknowledged, in this unlooked for help. The bitterest drop in the cup of suffering, which this husband, father, and son, was now tasting, was the thought of what his friends at home would suffer on his account.

Frederic well knew that his mother and Julia would watch carefully for news from him, and that they had doubtless heard of his sickness and subsequent capture. It was impossible that they should know all, and he was aware that they might conjecture much more that was painful than he had experienced, disagreeable as his experience had been. As soon as he was allowed to write at all, he wrote a very few lines to his family, to relieve their trying suspense. The care taken of him, and of everything that was his, by the lady of this aristocratic mansion, was indeed a boon from heaven.

He knew that, soon after his arrival, his hostess had given orders to her servants to see that the sick man's baggage was conveyed to a place of safety near his room, and that her orders had been obeyed; and he thought with pleasure of the privilege it would be to him, to speak to his Northern friends of the kindness he had received at the hands of this secession lady. Yet a sigh escaped him when he reflected that on one point she was infatuated, and that, strangely. He prayed that this might not be true of her, long.

CHAPTER XXX.

> "Alas! if we murmur at things like these,
> That reflection tells us are wise decrees,
> That the wind is not ever a gentle breath,
> That the sun is often the bearer of death,
> That the ocean wave is not always still,
> And that life is checkered with good and ill,
> If we know 't is well such change should be,
> What do we learn from the things we see?
> That an erring and sinning child of dust,
> Should not wonder and murmur, — but hope and trust!" — HALL.

WHEN Frederic had recovered so far as to be able to exercise in the open air, he was told that he would soon be sent to the barracks for paroled prisoners at St. Louis. Would I could go to my home for a time, thought he, yet he knew that the journey thither, would be too arduous an undertaking for one with his small amount of strength to endure, without injury. So he gave up the thought at once, and strove to content himself with his lot; but as the time drew near when he must leave this hospitable mansion, he felt regret at leaving a place where the bitterness of captivity and bodily suffering had been made endurable by the kindness of one, who was not only a stranger but a foe to the cause so dear to his heart; and the place was made sacred by the thought, that Israel's God had cared for him there. It was indeed a fit place to set up a waymark, to point out the power that had led him on thus far.

Frederic had conversed but little with his hostess, since that day on which she watched him when sleeping; but on the day preceding the one on which he was to set out for his new quarters, she met him in the hall, and invited him to take a seat in her parlor, saying, "I want to talk with you a little, before you leave us."

"I shall be glad to oblige you, madam," replied Frederic, as he accepted her invitation, and sat down upon a sofa, near which Mrs. Palmer had seated herself.

"You remember, I suppose," remarked the lady, "what you said about doing what you were called to do, thoroughly, when we conversed together, sometime since."

"I do recollect expressing myself in that way to you, and I feared afterwards, that you was offended at what I said, replied Frederic; "but I hope," he added, that you was not."

"I was not; yet that remark of yours did not suit me; at least, it was what I could n't be pleased with. Are you a fair specimen of the officers in the United States service?"

Frederic smiled at this question, and responded to it, by saying he hardly knew how to answer the question. "I believe that there are better officers, who are better men, too, than I am, in the Union service. Perhaps the average number are not all as conscientious as we could wish them. Some, I fear, have little fear of God before their eyes; I hate to have such go forth to battle."

"Our side do not fear this last-named class, terribly as they have at times fought, as they do such men as General Mitchel, Commodore Foote, and others, who fight from principle."

"Right is might, and a sense of right in what we are doing, strengthens us both to do and bear," said Frederic.

After a pause of a few minutes, Mrs. Palmer said: "I am very glad that I have made your acquaintance, Colonel Sedgwick. I have a better opinion of New England people now, than I had before you came here."

"Was brought here, you mean; it can hardly be said I came."

"Well, you got here somehow, you know; and I am not sorry that I have had an opportunity to show you that even an enemy can befriend you."

"I assure you, my noble hostess, that I appreciate the favors you have shown me, most highly, coming from such a source."

"What did you expect, Colonel, from the mistress of this house, when you came to it in such a state of extreme weakness."

"Indifference, at the best. Pardon me, madam, for saying this, but you certainly had a right to expect a truthful answer to your question."

"I like your candor, yet I am sorry you should have received an impression that Southern females were devoid of compassion. I hope I am not to be regarded by you as an exception, yet fear it will be so."

"I hope that there are many ladies to be found at the South, who are governed by motives such as influence you, madam, and I may become acquainted with more ladies like yourself; yet, thus far, I have n't met with a single secesh lady, who has treated me with common civility, excepting yourself, Mrs. Palmer. I regret that this is true, yet it is so, nevertheless."

"I regret it too, Colonel Sedgwick, much as I have been prejudiced against the Yankees. I have ever felt that every Southern woman should respect herself too much to stoop to the level of such females as use coarse, vulgar epithets, when conversing either with or about the opposing party."

"I agree with you fully, and I feel quite ashamed of women when they forget what is due mankind from their sex, which should be the gentler one, as it is called. I have seen Northern women, as well as Southern females, for whom I have blushed, when I have been obliged to listen to their vehement expressions, in denouncing what they dislike or think not right."

"I suppose it would be useless for me to attempt to persuade you to adopt my mode of reasoning in regard to things in the country, which has, until of late, been called the United States."

Mrs. Palmer said this with much earnestness; and Frederic spoke as earnestly when he said —

"It would be entirely so, my kind hostess; I should not dare think as you do, if I could."

"And why not?"

"Because I should fear the judgments of Heaven, if I set aside or overlook the teachings of the Bible, as I should be forced to in that case."

"Do you understand the Bible, sir?"

"I think I do its important precepts; they are so plain that 'a wayfaring man though a fool, need not err therein.' Have you studied the pages of God's holy Word, thoroughly, my dear madam?

"I cannot say that I have; I am not as fond of reading at all, as many are; but I have read my

Bible many times, because I felt it to be my duty to do so."

"Forgive me, Mrs. Palmer, if I assert what may seem to you fabulous, but to my mind it is a truth as clear as noonday, that neglect of God's Holy Word has been the means of bringing upon our once fair land this fratricidal war. The golden rule has been forgotten all over the country, both South and North. Had not this been true, we should be to-day a happy, united nation of freemen. Had not the sentiments of our dear old constitution been trampled under the feet of wicked men so recklessly, things would have been very different with us now. We are nominally a Christian nation, yet the majority of the citizens of this whole continent are unchristian in their practice, and fail to acknowledge God, even as a moral governor, much less a sovereign Father."

"But still, you think you Northerners ought to fight."

"True, we do feel that we cannot help it. We did not wish to fight our brethren at all."

"But our army has beat you so many times, that I should think you would get discouraged."

"We don't feel that we have been beaten very sorely, for we have been learning by experience so that we shall be better disciplined warriors, for each rebuff we meet."

"Don't you believe you will have to give up, Colonel?"

"I do not, and shall be slow to believe so, ever; and most ardently do I hope that it will never be."

"Well, if you and I should live seven years, and should at the end of that time meet each other again,

I believe you will be obliged to confess to me then, that you are now laboring under a strong delusion in supposing that the chivalric South will ever be conquered by military prowess. You will learn, by sad experience, that the Confederacy is invincible."

"What would you think if some of your strongholds should fall into our hands during the year 1863? For instance, Vicksburg or Port Hudson; possibly both may be ours before next September.

"Impossible, that such a disaster should ever befall us; you have done all you can in Tennessee; your army, I mean. Then look at your 'army of the Potomac.' See how easily General Jackson can route your forces; one would think Abe Lincoln would have more sense, than to keep his vandals on our soil. But I forbear, as you are my guest, and have not evinced any bitterness of spirit towards my party, to express my feelings towards your side, in this abolition contest, got up by fanatics."

"I have expressed the feelings I cherish habitually towards the South, since I have been under your roof, my kind hostess. I hate no one; I feel no bitterness towards a being God has made, and I repudiate the abominable sentiment that this war was inaugurated by the North. The people of the Northern States were driven to arms while the chivalry of the South were eager for it. I know that if the North had wished for war they could have done the same when President Buchanan was put into office, as the people of the South did, when Mr. Lincoln was elected. There was much heartburning felt, I assure you, when it was found that the man who was thought unfit to discharge the duties devolving upon the Chief Magistrate of our nation, by many thousands of the citizens of our country, was to be at the head of affairs for four years. Many felt it an indignity too great to be borne; still, they listened to the dictates of reason, and remembered the counsel of our national father, and thus their ire ceased to burn hotly, and they contented themselves by resolving to mend matters at the ballot-box, the next time they should go there to choose a President. Now suppose the South had pursued this course, and had borne what they considered grievances, as we mudsills, as you term us, did, where would have been the fighting, the terrible loss of life, the widows and orphans; the weeping mothers and sisters that now are found all over our land? All this, and legions of woe beside, would have been unknown to us as a nation."

"You think the South responsible, then, for all the suffering caused by this war."

"How can I think otherwise? and pardon me, if I say that it would be impossible for any one not blinded by prejudice, to think otherwise."

"I appreciate your compliment, certainly."

"And my candor, too, I hope."

"Yes;" and Mrs. Palmer smiled as she uttered this "yes." "Somehow I cant get angry as I ought, at what you say; but I wouldn't bear it from every——" she hesitated, and Frederic said quickly, Yankee. "That is not just what I was going to say; but that is a name I do not like, however; yet I meant to call the enemies of the Confederacy by a more disgraceful name."

Frederic wished to say, very much, "no name you could call us, would disgrace us," but he remembered he was conversing with a woman, and forbore.

"Let us part in kindness, madam," said he; "our next meeting may be on that great day —

'For which all other days were made.'"

"I hope we shall meet again on earth; I want you to tell me, some years hence, what you think about our losing Vicksburg, Port Hudson, and giving up to our opponents; and I shall wish you to be as candid then, as you are now."

"I shall be glad to talk with *you* then, too," said her guest with a smile.

Then, with many thanks for her kindness to him, he took his leave of her, greatly regretting that the judgment of one so kind-hearted should be so sadly perverted from right.

CHAPTER XXXI.

"We, ourselves, can never tell what is for our good."

Probably not one of the large family of human beings God has created, would ever think of a state of captivity as being anything but terrible. Nothing can be more abhorrent to a freeman, than the thought of being deprived of liberty. To become a prisoner of war is humiliating, and at the same time it is aggravating, because one is under the control, and at the mercy, of foes; yet life in a prison has, to some, been made tolerable, and the result of imprisonment has sometimes been anything but grievous.

Frederic Sedgwick was one who felt keenly all the ills of life. He was highly susceptible of both joy and sorrow. He, too, was possessed of large sympathies, and most keenly felt the woes of his fellow beings. He found himself on the way to the quarters for paroled prisoners, soon after his last conversation with Mrs. Palmer, and, while on that journey, had a mighty conflict with his own feelings, ere he could submit cheerfully to the idea of spending months in a monotonous state of waiting. His temperament was ardent, and his habits so active, that the state of usefulness which he was anticipating, looked dismal, indeed, and he felt that no selfish motive could reconcile him to it. "To face death upon the battle-field," thought he, "would be pleasure, compared with this lingering pain caused by having nothing to do. Lord, help me," he in his inmost spirit cried; and he felt that the cry was heard, for his spirit was at once cheered by the remembrance of those tender words of Holy Writ, "Fear not, I am with thee; I will never leave thee nor forsake thee;" and his desponding heart thrilled at the thought that his Saviour would go with him, and be with him.

"I can," said he mentally —

> ———"do all things, and can bear
> All suffering, if my Lord be there."

And Frederic, during his confinement, realized that he was not alone, but that he was supported by a strength not his own.

"If I may not do what I would, I can do something," thought he; and he did find employment that beguiled many an hour of its gloom. Very many of his fellow-prisoners were destitute of the support by which he was upheld. Some, to whom he had access, were sick or wounded, and were grateful for his sympathy and kind expressions, when he could offer them nothing more.

He had not long been at his new quarters, before his eyes were blest with the sight of his wife and little ones. How his heart leaped for joy when he beheld Julia and her children; she had not apprised him of her coming, for she would love to give him, she said, an agreeable surprise.

"But I have come to stay in this city while you are confined here."

She made this remark with some emphasis, in reply to Frederic, who told her he was very glad to have the privilege of seeing herself and the children, even for a little while.

"I can sacrifice home comforts as easily as you can, my husband, and shall contrive to feel at home, in a boarding-house, until you are exchanged. I think these quarters for paroled prisoners are good institutions, compared with some other places where our prisoners are kept. I felt happy when I knew that I could come to this city and be near you."

Frederic thanked his wife with tears in his eyes, on her arrival, but he felt that he had greater reason to be thankful, not only to her, but to God, as the weeks passed away, and he remained a prisoner. He was not idle, and as he was a lawyer by profession, his services were valuable many times at court martials that were held in the vicinity of the place where he was. Incidents of interest were daily occurring around him that were varied in character, and afforded opportunities for showing kindness to those who were less favored than himself.

The life here was altogether a new chapter in the history of Julia, or Mrs. Sedgwick, as she was called continually, in her temporary home. She marvelled at the strangeness of her surroundings, while she made herself contented with her lot, by striving to do all in her power to make those around her as happy as possible. Frederic brought to her notice many cases of sorrow and want, that gave her occupation for both time and thought.

One of these cases was that of a woman who had left her home in the South, because she could not live in her own snug little cottage in Texas, for reason of her attachment to the dear old stars and stripes. This was a case that deeply excited the sympathy and admiration of both Colonel Sedgwick and his wife. This woman had two young children with her, whom she had taken from the home of their infancy, that was now made by treasonable men a dangerous place to shelter them. So this proud and heroic mother took them in the darkness of night, and led or bore them beyond the terrible surveillance of those who ought to have guarded their helplessness with the tenderest care.

The husband of this woman, whom we will know as Mrs. Westcott, was a soldier in the Southern army. Long and earnestly did she plead with him to forbear, when first he proposed selling himself to traitors; for she felt that it was nothing but fear of losing his property, which made him dare think of using his strong right arm against the Government, under the auspices of which he had always been greatly blest.

"I must study my own interest, if you dont," was the reply he made to the pleadings of his agonized companion.

"I can't sacrifice all I have in the world, and my life too, just to keep along in the old way of thinking. You'll find you'll have to change your way of talking, or you'll get into trouble; in short, you've got to do it, to please me."

"I will do anything but sin wilfully, to gratify you, my husband, but that I dare not be guilty of, if I wished to; and I do not wish to turn against the Union cause, and, God helping me, I will sacrifice the last drop of my blood, before I will prove traitorous to the Government I have always loved and felt proud of."

"Ha! I didn't know you could make so fine a

speech; but I caution you against talking in that way where you will be heard by our neighbors. You might get into trouble by your speechifying."

"Is it possible that this is William Westcott, my husband, who is talking thus! O, why did I ever live to see this day!"

"O, you talk like a fool, Jennie; you can't suppose I would run the risk of having my property confiscated, and having a halter around my neck too tight for comfort, when I can prevent it, do you? If I don't enlist now, I shall be conscripted very soon, so I had better go now, and save myself some disagreeable consequences growing out of conscription."

"But, William, why not take our children, and go to the North? I have some friends in Conneticut, to whom we can go."

"What would you do with our home, in such a case? It wouldn't be easy to transport either the house, or the ground on which it stands."

"Of course, I should expect to give up our dear cottage home, and many other things that are very dear to me; but I should rather do so, than live here as things are now."

"You are nothing but a woman, and don't know anything about public affairs; you ought to put confidence in the leaders of the Confederate Government, and not hold on to your old-fashioned partiality for the flag and Government of the United States. This secession movement has commenced a new era in the history of this country."

"I believe your last statement, but what you affirm in regard to my ignorance, and in respect to the duty I owe Jefferson Davis & Co. I must dissent from. I will not sell my integrity, for the sake of preserving even my own loved home, and I feel ashamed that you, my husband, can think of doing it."

"If you persist in opposing me in this way, Jennie, you will make a hard bed for yourself to lie in, whether you believe so or not. I advise you to try and compromise matters a little with our acquaintances and friends, before I go away, for you will need their sympathy when I am gone."

"Is it possible that you can suppose for a moment that I will be governed by such motives?"

"To be sure; and you will find, to your cost, that you cannot breast public opinion without being a loser; but, Jennie, you can easily pursue a noncommittal course."

"Not if I don't wish to. If I am asked again, as I have often been, if I favor the old Union, I shall answer yes. I shall gain nothing by wicked evasions, but, on the contrary, should do violence to my own conscience. No, I shall never allow a Rebel flag to wave over my head, when you are away. The old rag shall be hauled down, speedily, when I am chief manager here."

"You talk like a crazy woman."

This was all that this deluded man said in reply to the frank avowal his wife had made in regard to her determination. Many such conversations as the one we have given was had by this husband and wife, ere the former went forth to fight against his early home, and the friends of his childhood and youth. Mr. Wescott was a native of New York State, and his wife was born in Connecticut. He had emigrated to the border of Texas a few years previous to 1860, and had been prospered in his industrial undertakings greatly, so that he had acquired quite a little fortune.

When our disturbances commenced, no man regretted the course the South pursued more than this man, for he saw clearly that nothing but unholy ambition urged men forward in their rash course. When South Carolina took herself, in form, out of the Union, he could not believe the mania of secession would spread as it did subsequently, and he hoped that the dangerous fever would not reach his place. In this we need not say he was disappointed, and his joints smote together, like the knees of one of old, when he found himself called upon to take a decided stand, either for or against this new movement.

Others might pretend to be neutral, but he was not allowed to cover his opinions with any such subterfuge. "The Union was well enough as it was; I wish it had been let alone, but these politicians have got up such a commotion, a man must do what he don't really wish to, to save his property and his neck; so I suppose I'll have to throw my lot in with people around me, to prevent my family from suffering from mob violence. It's too bad, that things have come to such a pass, but it's no use for a man like me to hold against such odds."

Thus reasoned William Westcott, and in the same manner argued many a Southern man, not considering that every fearful soul, who thus helped swell the tide of treason that was deluging the Southern States at that time, might have set up a standard of right, that would have proved an effectual barrier to the onward rush of these dark waters, that have since submerged the South.

What a blessing to this world is principle; firm, moral principle, based upon a sense of creature responsibility, to a benevolent, yet law-loving Creator. Mrs. Westcott was governed by a high and holy principle of right. She was left alone with her little ones, on the departure of her husband, in the midst of enemies; and enemies, too, who, but a few months before, had been friends. No friendly hand was now extended to grasp her own, by any, of all who had been ranked among the warmest of her friends. She was a doomed woman, and as the current of popular feeling, in the vicinity in which she lived, was turned against her, it was not safe for one or two, who did not wholly denounce her, to befriend her; for they would, by doing so, risk their own popularity.

So Mrs. Westcott went out, and returned to her home, without being, at any time, greeted with a word of kindness, or even a faint smile of recognition. Thus her days were passed in sadness, and her nights in apprehension of evil. The presence of her children was her only protection from violence, she well knew; and she shuddered as she thought that her little innocents might be taken from her. The terrible outrages she had witnessed, which had been perpetrated upon some of her neighbors, because they were Union-loving people, justified her in indulging such apprehensions.

Her husband wrote to her, and endeavored to persuade her to become a friend to the new bogus government. If his property should suffer in consequence of her unwillingness to have a Confederate flag float over the house, he should never forgive her. He thought she had acted like one bereft of reason, since the commencement of this war; but he had always thought her a conscientious Christian until then, and hoped she would prove herself one again, by renouncing her stubbornness. He was fearful, he said, that he should be captured by the Yankees, and then, he should not expect to see again his family or his home.

His wife wrote a kind letter in reply to this missive, which had been received by her just as all her plans were matured for escaping from Rebeldom, with her children. She told her husband that he had never had as much reason to believe her a Christian, as since she had been called to endure the bitter trials brought upon her by the secesh movement; and she felt that he would be convinced of the truth of the assertion, at some future day, if his life was spared. She expressed her perfect willingness to have him captured by the Federals, as she might, in that case, hope to meet him again on earth. She would not tell him that she was about starting for the North, lest something should prevent her setting out as she had planned, and some of her husband's relatives should learn, through his letters, what she intended to do.

Nobly she kept her own counsel, and began her perilous journey with a throbbing heart; yet, as she went on, the consciousness that she was being exiled from her own bright home, for the sake of right, sustained her spirit, and she felt that the covenant God, to whom she had committed her darlings and herself, ere she bade adieu to her own dwelling, was about her path continually.

CHAPTER XXXII.

*" Who then should fear the face of man,
When God hath answered prayer?
Away, away from men and towns,
To the wild wood and the downs,
To the silent wilderness,
Where the soul need not repress
Its music, lest it should not find
An echo in another's mind."* — SHELLEY.

MRS. WESTCOTT had a light purse when she quitted Texas. She had a small amount of gold coin, but the most of her funds was nothing better than Confederate money. She left her home in a light wagon, drawn by a mule, and travelled in this way for many miles. Her journey was prospered for a season, but she felt greatly discouraged when approaching, as she supposed, a bridge that she could cross quickly, and then secure a resting-place, to find that the bridge was gone.

"What shall I do?" was the anxious inquiry that arose in her mind, as this dilemma presented itself. "It is of no use for me to sit here grieving over this mishap, so I'll turn about the old mule and trot in another direction."

She was not acquainted with any other road, and was forced to inquire of a passer by, after turning about, which way to go. She asked with trembling, fearing she should meet with rudeness; for she had experienced so much that was disagreeable, she became in that *one* respect, a very coward. The person that she first addressed, could not give her the information she desired, but she ventured to inquire at the door of a farmhouse, where she was met by a man whose pleasant countenance encouraged her to ask several questions, in reply to which she obtained some important information. She was told that, had she been able to cross where she found the bridge had been burnt, she would have found herself surrounded by the Southern army.

"It will be some trouble to go around and reach the Union lines this other way," said the honest farmer, when he suspected from an exclamation that escaped her lips, when she learned how near she had been to the enemy, that she did not care to enter the Rebel lines; "but," he continued, "if you are trying to get to the North, you won't be troubled to find friends that will do all they can to help you."

The poor traveller looked earnestly into the face of this man, and she was sure she read sincerity in its expression.

"I am trying to get to the North," said she.

"Then it was providential for you that our bridge has been burned, for had you gone a short distance beyond, you would have been stopped, and your chances then, for reaching your place of destination, would have been small indeed."

"Thank heaven, I escaped that calamity," uttered Mrs. Westcott, with emotion.

"You have reason to," responded the other, "but come in and stop awhile here, to rest yourself; you look tired enough; we are all Union people in this house, and we all know how to protect friends. So come in and welcome."

With streaming eyes our poor wayfarer accepted the invitation of the good man, for his wife had approached the door, and become interested in the appearance of the stranger, and joined her husband in extending his hospitality to herself and little ones. Soothing indeed to the harassed feelings of this heroic woman was the kindness of these strangers. It was such a relief to be permitted to speak to an individual who was not hostile to the cause so dear to her heart, that the unlooked-for kindness she had met here quite overcame her. She wept long, ere she could command her feelings so as to keep back the tears that coursed so wilfully down her cheeks. Yet these tear-drops were not indicative of sorrow; they flowed from a superabundance of silent joy. Reader, if you have never shed tears like these, you are still a stranger to one of the most ennobling joys of earth.

"I must beg you to excuse my seeming want of appreciation of your kindness to me," said our traveller, when she could command her voice to articulate, "but it is so long since I have been addressed in friendly tones, that I cannot but weep for joy as I realize your kindness, and feel that I am no longer among enemies."

"Then you are one of those persecuted for fidelity to the old flag," said the host. "Well, you are not alone; many have been called to suffer greatly, since this reign of terror began. You are not the first that has rested beneath this roof, who have fled from the fanatical violence of Rebels, to the United States Government. Has your husband suffered, too?" asked the farmer's wife, compassionately.

How our traveller wished that this question had not

been asked; yet she answered it, though in a sad tone, and her answer was truthfully given.

"Poor child," said the other, while a tear bedewed her matronly cheek, "then you have indeed a bitter portion meted out to you; but if you only put your trust in God, you need not fear, even 'though a host encamp against you.'"

How sweet were those few words of pious consolation, to the heart of her to whom they were offered.

"O," exclaimed Mrs. Westcott, "how good is God, to bring me here; shall I ever forget His mercy, in this event?"

"His mercy is continual and never-ending," remarked the hostess. You need n't despair of yet seeing your husband an altered man; only pray for him, in submission to God's will. You may have to wait long for the blessing, but it will come at last, if your faith fails not."

"I should have fainted in despair," said her guest, "ere now, had I not been able to pour out my heart's anguish before the mercy-seat."

"That is a sure refuge, and never, since this world was made, has it been sought with more earnestness than it has been by many Christians since 'this cruel war' began. If you have lived near the borders of Texas, you know more, probably, or have seen more of the cruelty that has been practised upon Union-loving people, than we have here; though, for the sake of humanity, I hope that no greater atrocities have been committed in other places than have been perpetrated in our midst."

"I can conceive of nothing more terrible or revolting, than scenes that I have been obliged to witness in part in my Texan home. I had, at the commencement of the war, a neighbor; a kindly, good sort of man he was, but he loved the Union. No other charge was ever brought against him but this; he could not rejoice when the news of Sumter's fall reached him, for he was grieved at intelligence so sad to him. Yet, because he could not sympathize with secession, he was forced to submit to almost every kind of indignity that could be heaped upon him, and at last, having suffered the loss of all his property, he was seized by an infuriated mob, forced into a box, and pressed down into it with a board, which these demons in human shape nailed fast. The box was then trundled over and over until it was near the river, when it was opened, for it was their purpose to drown the unfortunate man if they found him alive.

"The air was rent with savage yells, when it was discovered that the spirit of their victim had fled, and only his bruised corpse was before them. After reeking their unhallowed vengeance upon these inanimate remains, these deluded victims of Southern demagogues, started again in pursuit of some other citizen, to whom popular frenzy had denied the very privilege these half insane men professed to contend that all men are entitled to, by birth. From that day," continued the narrator, "I felt that, somehow, I must get away. I had been threatened frequently, before, with a coat of tar and feathers, if I did not recant, and express myself in favor of the bogus government. I hardly replied at all, to any of the threats uttered against me, but I resolved to leave my dear home, that once was, and go in poverty, though not in disgrace, to New England, where I hope to find a relative, who, if not rich, can assist me, through his influence. The steps of my husband, I hope, may one day be directed to his family, and thus may we be enabled to live happily again, under the benign influence of the old flag."

Mrs. Westcott tarried for a day or two with these good Union friends, and was guided by her host, who himself accompanied her a short distance on her way. When she drew near the Mississippi River, and found that she would be obliged to travel upon a steamer, she disposed of her wagon and mule, and took passage in a boat. In this way, she journeyed to the place, where Frederic met her. She was obliged to travel by short stages, for want of means. At one place in the southwest, she spent some weeks, in order to earn money to help her on the way. Beg, she could not, though she would probably have got a free passage through, over most of the route, had her circumstances been known to many who had means and inclination to assist persons situated as she then was.

Many acts of kindness she did receive, and after she became acquainted with Frederic and his wife, and experienced their sympathy and assistance, she felt that her cares were greatly lessened, and her trials, wellnigh over. They enabled her to reach her friends in Connecticut; and we hope the story of her trials, as she rehearses it, from time to time, will open the eyes of some of the men and women in our land, to the truth, in regard to the atrocities committed by the enemies of our Government, upon such as have dared to continue faithful to the stars and stripes. Some we know, who pretend to have *hearts*, profess themselves skeptical in respect to Southern barbarity, while they are continually seeking for something that they can contrive to construe into wrongs done to their immaculate Southern brethren. Of this class, we are constrained to say, "O, my soul, come not thou into their secret; unto their assembly, mine honor, be not thou united."

CHAPTER XXXIII.

"Do they not err, that devise evil?"

"He hath indeed better bettered expectation, than you must expect me to tell you how."

WE left our friends the Murrays somewhat abruptly, and were led to speak of incidents in which others bore a part; but we expect to be pardoned by our readers if we do not come up to their standard, because we have not promised them much, as regards our ability to write a number-one work of fiction. We have only pledged ourselves to give incidents connected with this terrible civil war, which appears at the present time likely to afford many more circumstances of interest to the generations which are to follow this present one; therefore we have contented ourselves with stating incidents as they have been brought before our mind.

It will be recollected that Mrs. Murray and Clara were inmates at the house of the friendly Mrs. Adams, when we last looked in upon them. Mrs. Murray was some time in rallying from the great nervous prostration which had been brought upon her. Her constitution was never robust, and she was illy fitted, physically, to contend with hardships such as she had undergone. She strove against despondency, by looking at the bright side of her prospects; yet there were moments when she was overwhelmed with grief at the thought of her situation, as a deserted, unloved wife.

She was going back to the home of her girlhood,

and she was thankful too, that she could return to the dear old spot. But how different were her feelings at the present time, from what they had been when she left the home of her mother, nearly twenty years before. A feeling of proud exultation had predominated within her breast at that period in her history; but now the leading feelings of her stricken heart were gratitude and humility. Angels could joy over her now, but at her leaving the home of her girlhood, they might well have wept, if tears ever could bedew an angel's cheek.

Pride would sometimes whisper to the heart of this fugitive from her own splendid home, that it would be more than she could bear to meet her sister upon whom she had, in the first years of her wedded life, looked down, because she was less aspiring than herself. At such moments the conflict carried on in her heart, unseen and unsuspected even by Clara, was terrible; but she was enabled at these seasons to gain the victory over wrong, and each successive struggle was less severe.

"Thanks be to God, who giveth me the victory," was then the language of her heart. "I went out full," said she, as she was about starting for New England, "but I shall return empty; I went out proud and boastful, but I hope I shall return grateful and humble. I read in my Bible, such words as these: 'In all their affliction, he (Jesus) was afflicted, and the angel of his presence saved them;' it seems as if these comforting words had been put there especially to inspire my fainting heart with courage."

"This assurance will last you to your journey's end, my friend," said Mrs. Adams, "and, at the same time, it will sustain thousands of sinking hearts beside your own."

The parting with these friends of a short period was tender and affectionate, for the ties that bound them to each other were strong and enduring as the ties of sympathy must ever be. Clara promised to write to Mrs. Adams soon after her arrival at her aunt's, for thither their steps were to be first turned, because the residence of that relative was more easily reached, than the home of Mrs. Murray's mother. Their journey to that place was not marked by anything of importance. It was probably remarked, by more than one fellow-traveller, that these two ladies were very quiet and unpretending in their manners, as well as very reserved.

Some curious minds felt a desire to know something of their history; but every question addressed to either mother or daughter was politely answered, with such noncommittal reserve, that the most inquisitively disposed they encountered upon the whole route, thought it not worth their while to pry closely into their affairs. The heart of Mrs. Murray beat almost audibly, when she found herself seated in a carriage that was to convey her to the house of her sister. Clara noticed the agitation of her mother, and longed to relieve it.

"You are tired, my dear mother, are n't you?" inquired the noble girl, tenderly.

Her mother could not reply, for the deep fountain of feeling was broken up, and she could not control her emotions. She pressed her daughter's hand in silence, and the hand that held Clara's trembled so much, that the affectionate girl felt distressed at the disquietude of her loved parent. She made no attempt to console her again by words, but only put her arm around her neck, and laid her cheek close to that of her mother.

The distance from the depot to the place where our travellers were to stop, was not long. Clara wished it had been longer, as the carriage stopped before her aunt's door, for she wished her mother could have time to recover her self-possession before she met her relatives; yet every other feeling but joy, at the sight of her brother, was at once put to flight. Edgar was looking out at a front window in his aunt's parlor, as the carriage rolled up and stopped before the door. He was not certain, until he had reached the sidewalk and caught a glimpse of Clara's face, that this vehicle contained his mother and sister. But he had kept a lookout every time the cars came in, for some days previous, hoping they would arrive. Several times he had been to the depot, thinking to give his mother and sister a pleasant surprise; but having failed to meet them, he had, on the day of their arrival, concluded it would be better to stay at home.

Edgar's aunt observed that he ran to a front window, soon after he heard the car whistle of the midday train from Providence, or rather, the train that connected with that one.

"Do you think they will come at this hour of the day, my dear?" asked his aunt.

"I do, auntie; for the steamboat train starts so early from Groton, that I don't believe mother will be able to get up early enough to come on in it. You know she has been so sick she will get tired easy."

"That is true," replied the lady; "and Clara will

wish your mother to come with as little fatigue as possible; so she will be likely to learn the most comfortable way for her to travel, before she sets out."

"There comes a carriage, Aunt Jenkins, and it is coming near the curbstone; it is stopping; O, it must be my mother and sister!" and away flew the delighted boy, and paused not until he threw himself into the arms of Clara, who was the first to alight. His sister embraced him tenderly, and then hastily disengaged herself, and turned to assist her mother; but she had no need to do this, for Mrs. Jenkins had followed Edgar from the house, and took her sister's hand as she attempted to leave the carriage, and almost bore her in her arms while they ascended the doorsteps and entered the parlor.

Neither of the sisters were able to articulate a word. Mrs. Jenkins seated her sister upon the sofa, sat down beside her, and encircled her neck with her arms. Their tears mingled in silence for a while, and then the elder sister remembered that their mother was up-stairs in a remote part of the house, and could not know of the arrival. She strove hard to check her weeping, and speak cheerfully, but her efforts were unsuccessful; so she arose, saying between her sobs, "I will go and tell mother, myself."

Just then her son Willie entered the room, and stood near Clara, who had been escorted in by Edgar, who had also had a care to the baggage, which had been entirely unthought of by his aunt. Willie looked around upon the tearful faces in the room, for all had caught the contagion, and even the merry Albert was weeping with the rest.

"Mother," said he, "I thought you would feel glad

when auntie came; you told me that you should; and now she is here, you are all making a terrible ado about it, seems to me."

"We are only crying for joy," replied his mother, with a smile that did her own soul good, as well as her boy.

"That is queer, seems to me; I don't cry when I am glad."

"Because you never was glad enough, perhaps," answered Clara, as her aunt went to seek her mother, and apprise her of the coming of the daughter, who had for many years been as a stranger to her.

"There 'll be more crying when grandma comes down," said Willie, "for she sheds tears ever so easy, and so she won't keep them back this time, I know."

Willie's prophecy was fulfilled; his grandmother did weep long and tenderly, in the arms of her newly-found daughter.

"Do I indeed hold my long-lost Clara in my arms once more? How long I have prayed and waited in hope for this hour. Oh, what a prayer-hearing God is ours; the careless and skeptical know not what happiness is; how my heart rejoices at this answer to prayer, which I feel has been vouchsafed to me."

Mrs. Murray lifted her head from where her face had been laid upon her mother's neck, and looked earnestly and lovingly into her face. Then she spoke, although it was not without emotion; she uttered the words, "forgive my past ingratitude, my own dear mother."

"Forgive you, my daughter? You have ever been forgiven by me, for I have felt that, during all these trying years, you have not known what you were doing."

"It took Mr. Jefferson Davis & Company to open a way for mother to do her duty," said Clara, as she now approached her grandmother, and kissed her affectionately.

"And now," said Mrs. Jenkins with a smile, "it must be myself who opens a way to the room where supper is ready for these faint and weary guests of mine. They must talk no more, until they have had something to refresh them."

Mrs. Murray and Clara followed her to the dining-room, and were soon seated at a board, which in reality deserved the term social, as all these loved and loving relatives gathered around it, with beaming countenances, which expressed more forcibly than words could, the gladness of their overflowing hearts. All Mrs. Jenkins's family were present on this occasion, excepting Bessie, who was absent from home. In the joyous excitement of the hour, she was forgotten; though far otherwise would it have been, had it been thought by either of her family that her company would have heightened the pleasure of the interesting circle. But they knew her presence would only cast a shadow there, so she was unthought of, for the time, by this newly-united family. Yet it does not become us to forget Bessie, much as we should prefer to linger with these happy ones. We must invite the reader to follow the fortunes of this misguided young lady, with us, in another chapter.

CHAPTER XXXIV.

" But who shall so forecast the years,
And find in loss, a gain to match;
Or reach a hand through time to catch
The far-off interest of tears." — TENNYSON.

———*" I could sometimes die, life's changeless pulse*
Beateth so wearily." — WILLIS.

BESSIE's life was a burden to her; she had nursed her morbid feelings so constantly they had acquired great strength. Her health was impaired by her mental uneasiness, and she was, on the whole, an object of compassion, as she went about unblessing, and, we had almost said, unblest; yet this would hardly be true; though it was true that she was insensible to the blessings showered upon her, which is equivalent in a sense, to being destitute of good. Poor Bessie! poor, because she would be unhappy. She could find nothing essential to complain of, in her cousin Edgar; still, she declared he had been the torment of her life, ever since he had entered her mother's house.

"A great, hateful boy, to come here, when my brothers were enough to make me crazy with their noise." Bessie said this on the morning of the day on which the mother and sister of Edgar reached Oak Dale, and she spoke these unkind words, too, in the hearing of the sensitive lad.

Her mother replied by saying, "for shame, Bessie, how can you speak so?"

"I hate boys; you know I do."

As she uttered these hateful words she flung herself out of the room. When she had closed the door after her, Edgar approached his aunt, and laying his hand upon her arm, asked, while his lips trembled with emotion, " Am I so troublesome as cousin Bessie says I am, auntie ?"

"No, my son; don't give what Bessie says about your being a trouble, a second thought; you don't trouble us. Bessie is peevish and fretful, and I know that she is not well; yet that is no excuse for her ill-humor, and I am ashamed of her."

"But, Aunt Jenkins, has my sister done anything to displease Bessie?"

"No, indeed; why do you ask such a question, my dear?"

"Because I heard Bessie one day say something about not caring for cousins, that supplanted her in other people's affections. I thought from the way she spoke, she meant Clara, and I wondered what my dear sister could have done. I knew she had seen the young officer, who Albert says, is Bessie's beau, still, I thought this was not enough to make my cousin feel so towards her."

"You are right, Edgar; your sister has not done anything to injure Bessie; it was no fault of hers, that she became acquainted with Raymond Philips; neither was he to blame for doing all in his power, to serve your mother and sister, when they stood in need of a friend; I shall always respect him for it. Bessie does not view things as I wish she did; her temper is not pleasant, naturally."

Mrs. Jenkins sighed as she spoke, and felt a pang of self-reproach, as she reflected that, as a mother, she had been too indulgent, and too indolent. She had thought only of the present, in the training of her eldest child. Thoughts of how she was to get along in the most comfortable way with the self-willed little body, and keep her from soiling and tearing her clothes, day by day, predominated in her mind, and kept out more important reflections. Had she realized that she was rearing a woman, who was to act an important part in her sphere, on the great stage of life, she would have done differently. It was too late now, she felt, to interpose her authority, but she had repented of her former neglect of duty, and God, peradventure would hear her prayers, in behalf of her ill tempered daughter. These thoughts passed in the mind of Bessie's mother, during the few moments she was occupied in making the last remark to her nephew.

"I am sorry Bessie feels as she does," said Edgar; "I want her to be pleasant to Clara."

"So do I, very much; answered his aunt; "but Edgar, don't let her know that you think Bessie don't feel right towards her, on account of Raymond, will you?"

"Not if you would rather I would not, aunt."

"I should feel mortified to have her know Bessie is so foolish."

"I hope she will not find it out, without being told," remarked Edgar; and here the conversation was interrupted.

Bessie did not join the family again, that day; she merely looked into the room where her mother was busy at work, and said that she was going out, and might be absent during the day.

"Good riddance to ugly rubbish," muttered Willie, as she passed him on the doorsteps, as she was going out.

"You impudent rascal," exclaimed Bessie, glancing an indignant look, in his direction.

Willie chuckled and distorted his features, as all boys will, when they can think of no better way to vent their disdain upon one they feel has misused them.

"I wish I could die," thought Bessie, as she went out from the home her presence ought to have gladdened. "Why couldn't I have been one of those pretty doves, getting their living so easily by the wayside? I don't see what I was born for, I am sure. I know I have done wrong to Raymond, but I love him, notwithstanding, better than anyone else; I wonder why it is I won't let anybody love me. But I have been tried so much; if I was only loved by most people as Julia Sedgwick and Kate Sisson are, I should be happy. I wish Mrs. Sedgwick would come home; I feel lonely; nobody at home sympathizes with me, and no one excepting mother and grandmother knows that Raymond is hurt with me, so they cannot sympathize with me in that. If Julia Sedgwick was here, I think I might tell her, that is, if she doesn't form an intimacy with that cousin of mine, who has made herself such a heroine. She might have obeyed her father, and stayed in her rich home. What difference will it make to her in the end, whether Jefferson Davis or Abraham Lincoln is President? She's a foolish creature; I'd laugh to see myself setting up an opinion in defiance of others about the National Government, and running off and leaving my birthright. After all, it may turn out that all this heroism has been practised in order to attract the handsome Yankee officer. I know I shall never like Clara Murray; but anyhow, I wish I had not written that letter to Raymond; I'll not let any one know that I regret doing so, however. It's nobody's business but mine. If I am unhappy, I alone have to bear it."

In this Bessie was very much mistaken; others had to be burdened with *her* sorrows. She could not assume cheerfulness, or would not, if she could; and she cast a shadow of gloom along her pathway continually. She made several calls on the morning she left her home, in the unenviable mood we have described, then dined and spent most of the afternoon with a friend. Wearied with herself, and any object she met on the way, she returned home just in time to find our happy party at the table.

CHAPTER XXXV.

"For selfishness will ever send
Suspicious through the breast;
And makes man treat his truest friend
As an unwelcome guest." — M. HENRY.

WHEN Bessie entered the house, and heard voices, as she drew near the dining-room, that were not familiar to her ear, she paused a few moments to assure herself that there was company at the table, and then turned about and sought her chamber. Wondering who her mother's guests were on this occasion, she laid aside her shawl and hat and seated herself to consider what she should do about going down stairs to join the circle that she thought, from the cheerful tones she had heard, must be very happy.

"I wonder who these visitors are?" said she, mentally. "It cannot be that Aunt Murray and Clara have arrived, for they would have come early in the morning, and it was past the hour for the cars to arrive that would bring them, when I left home. It is, anyhow, persons who do not visit us often, for I should recognize the voices of mother's familiar guests. O, dear, what a bother it is to have so much company; mother might as well open a hotel at once, and then one could be more retired, because etiquette would not require us to provide social entertainment for our patrons. But here I am, more hungry than I ever was before in my life, and if I have any decent kind of a tea, I must go down. I wish I could have eaten more dinner at Mrs. Gordon's, but I couldn't force myself to eat *her* soup, and so I'm really faint. I suppose those horrid boys are all of them at the table; I wish mother did not care so much about having them practise table-manners; they are nothing but boys, and they ought to wait until the older members of the family have taken their meals, and then eat by themselves. Heigh ho! if I was only mistress in this house, I'd fix things to my own mind, I know I would; but I'm nobody, and my tastes are not often consulted, nor my wishes, either."

In a wonderfully short space of time, these reflections were indulged by Bessie, who was, as she said, faint, because she had eaten but little during the day. Then she arose and went down stairs, and, with a feeling of hesitation, entered the room where the pleasant group we have before looked in upon was seated around the supper-table.

"This is Bessie, my daughter," said Mrs. Jenkins, as Bessie advanced towards the circle of pleasant faces; "and these ladies, daughter, are your Aunt Murray, and Clara, your cousin."

Bessie was taken by surprise; she bowed awkwardly, and coolly offered her hand to the new comers, while her countenance assumed an unnatural whiteness. Her aunt observed her pallor, and instantly made the remark to her sister, that the young lady looked ill; upon which Bessie said in a constrained tone, "I am only faint and weary."

"Sit down, Bessie," said her grandmother, "and take a cup of warm tea; as you are not in the habit of drinking tea often, it will refresh you."

"I don't care what I have," was the peevish reply to this kind suggestion.

A cup of tea was accordingly passed to the morbid girl, and was held some little time before her; and then, as she did not condescend to take it, it was set down by her plate. After a few minutes, she took a teaspoonful of tea from the cup and tasted it; then hastily returning the spoon to the cup, she exclaimed impatiently —

"I can't drink such stuff as that; but if I had some coffee I might drink it; is n't there any coffee, mother?"

"There is n't any made, my dear; but you shall have a cupful directly, as there is boiling water in the kitchen. Willie, my son, won't you ask Pattie to make your sister a cup of coffee?"

"I suppose I must," said Willie, rising from the table; "but if she was only good natured, I would do it willingly."

"*You* hold your impudence," said his sister; but Willie had left the room, and did not hear this unlovely command.

"*Daughter!*" exclaimed Mrs. Jenkins, in a tone of expostulation, which the daughter did not heed.

All this time, Bessie's aunt and Cousin Clara sat, regarding her with feelings of mute surprise, which they unsuccessfully attempted to conceal. Edgar was past sharing their astonishment, for he had been shocked too many times to be disturbed by her fretfulness on this occasion. He regretted it, however, on Clara's account, more than for any other reason; he very naturally conceived the idea that it would be very gratifying to his sister, to be kindly welcomed by one so near her own age, as was Bessie. He saw and felt that the entrance of this cousin, had brought a shadow upon the brightness of the hour.

Willie felt it keenly, too; for he was somewhat older than when he was frightened out of bed by Bessie's sobs and groans, some months before. It mortified him, that his sister should deport herself in so unladylike a manner, the first time she ever met her relatives.. Albert was so merry a boy, that his keen sense of the ludicrous was more strongly appealed to by his sister's moodiness, than any other feeling; but Mrs. Jenkins and her mother, were really ashamed and pained at Bessie's conduct.

It was a great relief to all, but Bessie, to have Mrs. Sedgwick announced, just as they were leaving the table to return to the parlor. This lady sympathized so deeply in the happiness of the friends who had met after so long a separation, that her presence was a comfort to them.

"Had I known," said she to Mrs. Jenkins, "that your friends had but just arrived, I should have deferred my call until a later day; but as I did not intend to intrude upon you at this interesting moment, I know you will all accept my warmest sympathy, with my heartfelt congratulations that you have been permitted to meet again on earth, and under such interesting circumstances, too. And now I will bid you adieu, and call again to-morrow, or on some other day very soon."

"No, don't go, Mrs. Sedgwick," said Mrs. Jenkins. "You are the very friend whose society will do us good, this evening; so please sit down."

Mrs. Jenkins was joined by her mother, in urging this friend to stop awhile; while Mrs. Murray's countenance said plainly it was her wish she would comply with the solicitations of her relatives.

Had not Bessie thrown such a damper upon the good feelings of this party of friends, the society of one, even like Mrs. Sedgwick, would not have been desirable on this occasion; as it was, 't was truly a relief. After a few commonplace remarks had been made by several of the party, and Mrs. Sedgwick had answered several inquiries made by her friends respecting her son and his family, who were, as the reader already knows, absent from home at that time; that lady ventured to ask some questions about the state of things at the South, or that part of it which Mrs. Murray and her daughter had lately left.

Mrs. Jenkins had made Mrs. Sedgwick acquainted with some circumstances connected with the history of her sister. And as the heart of this friend was touched with pity for the mother, who had endured such neglect from a loved child, she could not but feel the most intense interest, in learning the manner in which this daughter had been led to see her errors, and renounce them. She was therefore gratified to find that Mrs. Murray did not shrink from speaking freely of the past, though she did so with an expression of touching sadness upon her countenance.

Any allusion to her husband was carefully avoided by her, after referring once to his being a Confederate soldier, and that, consequently, he was absent from his home and family. That Mrs. Sedgwick knew her position in Southern society, she had no doubt. She inferred too, from the reception given her by Mrs. Jenkins, and her mother, that she was a very dear friend, and that, with the sunny expression of her comely face, made her feel that this lady was to be loved and trusted.

"How I hope her smile will prove contagious to Bessie," thought Clara, as that young lady entered the parlor a short time after the rest of the little group had gathered there; and with interest she watched her, to see if Bessie would not welcome, cordially, the friend so dear to the other members of her family. "She will be glad to meet this lady, certainly," was in her thoughts, as Bessie moped along to that part of the room where Mrs. Sedgwick was sitting, and in return for the warm grasp of that lady's hand, gave her a hand passive and chilling to the touch.

"How can she?" arose to the lips of Clara, but she checked herself ere a sound escaped her.

"Sober yet, Bessie?" said Mrs. Sedgwick, as that young lady took a seat by her side. "I don't wonder that you feel anxious to hear from Raymond, now that he has been in a battle or skirmish; but you must hope for the best, and even if you hear sad accounts of him, you mustn't be in haste to believe such reports."

"Do you refer to Raymond Philips, Mrs. Sedgwick?" asked Mrs. Murray.

"I do; he has recently been engaged with the enemy near Kelly's Ford; and it is reported that some of the men he was with are prisoners, while quite a number have been killed."

Bessie's cheek paled as she heard this news; to her it was very sad intelligence. Her heart was pained at the thought that possibly Raymond was among the killed or wounded, and oh, if he should die, feeling that she was angry with him, she should never be happy again; and she shuddered at the bare possibility of such an event.

Mrs. Sedgwick was quick to discern the fact that she had been the bearer of unpleasant tidings to Bessie, and regretted having spoken of Raymond, without knowing that she was ignorant of his probable condition. She did not understand Bessie's feelings fully, because she was not acquainted with all the facts concerning this young couple. Bessie had risen in her esteem, since she had seen her part with Raymond in so becoming a manner. She could never have imagined that a tender-hearted girl could have written and sent him a missive to cause him pain; so she unwittingly probed deeply the wounded heart of the poor girl, by telling her that she had much to think of that was pleasant, in regard to her correspondence with Raymond, since he left his home, and that his letters would comfort her, even if he should never return.

"What a pleasant memento they will be of him, Bessie." As Mrs. Sedgwick said this, Bessie hid her face with her hands and groaned aloud.

"Bessie, dear, don't grieve so," said Mrs. Sedgwick, in a startled tone; "all may be well with Raymond, even now. You may receive a letter from him very soon."

Bessie could bear no more. Her friend had innocently inflicted a wound, when striving to comfort the misguided girl. She could not think that Mrs. Sedgwick had intentionally given her pain, but she wondered why this good friend had, on that night, stumbled upon the very subject she could not endure to have mentioned in her hearing.

"You don't know all the cause I have to grieve," said Bessie; "else you would not have spoken in the manner you have to me. Yet you are not to blame; sometime you may know more."

"It pains me to think I have hurt your feelings, Bessie," replied her friend. "I wanted to comfort you, and my desire to do so, has led me to say that which has given you pain. Innocently have I done this, but now I feel that I must know your great trouble, that I may be able to sympathize with you more deeply. It will never do for a young girl to go about with her head bowed down like a bulrush, when she is just at the age when cheerfulness, and playfulness too, is as natural to youth as the air they breathe."

Mrs. Sedgwick remembered the unhappiness of Bessie, at the prospect of Raymond's becoming a soldier, some time before, and she was fearful that she was augmenting whatever of sorrow she had been called to taste, by a sickly imagination; therefore when Bessie arose to leave the room, and remarked that Mrs. Sedgwick did not know that Raymond had become attached to another beside herself, she was less surprised than she would have been had she not been acquainted with these circumstances. With a smile she arose hastily and arrested Bessie, ere she had reached the door, by taking hold of her arm.

"Stop, Bessie," said she, "and let me say to you that I never expect to know that Raymond Philips loves any other object as he does you, unless you forbid his loving you first; and then, believe me, it will be some time before he could learn to regard another as he now does you."

"Oh, you don't know all," said Bessie, excitedly,

as she flung the arm of her friend from her and hurried from the room.

Mrs. Sedgwick returned to the seat she had left, remarking, as she did so, that something must be done for Bessie immediately, to divert her mind from the gloomy fancies she was indulging.

"I feel as you do about Bessie," said Mrs. Clement; "I don't think she has any reason to doubt Raymond's affection for her. She is indulging feelings that are hurting not only her own peace, but the happiness of a brave young soldier, who is entitled to her sympathy in his hardships, and who, too, ought to be cheered by the influence of her kind, cheerful letters. I pity Bessie, but not because she has heavy trials to bear, so much as because, poor child, she cultivates an unhappy disposition. I would not say this before these friends who do not know her, had she not manifested a most unamiable temper before them to-night. I must confess, I am ashamed of her behavior."

"And so am I," remarked Mrs. Jenkins. "I feel that this is a part of my chastisement for failing to do my duty by her in her childhood. I did not, until it was too late, discover my mistake. I misimproved the opportunity granted me, during the first seven years of this daughter's life. Those were the golden years for sowing seeds for a harvest of virtues in her womanhood. I did not know this fact when she was an infant; at least, I did not appreciate it as I ought."

The afflicted mother wept, as she confessed her short-comings.

"Dear auntie," said Clara, lovingly, "don't dwell upon the past, but let us look forward with hope to the future. I will try and make Bessie love me, and then I will help her overcome these pitiless feelings; I do believe I can."

"But, my dear girl," replied Bessie's mother, "you are the very individual of whom she is jealous; I fear you will be greatly tried with her."

"You need not fear, then, as that will be in my favor. I do not believe my cousin is entirely well, bodily; but I know that I can relieve her mental suffering, if I can gain her confidence, and I shall try hard to do so."

Mrs. Sedgwick regarded the young lady with a feeling of admiration as she spoke, while Mrs. Clement, who sat near Clara, put her arm around her neck and kissed her fondly.

Willie, who had quietly listened to the conversation, gave his opinion unasked, in boyish style.

"Plague take Bes! I say she is n't fit to be company for Clara, anyhow."

"That is not a very charitable speech, Cousin Willie," said Clara; "we must have patience with her, she is unhappy, and really believes that she is injured. We must do right ourselves, let others do as they may."

"But, Cousin Clara, how provoking it is to have her act so all the time; a fellow can't take much comfort, when a sister is looking so woe begone, and snapping him up so every time he speaks; for my part, I wish Bessie would be like Minnie Granger and other girls."

"Perhaps she will become just such a sister, some day, as you wish her to be; be kind to her, Willie, for the charms of kindness are oftentimes resistless; and you have reason to hope that, in your sister's case, this may be proved true."

"I hope Bessie will love you, Clara," said Willie, in a tone that implied he thought it a matter of doubt, however.

"I expect she will," answered Clara. It will not be long before she will be convinced that I do not stand in the way of her happiness, and that will make a great difference in her feelings towards me, and towards that young man, too, whom she thinks is partial to me."

"It will be a blessing to all this household if your sanguine hopes are realized," remarked Mrs. Clement.

As the newly arrived friends were wearied with their journey, Mrs. Sedgwick took leave of the family at an early hour, and all its members soon after retired to rest.

CHAPTER XXXVI.

"Resolve, the haughty moralist would say;
The single act is all that we demand.
Alas! such wisdom bids a creature fly,
Whose very sorrow is, that time hath shorn
His natural wings."— WORDSWORTH.

CLARA soon found that she had not appointed herself an easy task when she determined to make Bessie her friend. A letter written by Raymond to his mother, contradicted the report that had been current, in regard to his being engaged in the fight near Kelly's Ford. His regiment had not been in that skirmish at all; it had been employed in whipping and driving back a party of guerrillas, who had been making depredations upon our sutlers for some time. Somewhere in the vicinity of Antietam, Raymond had received a slight wound in his hand, which, he assured his mother was far from being dangerous. The tone of his letter was a shade less cheerful than his former letters, yet he did not, as he affirmed, regret that he had become a soldier. The most painful part of his experience was brought about by intemperance. Not the intemperance of privates, but of officers high in rank.

"It is galling, indeed," Raymond wrote; "to be obliged to submit to men, and be commanded by them, when they, almost every day, disgrace themselves in the eyes of their command, by drunkenness It was a great mistake made by the 'powers that be,' to trust spirituous liquors in the hands of commissioned officers; and those men who threw this obstacle in the way of the army, would be convinced that they had acted unwisely, if they could witness the drunkenness that abounds here, among men high in rank. My heart sickens as I write; I hope we may succeed better in our next attempt to dislodge the enemy at Fredericksburg, than we did last winter. We are soon to make another attack on that place, or I expect we are, for General Hooker is now ready to pass the Rappahannock. I only wish that all the officers would keep clear-headed during another fight, if we are to have another battle. I am sick, sick, sick of rum's doings in the army.

"How is Bessie? poor girl! she is morbid and unreasonable; but my dear mother, don't treat her coldly if you meet with her, but try to lead her to view things differently.

"When you see her, please give my love to her, and tell her I am Raymond, still."

Mrs. Philips called, taking the letter with her, at the house of Mrs. Jenkins, soon after she received it. She inquired for Bessie, and requested, on being told that the young lady was in her chamber, that she might be called down. This request was complied with, but Bessie refused to see Mrs. Philips. Clara had told her that Raymond's mother had a letter with her, from him, and that she wished to see her down stairs, very much.

"I dont care if she does," was the unkind response of Bessie.

"O, do go down and see this friend, cousin," said Clara, coaxingly; "you will regret not going, by and by, if you continue to refuse, and thus throw away the friendship of this excellent lady; do be persuaded by me, your cousin, just this once;" and Clara put her arm around Bessie's waist, and laid her cheek lovingly against that of this cousin; still, the misguided girl was obdurate and refused to go down.

"Will you consent to my inviting Mrs. Philips to come up-stairs and see you here, Bessie?" inquired Clara.

"If I must see her at all, I will go down; for rather than be obliged to see her alone, I would go on a long pilgrimage, barefooted; but I don't see why she cares to see me, I am sure."

"It is enough that she wishes to see you, cousin, no matter why; come, you will go down with me, won't you?" said Clara, encouraged by what Bessie had said, that the ice about her heart was beginning to melt a little.

"O, dear, I cannot; why need you say that I was at home?"

"Because it was necessary for me to reply to Mrs. Philips's question, both civilly and truthfully. And I shrink from the task of saying that to her, which will lower my cousin in her esteem, for I think she is a noble woman. No Roman mother ever could have excelled her, I am sure."

These cousins had known each other only a few days, at the time of which we are writing. With all Bessie's querulousness, she could not find fault with any trait she discovered in the character of her cousin, but the more she saw her, the more certain she felt that it was possible for Raymond to love one so amiable. The idea that Clara should care to have her preserve the friendship of Raymond's mother, interested her greatly.

"She cannot care about Raymond, as I do," thought Bessie, "or she would be glad to have his mother think less of me, instead of wishing me to preserve her good opinion."

Bessie was right in her judgment of Clara, for this noble girl could not love any one so selfishly as her cousin loved Raymond Philips. But we are digressing again.

Clara perceived that Bessie was beginning to falter in her purpose of denying herself to the mother of her best friend, and she availed herself of her irresoluteness to urge her to do right.

"Come, Bessie; you will be glad if you do go down; I know you will. I do want you to go so much; it will make me love you better, and I want you to let me love you a great deal."

"Do you, really?" asked Bessie.

"Yes, most assuredly I do, my dear cousin.".

As Clara uttered these words, she put her arms around Bessie, and moved towards the door of the room.

"'Come," said she in a low tone; "come cousin, you will be glad all your life, perhaps, if you conquer your selfish feelings on this occasion. Be morally brave."

As she was speaking, she was moving towards the stairs, and somehow, Bessie could n't tell how, she got down the stairs, and into the presence of Mrs. Philips, who was conversing with her mother, her grandmother, and aunt, in the common sitting-room of the family.

"How is your health, Bessie?" said Mrs. Philips, extending her hand kindly to the young lady, as she approached; "you are not looking blooming and fresh, as you ought to be, child; what is the matter, dear?"

All this was spoken in the kindest tone possible, and so quickly, that Bessie could not have answered the first question, before the last was asked. When the lady had ceased speaking, Bessie replied that she was not very well, but suffered considerably with headache.

"I am sorry," was the kind rejoinder of her friend.

"I did n't suppose you would care anything about me;" said Bessie.

"You did n't suppose I would care anything about you? A very erroneous idea of yours, is that certainly. Let me tell you then, Bessie, child, that I do care to have you just the pattern young lady, physically, mentally, and morally, that Raymond wishes you to become. O, I must not forget to give you the message he sent in his last letter to me."

"What word did he send me?" inquired Bessie, eagerly.

"He requested me to give his love to you, and tell you that he was Raymond, still."

Bessie did not reply immediately, and Mrs. Philips asked her what word she should send to Raymond, in answer to his message.

"O, I don't know," said Bessié; "I must consider what to say."

Mrs. Philips left her to consider at her leisure, while she conversed with others of the little circle. The conversation soon became general, and the mention of one topic led to the introduction of others, until incidentally the name of George Ashley was spoken by Mrs. Philips. Clara started at the sound of that name, and longed to ask where this young gentleman lived when at home; she forbore, however, and listened attentively, hoping to hear something said that would enlighten her upon the subject. She was not disappointed, for Mrs. Philips gave a brief account of the circumstances which had compelled George to leave his home, and resign all claim to the portion of his father's estate that belonged to him, because he could not consent to aid the Rebellion against our Government.

"Where is this young man?" inquired Clara, eagerly.

"He is at present in Boston, where he has been fortunate enough to obtain a situation as clerk in a mercantile house."

"Has he ever been in Oak Dale?" asked Clara.

"He stopped here a few days, before he obtained the situation, and stayed at my house," said Mrs. Philips.

"Then you are acquainted with him."

"I am, and I esteem him very highly, too."

"It seems that this young man is not a stranger to you, Clara," remarked her aunt.

"He is not; I have known him long."

"And you might add, Clara," said her mother, "that you are greatly interested in him."

"I might, had you not added it for me, mother," Clara replied.

Bessie did not lose one word of this conversation. Was it true that Clara was attached to this gentleman? It might be so, Bessie thought. She hoped it was, at any rate, and she would know before long, for she would contrive to learn if such was the fact from her cousin's own lips.

"Then, after all my worrying, Raymond may not be so much interested in Clara, as I feared," thought she; "it's a pity, then, I wrote that letter to him, but I've done it, and it must remain as it is, with Raymond and myself. I wish I had n't been so hasty, but it can't be helped now."

Thus Bessie reflected, until her thoughts were disturbed by Mrs. Philips, who had risen to take her leave, and asked her again, what message she should give Raymond from her.

"Please tell him that I am not Bessie, now."

Mrs. Philips, after waiting a little time with the expectation that Bessie would say more, and finding that she did not, asked, "What more?"

"Only give him my regards," was Bessie's answer.

All her friends were glad that she had not refused at the last moment to see Mrs. Philips. That lady more than suspected that Bessie had left her chamber with reluctance to comply with her request; still, the fact that she had crossed her inclination to meet her, gave this kind mother pleasure. She knew that the happiness of her son was connected with the welfare of Bessie, and besides her love of benevolence, that led her to desire the highest good of all, she felt a special interest for the young lady who was to be to her at some future time a daughter. It was true she often wished that Bessie was a different character, for she was too much governed by impulse and too much inclined to excuse herself for wrong doing, by saying she was so constituted she could not control her feelings easily. Mrs.

Philips longed to have her see these faults, yet feared giving offence by kindly speaking of them to their victim.

She was ignorant of the unkindness of the infatuated girl, in writing to Raymond a letter filled with accusations and reproaches, for he would not speak of what had given him so much pain, even to his mother, therefore the conduct of Bessie had recently perplexed Mrs. Philips greatly. She feared her son would, at the best, lead a checkered life with Bessie, and that there would be more shadows than lights along his pathway, if he became connected with such a being of mere impulse. But she was determined to lead the selfish girl to be governed by higher principles, and leave the result with the All-Powerful One above.

CHAPTER XXXVII.

"And slight withal may be the things which bring
Back on the heart the weight which it would fling
Aside forever; — it may be a sound, —
A tone of music, — Summer's breath, or Spring, —
A flower, — a leaf, — the ocean, — which may wound,
Striking th' electric chain wherewith we are darkly bound."— BYRON.

"AND so I have come home, to find myself a deserted husband and father; I did not think my wife had courage enough to leave her home and my protection, she has always been so passive in regard to my wishes. It is that girl, Clara, who has brought about this state of things; I am sure of that. But where can they have gone, and where is Edgar?"

Thus mused Colonel Murray, as he sat in his library, a fortnight after the departure of his wife and daughter, for the North. He had returned to his home, with his heart full of angry feelings towards Mrs. Murray and Clara, and with a firm resolution, also, that he would find his son. He entered his dwelling, and saw several of his servants, who accosted him with deference; yet he asked no questions, but proceeded to the library at once, and from thence to the sitting-room of the family; but not discovering any signs of its having been inhabited very recently, he took himself to the chamber of Mrs. Murray. He listened at the door for a moment, and then opened it, and walked into the deserted apartment.

Colonel Murray looked around in astonishment for a little time, feeling bewildered in his surprise.

"What can this mean?" asked the proud man, mentally; "these rooms, where my wife and daughter have always been found, when at home, look as if no one had occupied them lately; but I shall find out, by the servants, how things are. Perhaps my gentle wife and daughter are practising some ruse, thinking to annoy me, for it cannot be that they have left these premises privately, when they were so closely watched."

Thus musing, Colonel Murray entered his library, and rang for a servant. Sam obeyed the summons, and stood before his master, with an expression of gravity upon his sable face, such as few could assume.

"Where is your mistress?" demanded Colonel Murray, in a stern voice.

"De good Lor' knows, massa, I spose; but none of de niggers here has n't seed her sence dat orfullest night I ever seed."

"What night, you black rascal? tell me, and don't dare to talk any of your cursed nigger nonsense to me, for you shall tell me all you know, or I will punish you, until you will be glad to."

At this juncture Mr. Smith was announced. This mercenary tool, we cannot call him a man, had heard of the arrival of his employer, and hastened to clear himself from blame, in regard to the disappearance of the two ladies whom that dignitary had placed in his custody.

"Good day, Colonel Murray," said this obsequious vassal of "chivalry;" "good day, sir," he repeated, as he perceived, by the expression of the Colonel's countenance, that a storm was brewing, which might burst on his shallow pate. Sam was ordered from the room.

"I'm very sorry, sir; I was as vigilant as a man could be possibly, and yet, somehow, your wife and daughter got out of this house, and away from the place, at a time when nobody would have supposed they would dare to go out of doors, for there was the most terrible tempest, on that night, I ever knew. They must have gone while the storm was raging, for they were here when it began, and I came here just as soon as it abated a little, and found the door that we usually enter, unfastened. You know, Colonel, that door which opens upon the piazza, on the east side of the house, is fastened with a bolt, and must have been opened on the inside. I didn't suspect anything had happened, until after the breakfast-bell had rung, and no one came down. I stopped to breakfast that morning, and after waiting ever so long for the ladies to present themselves, and ringing repeatedly, Hannah went up to her mistress' room, and found it vacant."

"How did the servants appear?" inquired Colonel Murray.

"They looked dismayed."

"Then you think they did n't know of the departure of my wife and daughter until after you came here, on that morning."

"Yes, I feel sure that they could not have known anything about it. The idea that the ladies had gone away in such a terrible thunder-storm, frightened them. It was hard for them to believe they had not been carried off forcibly, at first. Hannah was the first to admit that they might have gone off voluntarily, yet I do not believe she suspected they thought of going at the time they did go, though I am not certain but she had an idea that they would take themselves off, some time, to the North. I questioned her, but I could n't get much out of her yet; as far as she answered my questions, I think she told the truth; she seems to have considerable conscience about what she does tell."

"Hang her conscience; I 'll make her tell me all she knows, and Sam, too."

"That Sam, I don't know what to think of him; he's one way one minute, and some other, a minute after."

After a long pause, Colonel Murray rang the bell loudly, and Sam again thrust his shining face within the library door, asking, "What does massa want?"

"I want you to come here," said the Colonel.

"Yah, massa," said the slave, as he again presented his *very* grave countenance to his master. As he stood before the man who he well knew had unlimited power over his person, Sam did not tremble, or manifest any other sign of fear, and Colonel Murray was more puzzled by the expression of his face than he had ever been before.

"Sam," asked he, "did you tell me the truth, when you said you did n't know how your mistress left the house?"

"Sartin true, I did, massa. I hope to die dis minute, if I did n't tell de truth 'bout it."

"You did n't see her go, then?"

"Lor', no, massa. Why, 't was de orfullest night dat eber was seed. I's so skeered, I kep my head kivered up 'n bed. I hope nobody come and took Missus and Miss Clary off, that's all."

The Colonel studied the face of his servant, while

he gave the foregoing account of what had occurred, but could make out no more than he had often done when Sam had before mystified him.

"If I find out that you have lied to me, Sam, it will go hard with you," said the Colonel.

"I reckon Sam knows dat ar wal 'nough to tell de truth; but massa neber 'd find out Sam lied dis time, dat's sartin."

The Colonel had Hannah summoned before him.

"Now," said this chivalric gentleman, "I must have you tell me the truth about your mistress. Did n't you help her and Clara dress, to go out that night?"

"No, massa."

"Did n't see or hear them leave the house?"

"No, massa; I never seed um go, an' nothin' could be heerd, the thunder was so loud;" and the servant cried, "so dar was no hearin' nothin'. I never 'spected dey 'd go off, when it rained an' lightened so dreffully, I's sure."

"Then you expected they were going away sometime, did you?"

"I's kinder 'spected it, 'coz I heern missus say, one day, 'Oh, how I wish I could get to my mother and sister in Massachusetts.' I blieve dat was de place she told on. She did n't know 's I heerd her, but I 'spected she meant to try to git to dat place, sometime. I hope de good Lor took care ob her, and Miss Clary, in dat orful storm, if dey was trav'lin in it; anyhow, I's asked him to look arter 'em, soon's I knowed dey's gone; dat's all I could do for 'em."

"Did n't you pray that they might return to their

home, Hannah?" asked Colonel Murray, thinking he should learn something by her answer.

Hannah did not reply immediately, and the question was repeated with emphasis, and she was threatened with punishment if she did not tell the truth.

"'Pears like I could n't tell nothin' but dat is right 'bout it, massa; and de bressed Lor knows I did n't tink to pray dat ar, no ways."

"You are glad, then, to have your mistress away, are you?"

"No, massa, not dat; I's sorry like, as dey did. Massa Jones, a while back, Sam heerd 'em say dey was comin' dat night, so it made me glad to have de tunder and lightnin' cum dat ar night. I tole Miss Clary all Sam heerd, and I was so glad dese men did n't cum, I e'en a'most cried for joy, 'til I find out Missus had dun gone off somewhar, and den I feel bad 'cause I dunno whar she be."

There was an air of Christian sincerity about Hannah, which inspired trust, even in the hearts of the most suspicious. Colonel Murray did not doubt her word on this occasion; the revelation she had made, however, was mortifying to him. He dismissed her from his presence, and then interrogated Smith, in regard to what had transpired in his absence. This apology for a man was forced to admit that Mrs. Murray and her daughter had doubtless escaped insult, if not injury, by leaving their home at just the time they had done so. The indignation of the Colonel was roused by hearing this statement, and his pride was sorely wounded besides.

"To think," said he, "that any of *my* family should have been exposed to the violence of a mob. Worse still, to be obliged to feel that their perverseness in maintaining their own ultra opinions has brought disgrace upon me."

"People can't be blamed for becoming excited in such times as these, and it seems strange that women folks don't fall in with others, in their way of thinking."

"A d—n mean piece of business, this, to be transacted on my premises. How did you convince the men that assembled here, that there were no tories here?"

"I happen to have some influence with one of the leaders, and he kept the rest back, while I went through the house and over the place to convince him that the birds he sought, were flown. He stated this fact to the men who were waiting, and asked me to offer to treat them to a drink if they would go away quietly. They swore a strong round at first, but, after being told that they should have plenty of liquor, they were pacified, and having drank full as much as was good for them, they went away."

"Too bad, too bad," said Colonel Murray, "too bad, that a man must be mortified so."

"Men will go too far sometimes; I know it's too bad," replied Smith.

"True, but we here at the South have had such great provocations," said the other. "I don't know," he continued, "what has possessed my wife and daughter to adopt sentiments that I abominate; and now too, both have deserted me, and, not content with that, they have contrived to get Edgar away, before they went themselves. I shall let them feel that I am not to be trifled with. They will be glad to get back when their money is gone; they cannot have much with them, and their Yankee friends are not wealthy."

With this reflection, this lonely lord of his mansion consoled himself for a time, yet there came to him moments when the sight of objects about the house, which were associated with the remembrance of a wife and daughter he had unkindly treated, brought a sting to his bosom. He could not bear to look at anything that had been used by either his wife or children, and ordered every such article to be removed from his sight.

Conscience, that faithful monitor, more than once whispered to this forsaken father and husband, that he had driven his family from him by unkindness, but these gentle whispers were at once silenced by the man who had madly and blindly risked everything that ought to be dear to him, for the sake of the bogus Confederacy of the South. This was the hobby he had begun to ride with the hope of aggrandizement, and he would continue to ride it, too, even if he failed in realizing his own ambitious wishes for a time; he would, in the end, become a great man, and belong to a great country, that he had assisted in making independent of everything, even the law of God.

Colonel Murray did not say this in so many words, it is true; still, this was the result of his reasoning, and also of the reasoning of every other secessionist, or secession sympathizer, in our land. Are not such deluded mortals entitled to our pity? Yes, we must pity their infatuation, while we blame their faults, and sustain the glorious Government, which they would overthrow, by "the sword of the Lord and of Gideon." We must battle for the right, in humble dependence upon God, if we would succeed in our efforts, for God will be acknowledged by the creatures of His sovereign power.

Colonel Murray did not think to look for a letter or some communication from his wife, until after all his inquiries respecting her, had resulted in disappointment. He then bethought himself to look in her chamber for something which might enlighten him. He entered the room where, during many of the recent years of his life, he had seldom failed to find her. He searched the drawers of her bureau, but found nothing; then took up a book that lay upon the top of the bureau, and, on opening it, found a letter, superscribed to him, in the handwriting of his wife. He sat down, took the letter from its envelope in haste, and read as follows: —

MY OWN, AND ONCE VERY DEAR HUSBAND : —
When your eye rests upon these lines, I shall be far away from you; also both our children. I cannot go without informing you of my place of destination. I shall endeavor to reach my friends in Massachusetts, as soon as possible. It is not in anger that I leave you, but in sorrow; my heart bleeds as I reflect upon the cause of our separation. It is so unholy, so base, so heaven-daring. Would you could see treason in the same light in which I view it; then would the right arm you raise against our Government, be unequal to striking a blow against the dear flag of our Union. But you will not see; and all that remains for your poor afflicted wife to do, is to wait and pray for you, my misguided husband. Do not throw aside this letter in anger; do not spurn the memory of one who is still faithful in heart to you. You well know that my person is not safe here amid the clamor of an excited rabble, who rush recklessly on to accomplish

their terrible purposes. Judging from what I have witnessed of outrage perpetrated upon others, for their love to the Union, I cannot suppose I shall remain much longer unmolested. I, or we, for Clara will go too, shall therefore avail ourselves of the first thunder tempest that rises mid the darkness of night, to leave unseen a home, which, but for this frenzy of the South in withdrawing from the loved Union, might now be a happy one. If you spurn us for this act forever, it must be so, and I must live without you; but if you ever change in regard to the views you now entertain, and wish to rejoin your family, you will find your wife ready to welcome you, and forget all these dark and trying days, in the happiness of a pleasant reunion.

Do not blame any of the servants for any part you may imagine they have taken in assisting us to leave, for the poor affectionate creatures are innocent, and no doubt will feel anxious about our disappearance. If you ever wish to hear from us, it will be easy for you to get word to me through some Massachusetts soldier; that is, any word which it would be desirable for you to send. And now I must bid you adieu; yet not forever, unless you choose it shall be so.

Your afflicted wife,
CLARA MURRAY.

October, 1862.

"Humph!" said this fancied Lord of creation, when he had perused the letter. "She can stay with her plebeian relatives, for I shall never notice her more. 'T is too bad, however, for a man to be robbed of his children in such an underhanded way; she don't say that Edgar is with her, but I've no doubt she's contrived before this, to get him to that infernal State, the very last place where I'd wish my boy to finish his education. However, I can do nothing now; but by and by, if our forces invade the North, I'll make that insolent woman, and Clara, too, eat humble pie for their perfidious actions."

Having relieved himself by muttering the threat he could not expect to execute, he looked at the missive of his wife a moment, hesitating whether to destroy, or leave it for a future perusal. He then threw it into a drawer, and turning the key upon it, which he afterwards hid, he left the room to attend to whatever business he might find had accumulated during his absence.

We will leave him thus employed for the present, to mingle in scenes that are not overshadowed by his dark presence.

CHAPTER XXXVIII.

"But gratitude still lives, and loves to cherish
The patriot's virtues."

"Not for myself did I ascend,
  In judgment, my triumphal car:
'T was God alone, on high, did send
  The avenging Scythian to the war;—
To shake abroad, with iron hand,
The appointed scourge of His command."

WE must now follow the fortunes of our friend Raymond, for a while. At this period in our story, he is as valiant for the right as ever; and as cheerful in the performance of duty, as if there were no feeling of sadness lurking in his breast, on account of the perverseness of the object of his affections. He is now anxiously awaiting a summons to the field of strife, and he wonders whether General Hooker will be any more successful in attacking Fredericksburg, than was General Burnside.

He had not long to wait, however, before a forward movement was made, by the Army of the Potomac, and our forces were met by that renowned Rebel, known to the world as Stonewall Jackson. It is not for us to give to our readers an account of this battle, or its result, farther than it concerned Raymond. It will be remembered by all interested, that the greatest of Rebel generals received his death-blow during this conflict.

His fall was a severe blow to the Confederate army; they could illy afford to lose him, and they felt his loss severely, not only at the time of his death, but subsequently, when they were made to feel the need of his sagacity and iron will. General Lee has never filled his place.

Many hearts were made sorrowful by that battle, and some, in such a way, that the wound then given cannot be healed by comfort coming from any earthly source. Of some, it has been said, ever since that sad period, "They are missing." Missing, but where can they be? ask the fond hearts of mothers, wives, and sisters. But only echo answers, Where? to the sad and oft-repeated question. Some there are, who have suffered from cruel suspense, since that battle, and some too, there are, who have not heard from their friends since the first battle that was fought at Fredericksburg.

Who shall attempt to comfort those, thus bereaved? We are coldly told by some, that such calamities are the fate of war; that we ought to have expected such trials, when we gave our loved ones to our country. We do not need to be told this; we acknowledge, that when we laid our friends upon the altar of our common country, we felt that we might be called to great suffering, on their account; still, we feel as acutely these tortures of suspense, as if we had not long ago, at times, pictured such trials in our imagination. But here we are digressing again, without intending to do so.

Raymond Philips was wounded on the same day that Stonewall Jackson fell. He performed his duty bravely, until a shot from the enemy laid him low. He was borne from the field weltering in his blood, the loss of which prostrated his strength rapidly. He was placed in a hospital tent, and his wound, which was in his left arm, dressed as soon as it could consistently be attended to. Every attention was paid him that the circumstances allowed, for he was greatly beloved by the men, as well as by his brother officers, and no pains were spared in administering to his comfort. Still he lingered, even after he was carried to a hospital near Washington, where could be found greater facilities for procuring necessaries for the gallant soldiers, who were suffering from sickness or wounds, far from home and friends. Yet not far from friends were all, for some had made many friends during the months they had spent on the tented field.

Among these was Raymond Philips. His kindliness of manner pleased, while his straightforwardness gained him the confidence of some, even, who thought him too puritanical in his notions of right. Raymond strove to maintain his profession of love to his Saviour, consistently, amid the temptations of camp life, as well as in all other places to which duty called him. His presence in the hospital cheered many a poor soldier, for he was patient and cheerful, and as soon as he regained strength sufficient to enable him to converse, he used it, to comfort if possible, the sad and desponding, about him. We scarcely need tell our readers, that he was one of those to whom it afforded comfort to lady visitors at the hospital to minister. These attentions, which he received in the guise of little delicacies, were most grateful to his heart, still he felt that he could not enjoy them fully, unless the men, whom some have termed "only privates," could share them with him.

"These are they," said Raymond one day to some ladies who had kindly brought him some tempting articles of refreshment, "these are the men who have devoted their lives to their country, and they merit all the attention you can bestow upon them. I would deny myself anything I crave, rather than have these noble soldiers do without what is essential to their comfort;" and many a luxury was given to the privates through his instrumentality.

The first duty required of Raymond, after he was able to converse, was to dictate a letter to a fellow-soldier who consented to act as amanuensis, to be written to his mother. He knew that reports of his case must cause her great anxiety, and therefore he told her in the most cautious manner, that although he was weak, he was fast recovering and might possibly obtain leave of absence, to allow him to visit his home for a few days, ere he returned to the post of duty again.

Having seen this missive despatched, he gave himself up to the performance of the duty of the hour. As soon as he was able to move about a little, he sought out, as far as practicable, those who seemed most in need of sympathy and kindness. Everywhere his presence was greeted with a smile by the poor and distressed, for he was known as a friend to suffering humanity; one who was not afraid of being contaminated if he approached *very near* the couch of a sick or wounded fellow-man.

This could not be said truthfully of all, even of woman; for some of the gentler sex, as we are called, dare not visit a hospital, and walk through the different wards, without keeping a smelling-bottle at their nose, thus wounding the feelings of the men, who have fought and bled to save, if possible, our dear land from ruin. Such had better never intrude their presence into these habitations of distress, for the noble boys who have been made to suffer from their love of country, ought not to be treated thus by those for whose welfare they have fought. If women or females, who are so strangely devoid of feeling as to act thus, could only see how ridiculous they appear, we are sure they would never play so ludicrous a part, with a hospital for a stage, again.

One young man, who suffered long and terribly from a wound in his leg, has expressed himself very feelingly upon this subject to a lady living in Rhode Island, who became his friend, by visiting the Asylum where he was confined, and offering her services in administering to the comfort of the patients. A matron requested this lady to assist her, by holding the wounded limb of this young man while it should be dressed. The lady did not shrink from the task, trying as it was to the feelings of one like herself, who had never beheld so bad a wound before, but she wisely reflected that if the patient could bear the pain of it all the time, it was little in comparison for her delicate nerves to sustain the shock of looking at this mark of a soldier's honor for a little while. And she performed her part well and creditably to her sex.

By that soldier she will never be forgotten, or by others whose burning brows she bathed with cold water, and whose parched lips and tongues she refreshed, by administering, in gentle kindness, some cooling draught to quench their thirst. This lady was afterwards told by the soldier who was her first care on the occasion of the visit alluded to, that he knew when his eye first rested upon her countenance, as she approached him, that she had not come in to gratify an idle curiosity, like those ladies who find a smelling-bottle an essential attendant on their visit.

"We poor fellows," said the young man, "wish these ladies would stay away; we don't care to be made a spectacle for the curious. Some of us have wives, mothers, and sisters, more refined than these butterfly women ever can be. We know what belongs to good breeding, if we are only privates. It amuses us boys, to see these would-be-nice ladies come along, and look at one poor fellow after another, as they trip disdainfully through the wards. One day, I almost laughed in the face of one of these visitors, who came along and spoke to a poor boy near me, who was very sick. Said she to him, 'Are you very ill?'

"'Yes, ma'am,' was the feeble answer, and then the twist of the lady's nose, and her 'O,' as she passed him with her aromatic bottle in use, upset my gravity entirely, so I could scarcely reply at all, when she put the same question to me, a minute afterwards. I suppose she thought me a graceless fellow, but I could not command my feelings or muscles for the moment. My sense of the ludicrous is too strong to admit of my being brought in contact with such females, without having it provoked."

Raymond not unfrequently witnessed such scenes as this young man described, and, like him, wondered that such women should at any time enter a hospital, unless summoned there to see a dying friend. He also noticed that the soldiers, as they lay upon their beds, studied habitually the countenances of visitors, and they seldom judged incorrectly, in respect to the characters of persons who came near them.

"We know very soon, when a lady comes in, whether we are to be any better off for her coming, for her eyes always tell us at once. It is so pleasant to have a fellow's head bathed, and have words of kindness spoken to him, that we watch anxiously for the coming of such every day."

These remarks of the sick man Raymond stated in a letter to his mother, for he wrote often, after he had strength enough to write at all.

"Mother," said this Christian patriot, "I have been learning in this hospital, and some of the lessons taught me here, will, I trust, do me good always. There is one thing which I have learned, that I want to have you teach to all, especially the young people whom you can influence, and that is, the very great value there is attached to very trifling things. I presume, my dear mother, that you have learned this long ago, for I remember you have tried to impress the importance of this fact upon my mind; yet I have never fully realized it until now. I here often see gladness depicted upon the face of a man, by a seeming trifle; a look expressive of sympathy, a tear it may be, or a hand laid tenderly upon a burning brow. Sometimes a pleasant smile, even, will act like a charm upon a desponding heart. These little things, which are in the power of all to give, are invaluable to the suffering. Do not the ladies of our land owe something to these brave ones, who have perilled life, health, and limbs, to help secure to them the blessings of our benign Government?

"I feel assured that every reflecting person will admit that they do. Then let each and all the ladies of the Union, practise a small amount of self-denial, to do something for the sick and wounded soldiers. Do any think that they cannot make farther retrenchments in their expenses? Let them reflect long and seriously upon this subject, ere they decide to do no more for those who are so richly entitled to their kindness and gratitude. It must be kept in mind that it is the privates who fight our battles. It is true we have many brave officers, yet what would they do without the men to breast the foe? You will, my mother, feel that I have spoken earnestly. I grant that I have, for I feel intensely upon this subject; and could you, and many of the ladies of our land, spend but one day, where I have passed weeks, you would not be surprised at my earnestness; you would rather wonder, perhaps, that I feel no more. I may see you erelong, dear mother, and then I will tell you of much, that will incite you to act for the suffering soldiers."

CHAPTER XXXIX.

"One part, one little part, we dimly scan
Through the dark medium of life's feverish dream."

Some there are, who can bear to be unwelcome guests.

"There comes Aunt Amey Benson, if I live," said Minnie Granger, one afternoon in the Spring of 18—. The mother of Minnie raised her eyes from a piece of work she was in haste to finish, and saw the veritable Aunt Amey approaching the side door of the house, by coming through a little flower-garden, which was the pet care of Minnie. Mrs. Granger sighed as she beheld her visitor approach; she could not help it; for she knew full well that the presence of this relative would bring a shadow over her now bright home. She was, however, a Christian, and endeavored to be guided by the golden rule, in all her acts toward her fellow-beings.

She met Aunt Amey at the door, and offered her hand cordially; then, perceiving that the old lady was out of breath, and greatly fatigued by walking, she put her arm about her, and supported her to a seat that was near, kindly bidding her rest awhile before speaking, or taking off her bonnet and shawl.

"O dear," said Aunt Amey, "I am a poor creature; I don't know as you are glad to see me, but I've come to plague you for a few days. You'll let me stay, won't you, Minnie?"

This speech was addressed to Mrs. Granger, who answered that she would try and make her comfortable for a few days, notwithstanding the family were much engaged in sewing, which they must accomplish without delay.

"Well, I supposed you would n't be glad to have me come, but I shall stay, if you have n't told me you are glad to see me."

Mrs. Granger did not know how to reply truthfully to this tirade, and therefore remained silent. Minnie had heard this conversation from an adjoining room, to which she had fled ere Aunt Amey entered the house. This lively girl was both amused and annoyed at the prospect which had so suddenly opened before her, of having to practise great self-denial for an indefinite period, for she had good reason to fear that Aunt Amey's few days would not end until some weeks had gone by. She had been congratulating herself mentally, only a few minutes before this old lady came in sight, that her family would escape the trial of a visit from this uneasy relative that year, for she was too far off to reach them.

Minnie believed Aunt Amey was regaling herself with rural sights and sounds in Minnesota, where the spring season opens most beauteously, and her disappointment was great to find it was otherwise. But Minnie Granger was her mother's own child, and she had only to combat inclination a few minutes, ere she resolved to make the best of a bad case, and receive this relative, whom she could not really love, with the respect due to her age. She soon emerged from her hiding-place, and saluted Aunt Amey with respect, offering her hand at the same time, which the old lady grasped so warmly, that the want of cordiality on the part of the young girl was unnoticed by her.

After tea, she informed the family that, after resting a while, she wished to hear the evening paper read by some one. "I prefer to hear you read, Minnie," said she, addressing her niece, or grand-niece, rather, for the old lady was aunt to Minnie's mother. The unfortunate girl could offer no reasonable excuse for refusing to comply with the wishes of Aunt Amey; she therefore seated herself by the table as soon as the paper arrived, which proved to be the *Boston Evening Journal*, and commenced the Herculean task of reading through its four large pages of finely printed matter, for she had been instructed by her "big aunt," as she playfully termed Aunt Amey, to commence reading at the beginning of the paper.

Minnie at first remonstrated, by asking if it would n't be best to read the "war-news" first. But this did not avail her much, for the old lady declared that there might be a great deal lost by reading a paper in that way; still, if it was a great bore to such a *smart* young lady as she was, to read an hour or two, she would n't ask her to read again very soon.

"Oh, don't say so, Aunt Amey; I can read all you wish me to," replied Minnie. Accordingly, she commenced at the head of the first column of the paper, and plodded through it, with an aching throat. She did not accomplish this task without interruption, however, for it was wellnigh impossible for Aunt Amey to listen patiently to any statement that was made in her hearing, without contradicting it; much less could she admit by becoming silence, when hearing newspaper reports, that she believed such doubtful statements.

"That's a lie. I know better than to believe such

stuff as that," were the frequent responses to Minnie, as she read the many items of news the *Journal* contained. Minnie's mother pitied her daughter very much, yet was pleased to see her bear herself nobly, through this torturing trial.

A letter was brought in and handed to Mrs. Granger, while Minnie was striving hard to preserve her equanimity, and satisfy her auditor with news. This afforded her a rest of a few moments, for Aunt Amey eagerly inquired about the letter, who and where it came from, with other rapidly repeated interrogations, to which her niece responded by saying, "I will read my letter soon, after I have first looked it over. It is from Aleck; so we can expect to hear from Charles Abbott, also, as Aleck generally keeps us advised of his whereabouts and condition.

Minnie, as might be expected, was delighted to hear from her brother, and not less so, to receive tidings of Charles Abbott. Both these young men were in General Banks's division, and the thoughts of all who loved them had begun to turn anxiously towards the vicinity of Port Hudson. Every paper they read contained some item in regard to this dangerous expedition, and Minnie felt it was a matter of rejoicing, that her brother had been in a condition to write as recently as ten days before that evening. She waited in silence for her mother to look over her missive; yet not so did Aunt Amey.

She merely allowed the mother to take the letter of her son from the envelope that contained it, and glance at the date, before she began to pull at her sleeve, and ask her to hurry and read the missive aloud. "Come, you need n't mind me; you know I am interested in all that relates to the war, especially all that concerns Aleck and Charlie. I know all about it, Minnie; you can't tell me anything, I guess, so you may as well let your mother read the letter aloud."

"I wasn't doing anything to hinder her reading it, auntie, did you think I was?"

"I thought you wouldn't be willing, perhaps, to have your old auntie know about Charlie; but I do know."

"I will read this letter aloud now, if you will listen, Aunt Amey," said Mrs. Granger.

"Do," said the other; and she listened quietly until her niece had nearly perused the first page; then her combativeness would not admit of her being still, longer, for Aleck had said that, on the last few lines, which her faith could not grasp.

"We shall have Port Hudson," wrote the young man, "the Rebels may say what they will. The sons of rocky New England which are here, are not to be daunted. The star-spangled banner *must* and will float to the breeze, over the enemy's works here, before next August."

"Pho," said Aunt Amey; "that's all nonsense; they won't do any such thing, I know."

"How do you know, auntie?" arose to the lips of Minnie, but she forbore to speak the words, and her mother proceeded with the missive. She read farther this time, without interruption, for Aunt Amey had a feeling heart, and the silent tear coursed down her cheek, as she listened to accounts which Aleck had penned, of the sickness and death of some of his brave comrades. After Mrs. Granger had finished reading, Aunt Amey said, sorrowfully —

"When will this terrible war be over?"

"If you mean to ask me when," answered Mrs. Granger, "I shall be obliged to reply that I cannot imagine when it will cease; but, Aunt Amey, our affairs are under the direction of an infinitely wise Being, and therefore all will, in the end, be well."

"I don't see the well, Minnie Granger; I know Christians pray, but how do they know that their prayers will ever be answered? It is all of two full years, now, since this Rebellion began."

"It is more than two years, Aunt Amey," said the younger Minnie; "it is two years since the enemies of our Government resorted to arms. They rebelled long before; treason is an old crime in our land; twenty or thirty years old at least."

"I suppose what you say is true, Minnie, but I am perplexed greatly with the way in which things go on in this country, and I'm perplexed more yet with the thought that a holy and sovereign Being disposes the events which are daily occurring. Think what these events are; think of the bloodshed, the pain and suffering caused by this war, and reconcile yourself as well as you can to the doctrine, that a holy God doeth all things well. For my part, I can't do it at all; I don't see the reasonableness of such a belief."

"Were it not for my faith in a sovereign, wonder-working God, I should be wretched indeed," responded Mrs. Granger.

"And so should I," said her daughter, with deep feeling.

Minnie was a lovely girl. We have said this in substance before, and our readers learned something of her character at the time Charles Abbott and Frederic

Sedgwick were getting ready to go to the war. It was this same Minnie, who strove to persuade Bessie Jenkins to be reconciled to the departure of her lover.

Minnie had never wearied in her efforts to convince Bessie that she was doing herself an injury by cherishing the selfish feelings she manifested on the occasion alluded to, and it really rejoiced her noble young heart to find that Bessie submitted quietly to the trial of parting, when, at length, Raymond was enabled to break the spell of enchantment by which he had been held from duty, and depart, leaving Bessie for an indefinite period. She was aware of the fact that a cloud had enveloped this impulsive girl recently, for a season, though she did not fully understand the nature of the vapor with which this cloud was surcharged; yet she had not the remotest idea that Aunt Amey was acquainted with the history of Bessie during the years she had been at the West, and was surprised, therefore, when the old lady inquired, how Bessie Jenkins got along with her sulks.

"I've heard about her jealous fever, and I want to whip her, and shut her up in a dark closet."

"Why, Aunt Amey, who could have told you about Bessie?" exclaimed Minnie.

"O, I heard about her hateful actions, while I was at the West. She does n't deserve the good will of that young Philips, and I would break up this anticipated match, if I could; for I hate to see a man, or woman either, jump right into a fire that must burn forever."

"Don't say so, auntie; everybody can overcome what is wrong in their temper, and I trust Bessie will overcome all her naughty feelings. Think what a bright crown she will wear in heaven, if she is enabled to conquer all her wicked feelings."

"Talk about *her* conquering anything ; she's nothing but a great simple bunch of nerves and selfishness ; she'll never be any different, unless she goes away from this world, and comes back again after a while. But it is not probable that she will do any such thing as that, and so I see no help for her."

A few days after this conversation took place, Aunt Amey proposed making Mrs. Jenkins a visit. Mrs. Granger offered to send word to this lady, that Aunt Amey would spend a day with her, soon.

"Shall I send word, auntie, that she may expect you to-morrow?" asked that lady.

"No, it's not necessary to let her know beforehand that I'm coming. I wish to see Bessie and all the rest of the family ; but, if I apprise them of my coming, a part of the household will be 'skedadling,' as they say, nowadays. No, I'll just go and surprise them with my presence."

Mrs. Granger turned from the old lady to hide a smile, wondering mean time, how it was possible for Aunt Amey, or any other person, to take pleasure in visiting a family under the circumstances she had stated.

CHAPTER XL.

"How wondrous are God's secret ways; —
The chastening furnace of affliction,
Taught this young maiden's heart to praise
Her Lord in streams of benediction!"
E. L. NIGHT WATCHES.

THE next morning, bright and early, Aunt Amey arrayed herself for a walk, and having bespoke the attendance of Minnie, started on her errand of curiosity; for it must have been her desire to be acquainted with the affairs of all mankind, as far as possible, that induced her to visit persons whom she was fearful would leave their homes if they expected her to appear in it. Many things went wrong with Aunt Amey, while she was on the way to Mrs. Jenkins.

There had not been any rain for some little time, and the road was dusty, therefore she blamed every man who drove a team along the road, and thought if Oak Dale was a country village, the people might be enterprising enough to have the streets watered, so as not to have folks who walked through the *little mean* place, covered with dust. No one thing beneath the sun, was ever made to suit Miss Benson's taste, exactly. The road was always either too rough, too smooth, or too sandy; and, worse than all, it would be wet sometimes when the clouds poured out showers.

Minnie knew her great aunt very well; she had spent months together beneath the same roof that had sheltered the old lady, almost every year since her remembrance, and she would gladly have loved this relative dearly, if she could have been allowed to, but Aunt Amey did n't care a groat for love; she liked to fidget, and make herself and all around her uncomfortable. As she drew near the house of Mrs. Jenkins, on that morning, Minnie saw Bessie look out of a chamber window for a very few moments, and then move hurriedly away. The young lady resolved not to speak of what she had seen, but, scarcely had she done so, ere Aunt Amey exclaimed, "I told you so; I knew they 'd scatter if they found I was coming. But Bes was n't quite quick enough; I saw her, and now she 'll have to see me."

"I should n't think you would like to go where you suppose some of the family dislike you, auntie."

"Pho! what do I care for such little upstarts as Bessie."

While thus speaking, she opened the door and walked herself into the sitting-room of the astonished Mrs. Jenkins.

"Why Miss Benson, you are a great stranger; when did you arrive? I suppose you came from the West."

This was the salutation of the lady, who, not having heard of the arrival of Aunt Amey, was quite taken by surprise at her sudden appearance.

"I did n't come from the West this morning."

"So I perceive, by the company you come with."

Minnie had been kindly greeted by her friend, as she stood in the hall after the ingress of Aunt Amey into the room, where the old lady was soon comfortably ensconced in a rocking-chair, and feeling relieved;

Minnie, at the suggestion of Mrs. Jenkins, proceeded to the chamber of Bessie.

"I've come to spend the day with you, though I don't suppose you are extra glad to see me," said Aunt Amey; then added in a deprecating tone, "nobody cares for me."

"I am sure that I am glad to see you looking so well," answered Mrs. Jenkins.

"Looking so well, indeed; why, there's nothing of me. I'm worried to death all the time, with the plaguy actions at the seat of war. I'd manage affairs, if I could go out there and have control."

"Pity you could n't go, Aunt Amey," said Albert, who just then entered the room, and offered Miss Benson his hand. "How do you do, Miss Benson?" said he, hoping to atone for the slip of the tongue, which had caused him to say "Aunt Amey," by being very polite to his mother's visitor.

"I'm as well as I can ever expect to be; but I'm not Aunt Amey to you, my lad."

"O, do excuse me, Miss Benson, for that slip of the tongue, just once."

"Do you wish to be excused for calling me so, behind my back?"

"O, no, ma'am; only for this once."

"Then the other times, you don't care for; it's only because I happened to hear you taking such a liberty with a person old enough to be your grandmother."

"I would not speak disrespectfully of you," began Albert.

"Hush! I know very well all about it, and I suppose it's no matter, being it's me who's treated so."

"Well, please shake hands with me, Miss Benson, and then I'll try and not do anything to hurt your feelings again."

Aunt Amey allowed Albert to shake hands with her, and he then ran off, glad to get away without a long lecture from the woman who had often provoked his risibility in days past.

Minnie persuaded Bessie to break a resolution she had hastily formed, to keep out of sight while the disagreeable visitor was in the house.

"You have been seen by her," said Minnie, "and you must go down stairs to please me. I want to see your cousin Clara, very much indeed. In short, I want to see as many of the household together as I can while auntie is present. Remember, age is entitled to deference."

"Not hateful old age; but I can go down, and be bored to death by the woman I hate worse than all the world beside."

"Come, Bessie; try and look better feelings," said her young friend.

"I don't care to," was the brief response of Bessie, as she entered the room where the visitor sat, with the pleasant family circle of Mrs. Jenkins, which had gathered to entertain the guest.

"How do you do, Miss Bessie?" was the rather stiff salutation of Miss Benson, as Bessie approached her, and without waiting for the young lady to reply, she continued, "you look just as if you'd been worrying yourself to no purpose; just as you do about Raymond. But I can tell you it's wrong for you to be jealous of a young lady, who is attached to another young gentleman, and has been for years."

"You mystify the company, auntie," remarked Minnie, who found it difficult to keep her countenance from betraying the amusement she felt.

"Do I? well, I can't help it. I am mystified myself, with some things."

Now Aunt Amey had a way with her, that was not pleasant to any one; but it was intolerable to young people; a certain mysterious air, which is indefinable, save that she would toss her head in such a peculiar mode, that no one was able to tell just how she did it.

Minnie knew that Bessie was both vexed and interested by what this lady had just said, for she had observed her closely, while Aunt Amey was talking, and saw that Bessie looked at her attentively, while she was speaking, with an expression of countenance that seemed to desire her to say more. Mrs. Jenkins too, was interested, for she knew that Aunt Amey was a great newsgatherer, and she recollected the words which had fallen so unconsciously from the lips of Clara when the name of George Ashley had been mentioned in her hearing, and therefore she remarked to Aunt Amey, "so, Miss Benson, you intend we shall infer that our Clara has a beau."

"I didn't say anything about Clara; I was speaking of a young lady of whom I heard that Bessie was jealous. I didn't say what young lady I heard she was jealous of," replied Aunt Amey.

"But you will tell us, will you not?" asked Mrs Jenkins, "provided you know," added she in a low tone.

"Perhaps you doubt my word; but it's only me, and so no matter," answered Miss Benson, a little piqued at the idea that there existed the possibility of a doubt in regard to the truth of what she stated.

"No, Miss Benson; I only think it is possible you may have been misinformed in regard to the subject before us."

"That's all you know about it; but I know the whole," said the old lady, with that significant, yet unbecoming toss of the head, before alluded to.

"I suppose she must have told you something about it, before now," said Mrs. Jenkins, addressing Minnie; but, before that young lady could reply, Aunt Amey spoke in a hurried, sharp manner, which people declared was natural to her, — saying, "of course she don't know anything about it; how could she, when nobody in these parts understand how things are, but me, except one of the parties concerned. I have n't told a soul, because I wanted to see, and tell Bessie myself. I don't like the girl, if I do like her mother. I always said she'd be a spoiled child, and I guess her mother is forced to think sometimes now, of what I used to say to her, when she was letting Bessie have her own way. I knew she was making herself trouble, but as folks will make their beds, they generally have to lie in them."

Mrs. Murray was very uneasy while listening to this speech; she saw that her sister was far from pleased with it, though she felt that a part of it, at least, might be true; therefore she moved her chair very near to Aunt Amey, and seating herself, with her knitting work in her hands, said pleasantly, "I am interested in this affair, for I am acquainted with a young gentleman, whose name is George Ashley, so you will allow me to ask some questions about the individual you know by that name."

"I don't know this young man, only by hearing others speak of him. A friend of mine, who lives at the West, is a relative of George Ashley's mother, and she corresponded with an aunt of his, who gave her an account of some things that have occurred. overheard her talking with her husband about the dark fortunes of young Ashley, one day, so I told her I'd just heard enough, to make me want to know more; then she told me the whole story. It may be told in a few words, so I'll tell what I know, without calling names, and then nobody can accuse me of being personal."

No other person could be so utterly regardless of hurting the feelings of their fellow-beings, as was this woman. She appeared to take advantage of the fact that she had lived upwards of threescore years, and had been called to suffer bereavement in the death of all the very near relatives she ever had had. A nephew, who had always compassionated her lonely condition, had died soon after this war commenced. He had held some office in the commissary department of the army, and had been in the habit of remitting money to Aunt Amey, until his death. Deprived suddenly of the sum he had given her, her means were rather limited, therefore she felt, ever after her nephew died, that all mankind were under obligations to contribute to her means of support.

If the old lady had ever tried to conceal this feeling, she had been very unsuccessful, for it was made manifest, in her actions, every day. She had not been in the house of Mrs. Jenkins two hours, on the day of that visit, before her character was understood by all who were in it. All the ladies were interested in hearing how Aunt Amey would tell her short story, and yet they dreaded to know what it was.

"All I have to tell," began the old lady, "is, that once upon a time, a soldier picked up a letter which had been dropped accidentally by a young Lieutenant, belonging to a Massachusetts Regiment. The letter had been opened and read, before it had been lost, and the man who picked it up, looked at the inside, to ascertain the owner's name, if possible, as the envelope was so covered with mud, the writing was unreadable. He at once discovered that the first name of the person to whom the letter belonged, was Raymond; then curiosity prompted him to read farther, and the spirit of the letter so surprised him, that he read it to the end. He perceived that a young lady, whom he had ever had reason to respect, was referred to in the letter, and this surprised him greatly, for she was named as a rival of the writer. Bessie may try and guess,

"The contents of this letter so troubled the mind of the man, that he copied it and sent it to his mother. She let me read it, and such an abusive missive is n't often seen as that was. We knew the writer's name, for she signed it in full; and as I thought it might do her good to see a copy of it, I got one of the young ladies I knew to copy it for me, so that I could have it to bring to Massachusetts with me. Here it is," said Miss Benson, putting her hand in her pocket; as she did so, Bessie arose, and almost flew from the room.

"You need n't run so, Bessie," called the old lady, but Bessie was determined not to hear her call.

"Never mind," said Aunt Amey, "I'll read it to the rest of you. Here it is," said she, as she succeeded in her attempt to extricate it from the depths of not an easily-fathomed pocket. "It is n't a long letter, and so it 'll soon be heard."

"My once dear Friend Raymond: —

"I never expected to come to this; to be obliged to feel that some other woman has taken the place in your heart which I once thought I occupied. You speak, too, in your letters to me, of my rival, and imagine that because she is my cousin, I shall be blind in regard to your feelings towards her. You don't know me, if you think I am such a fool as to bear your mentioning the name of Clara Murray in your letters, every time you write, with so much interest. I don't intend to bear such treatment; you need not try again to make me think that you care more for me than any other woman, since you have said so much about Clara Murray. I thought, when you first alluded to her, that I should like to know her; but I soon saw through your disinterested, patriotic, gentlemanly efforts to do all you could for her mother, for her sake. And now, I don't care if I don't see you ever again; and less than that do I care for her.

"So no more from —"

"I will not say who;" and Miss Benson did not need to read the name of the writer of this shameful missive, for her grandmother and mother knew full well, and Mrs. Murray suspected very strongly, while Minnie and Clara thought it must have been written by Bessie.

Minnie felt inclined to ridicule the production, but Clara was differently affected, She had listened to it with mingled emotions; she was pained that her cousin could have written such a production, but glad that her having been obliged to hear it read, had opened a way for her to converse with Bessie upon a subject she had long wished to introduce.

CHAPTER XLI.

"Oh, there's a grief, so with the thread of being
Ravelled and twined, it sickens every sense."

" The sorrow of the world worketh death."

LIKE all other days that have thus far dawned upon this world, the day on which Miss Benson visited Mrs. Jenkins, came to an end. The sinking of the sun when it began to set, on the evening of that day, was a joyful sight to all the members of that household, for the visit of Aunt Amey was almost over then, and when the curtains of night were closely drawn over the light, and the old lady took her leave of the patient little circle, and withdrew, a feeling of relief was felt by the whole family.

"The thing is over with; are n't you glad, mother, that she will not bore us again this year?" said Albert, as soon as Aunt Amey had gone.

"I wish Miss Benson was a little different," said his mother in reply, "that we could love to have her stay longer when she visits us."

"She is an intelligent woman," remarked Mrs. Murray, "but has failed in overcoming what is wrong in her character. I suppose she must have indulged unhappy feelings in her youth, so that now this unpleasant, sharp, unfeeling manner that characterizes all she says and does, is a kind of second nature to her. I cannot imagine that she is aware how often she gives pain, when conversing. How often *devil*, that strange word for a lady to speak, escapes her lips. I pity her, because she has not controlled herself more when she could have done so."

"When do you think she could have made herself a more agreeable person, aunt Clara?" asked Albert.

"When all was new, and life was in its spring," responded Mrs. Murray, in the language of H. K. White.

"I wish our Bessie would begin in a hurry to overcome her evil moods, if she is now growing into a character like that old fudge, who has been here to-day," said Albert.

"Don't speak so disrespectfully of a person as old as Miss Benson again, my son."

"How can a person expect to be spoken of respectfully, when their deportment is such, all the time, that it is impossible for a fellow to feel any respect for them."

"You should respect yourself too, not to do what is wrong because others do."

"I'll try and remember, when aunt, I mean when Miss Benson comes again," said Albert, as he went out.

Mrs. Clement had not enjoyed the visit of Aunt Amey more than the other members of the household, yet she was glad she came there with her disagreeable queer ways, because she hoped Bessie would see herself in the mirror held before her by Miss Benson. She hoped, too, that what Aunt Amey had said to her grand-daughter, would not be lost upon her; Bessie's knowledge, too, of the fact that the old lady was in possession of a copy of the letter she had in her anger addressed to Raymond, would, her grandmother thought, do her good. She felt convinced that she was not wrong in thus thinking, when Bessie entered the room where the family were assembled about an hour after Miss Benson had taken leave of them, with a more cheerful face than she had worn for a long time. She had not been there long, ere she asked the very question aloud which some of her friends had asked mentally, many times during Aunt Amey's stay. It was asked by Bessie, earnestly —

"Shall I ever become, if I live to be as old, as disagreeable a woman as Aunt Amey?"

A smile went around the whole circle, as this question was asked.

"It depends upon yourself," said her mother, "my dear Bessie, whether you will be or not. No one can answer this question for you. Much as we wish to have you unlike her, we fear for you, in regard to your prospects in after years, if you do not cherish friendly, cheerful feelings, now that you are young."

"But Aunt Amey looks with suspicion upon every one," said Bessie. "I don't believe she really feels that she is loved by any one; I hope I shall not feel so when I am old."

"Then don't allow yourself," said Mrs. Clement, "to feel so now. It is much better to be sometimes imposed upon, than never to trust. We make people our enemies often, when they would gladly be our friends, by being suspicious of them. I would not entertain distrust in my heart, at all, unless I was forced to. I think it will be well to remember Miss Benson, when we are tempted to feel distrustful," said Mrs. Murray, "for if habitually cherished, distrust has made her what she is; thoughts of her unhappiness may do us good. I pity that young lady who was so patient towards her, for Miss Benson informed me, that she was intending to make that young friend's mother a long visit."

"You need not pity her mother; she is one of the most cheerful beings I ever saw, and she has very dear friends at the war too," said Clara.

"That is always her way," remarked Bessie; "I don't believe anything could make her sad very long; she is always making amusing remarks, which make others laugh. I don't understand how she can feel so light-hearted, in such a gloomy world as this."

"Don't let that part of the world be gloomy, which you inhabit, cousin Bessie," said Clara, "for I want you to laugh with me; I like to be cheerful, and have cheerful people about me."

"O, I'm not constituted like you and Minnie Granger; I wish I was."

"No matter how you are constituted; you can purpose to do a right thing, and then do it. You can say depart! to gloomy feelings, and they will not be so very impolite as to tarry, when you wish them gone."

"But I have one great grief, Clara, that is sapping my young life away." This was said by Bessie in a low tone. As she drew near her cousin, she added, in an almost whisper; "I will tell you of my troubles, sometime."

"Then we'll be friends," said Clara, "and I'll tell you my story, for I've had an experience, as well as yourself."

These few words, softly spoken, laid the foundation of a friendship between the two cousins, which was pure and lasting. It was pleasant to see the untiring patience of Clara, towards Bessie's faults; she regarded her as a spoiled and petted child, and she had felt anxious, since the first time she beheld her, to assist her to mend her ways. Surely, it is worth the work of a lifetime, to win one soul to Jesus, thought this good girl.

"Angels rejoice in heaven, over one erring one who repents, and it will be glorious work if Bessie will only allow me to assist her to drive the demon of jealousy from her heart."

But this evil spirit of jealousy did not come unattended into the breast of Bessie. It seldom, if ever, goes alone; what the poet Young says of woe, is true of this monster. "It loves a train," for it is impossible for it to dwell in the heart of any being, unless it is preceded and encouraged by other sins; sins of omission, it may be, sometimes help to foster it. Clara felt that this might be true in Bessie's case. It was true of Bessie, that she was sometimes very zealous in a good cause, but her zeal would soon grow cold, because it was not kept glowing by generous principle. Benevolent impulses are beautiful in their effect, oftentimes; we would not undervalue them, but would have every good impulse strengthened, until it becomes a principle of character. All we contend against, is the habit many people indulge, of being led by impulse.

"I'll do so, if I feel like it," says one. "I know I'm not doing right, but I must act as I feel," says another.

"I knew one person," said Mrs. Clement on that evening, after Aunt Amey visited Mrs. Jenkins, "who was governed by feeling, who seldom performed an act of charity, unless he yielded to some sudden impulse." "I have," she said, "known his wife to put herself to much inconvenience in order to dispose of a few dollars, that had been given to her by her husband, before he should take them back, when his kindly feeling had passed away. He had changed his purposes so many times, in regard to bestowing a small sum on charitable objects, that his benevolent wife was fain to place money given thus impulsively, immediately beyond his reach. I have watched the conduct of this man for years; he has followed impulsively, for a short period, a great variety of vocations. He liked each one at the onset, and was sure of getting rich, by pursuing it; but O, he would soon change, and then another impulse would govern him for a time.

"Soon after the war commenced, he was led by a strong impulse to join the army, and he did become a soldier, and went forth, taking with him the good wishes of many. 'Now,' thought his friends, 'Mr. Jones will be suited with his occupation, because, it is exciting, and he will serve contentedly, during the term of his enlistment.' But lo, how unwisely they judged; he did not stay until half the three years, for which he enlisted, had expired. Becoming very unhappy, he found out, all on a sudden, that he was unfit for Government service. His health was good, very good, — he boasted often that it was excellent; still, he contrived after much manœuvring to get discharged and return home. Since that time he has continued his favorite course, and I fear he will go through life acting in the same unstable manner. It is not safe to be guided by our inclinations, without a higher standard of action."

"I wish I could be different," said Bessie to Clara, after the two cousins had retired to their chamber that night. "I know, very well, they all mean me, when they make their remarks, and tell their stories about impulsive people. I wish I could be different, so as not to be the butt of all the household; even my young brothers treat me with contempt."

"Not you, cousin Bessie; I am sure your brothers love you, but some of your moods they do not like, neither do I."

Here Clara paused, fearing she had gone too far, and both Bessie and herself were silent for a time.

"We will be the best of friends to each other," said Clara, at length. "At least, I hope so; I hope we may be faithful friends and tell each other our faults. Will you be such a friend to me, Bessie, while we are near each other?"

"I am afraid to promise; I can't never do anything I wish to."

"You must not feel so, Bessie," was the kind reply of Clara, while she put her arms lovingly about the neck of her cousin. "You must let me love you and help you to get above some of your miserable feelings. I've been thinking we can be very happy together if we are not afraid of each other."

"But this one great trial of mine, you do not know, and I do not like to tell you what it is."

"Supposing I tell you that I have an idea that you have hurt the feelings of a young man, who is your best friend, by writing a letter to him when you were in a bad humor; what would you say?"

"I would ask what you think about it?"

"Then I would say you ought to feel sorry that

you had done wrong; but instead of sitting down to think about what you have done, you should do all in your power to make restitution for the wrong, while you ask help of your heavenly Father to save you from a repetition of the offence."

"But I don't know what to do about that hateful letter; I wish I had not written it."

"Still, it is true that you did write it, and it appears that it has travelled a long way towards the setting sun. It is amusing to think of the manner in which that letter came back to your home, Bessie. I believe its appearance here was to do good to the writer of it; no accident brought it, for all things are controlled by Omnipotence."

"But to think of Miss Benson's bringing it here; the woman I dislike most of any being in the world. This is terribly mortifying."

"Let this mortification be the means of making you wiser, Bessie."

"I hope it will teach me wisdom, and teach me also that it is best to wait long enough to find out the truth in regard to what I suspect, before I settle in my mind, as a fact, what I only fear may be one."

"It is strange, cousin, that you could have thought of me as a rival."

"It does n't seem strange to me; I only wonder that you did n't supplant me in Raymond's affections from the first moment of your acquaintance; you are so much more lovable than I am, or ever can be."

"O fie, don't entertain such a foolish thought one moment. God has given you great capacity for happiness as well as for misery. It is for you to choose whether you will cast a gloomy shadow wherever you go, or whether you will be happy yourself and make others so. It is of no use, dear Bessie, to talk about constitutional infirmities, when we have the word of God, that His grace is sufficient for us in every emergency."

"But you forget, Clara, that I don't profess to be a Christian, and the promises in the Bible are made to Christians."

"I didn't forget, cousin, and there is no reason why you should not be a Christian to-day. Every creature that God has made is commanded to love Him, and also all mankind. There is not a shadow of excuse for the neglect of this duty in any case."

"But how much one has to give up to become a Christian."

"True, some sacrifice is required of all who would walk the road to heaven; but no one who sets out in earnest to travel the way, will tell you that they have ever lost one real good. They speak of pleasure the world had not power to bestow, which they have tasted in the service of Jesus."

"Didn't you make great sacrifices, Clara?"

"The sacrifice I made did not seem great to me."

"Suppose you felt obliged to do something that would mortify your pride very much indeed, then what?"

"Why, if it was right I should do this humiliating thing, I would pray for strength to do it, and cease not to struggle against my pride until I had been enabled to take up the cross, however heavy it might be. I could not be a child of God, if I refused thus to mortify self."

"I shall never, never be a Christian then; for I never can confess to Raymond that I am sorry I wrote that unpleasant letter, and ask him to forgive me for having sent it to him."

"You feel that you did wrong to write it, and that which was worse still, to send it to him; then why not tell Mr. Philips you feel so? I have n't a doubt, from what I know of him, that he would gladly forgive you, and rejoice, too, that your feelings had led you to acknowledge your error."

Here the conversation was ended for a time by a summons these two cousins received, to go down stairs.

CHAPTER XLII.

"Go, beside all waters sow,
 In the morning scatter wide;
Liberal bid thy hand bestow,
 At the fall of eventide.
What shall spring, or where, or when,
 Thou art not concerned to know;
Quickening sunbeams, genial rain,
 God in his own time will show."

"Why should we be called down stairs in this peremptory manner, I wonder," said Bessie; "I'm half inclined to disregard this call to join the family."

"You must not, Bessie; we must both go down, for I dare say we shall find some pleasant friend has come in."

"Mrs. Sedgwick perhaps has called," said Bessie, as she followed Clara mechanically down the stairs. "I don't care to go in, now," was on Bessie's lips, but Clara, suspecting her disinclination for company, opened the door of the parlor, where the sound of voices told her the family had assembled. The first person Bessie saw upon entering the room, was Raymond Philips. She would have retreated immediately, had she not been noticed by the mother of Raymond, who extended her hand to Bessie, and thus prevented her intended exit.

Raymond arose and shook hands with the downcast girl, as cordially as if she had not given him reason to treat her cooly. Clara grasped the hand of this friend, with too much warmth and frankness to leave any room for the suspicion that she was *tenderly* attached to him.

"I am very, very glad to meet you again," said Clara, "and the more so, because your visit was so entirely unexpected."

Raymond returned her kindly greeting, with great sincerity, and with as much affectionate regard as if he had not known that Bessie was taking cognizance of all his acts. A close observer would have seen a shade of anxiety resting upon his open countenance, but his manner was as free from embarrassment as possible, and having saluted the young ladies courteously, he resumed his part of a conversation which their entrance had interrupted.

"You asked me, I think, Mrs. Murray, my opinion in regard to the fall of Vicksburg. I must say, in reply, that I believe General Grant will have the place sometime during the coming summer. He has much to contend with; subordinate officers are a great obstacle in the way of a General; and I have pretty good reasons for believing that all the Captains and Lieutenants in his command are not temperance men, and the General is often nonplussed for a few hours, by the want of sobriety among his inferior officers. Drunkenness is so common a sin, among the commissioned soldiers in the army and navy, that there is little hope that it will ever be entirely banished from either."

"This is a lamentable fact," said Mrs. Clement. "It puzzles me," she continued, "to conjecture the reason the Government seems to see existing, for commissioned officers to have spirits at their control. It appears to me it would be quite as sensible to let them have arsenic, or any other poison, to tamper with, while as a body they are less fit to have access to spirituous liquors than the private soldiers and sailors; and, very wisely, Government forbids this last class the free use of strong drink."

"I think that Uncle Sam should care as tenderly for the morals of the officers as for those of the men," remarked Mrs. Phillips, by way of replying to what Mrs. Clement had said.

"Do you think the Rebel General will attempt to invade Pennsylvania?" inquired Mrs. Jenkins, addressing her question to Raymond.

"I am inclined to believe he intends trying the strength of our forces in that direction. Many differ with me in thus thinking; but I should not be surprised if some of our friends in the keystone State should receive a visit from a portion of his army, before long."

"O, I hope you will be proved, by time, a false prophet," said Mrs. Jenkins. "I cannot bear the thought that this war will ever be brought so near the New England States."

"But if the greatest good can be accomplished by our submitting to the trial of having our own homes become the theatre of military display, we ought to be willing that this war should close, even at our own doors. The people need to be aroused again as they were by the first blow that was struck by the Rebellion."

"Then you don't dread the approach of Lee's army into Pennsylvania," said Mrs. Murray.

"I cannot say that I do, on all accounts. I should dread the loss of life which would follow in the footsteps of this Rebel General, if he should plant his treacherous feet upon the soil of that State. He would have everything at stake if he should advance so far Northward, and the very risk he would run would make him desperate; still, the effect upon the loyal North would be to fire the hearts of the people anew with patriotism. Some men need to have an object right before their eyes, in order to be convinced that it has an existence; and some really loyal men are resting as contentedly, after having given a few dollars to the Union cause, as if they thought there was no more to be done. Our foes are more vigilant at present than we are."

Bessie did not lose one word which fell from the lips of Raymond. She scarcely spoke at all, herself, but her countenance expressed no displeasure at anything that was said by any of the company. She wondered if Raymond would go away without asking for a private interview with herself; and Clara was anxious to know, also, whether he would, during all his visit, bear himself toward her cousin as he had thus far. No one, not acquainted with the parties, would ever have imagined, judging from the manner of this young couple toward each other, that they had ever been more than common friends.

When Raymond took his leave, he shook hands with Bessie as he did with the rest of the company, and no look or word from him, said more to her than to the others. When Mrs. Jenkins invited him to visit her house again, he thanked her, and then said, "I should be happy to come again, if my stay at home was not very limited indeed. My visit home is necessarily birdlike at this time. If I live, I shall probably be able to get leave of absence for a longer period before many months have gone."

His "good by" to each was cheerful, and Bessie was almost hurt with him because he was not unhappy. She expressed this feeling to Clara, who asked her, playfully, if it was because misery is fond of company, that she was disturbed by the cheerfulness of the young Lieutenant.

"I don't know as I am disturbed by it; I don't know exactly how I do feel; I only wish I could know that he cares for me."

"Try him, cousin, by telling him that you feel you have treated him ill."

"I dare not; if he should repulse my offer of reconciliation, I could not bear the pain it would cause me, Clara; I dare not try him."

"Your distrust is not very complimentary to Raymond, cousin Bessie."

"I know it, Clara; but then, to see him shake hands with me so calmly, while I was trembling like a leaf in autumn, shows plainly that he has thrown my love aside. I suppose his country takes the place in his heart which I once held."

"Jealous again, cousin; I should think you would be glad that he does love his country; I cannot easily love a person who does not care a great deal for our Government, for I feel that those who can be indifferent, even, to the claims which the land of their birth has upon them, lack the requisites for making a true friend."

"I have not, until within a year or two, ever given a thought to what has been going on in the land. Mother never said anything about public affairs; she did not even read the papers. I have often heard mother say that Uncle Sam was big enough to take care of himself, when our grandmother has tried to get her interested in some matter that was popular in the nation. Nowadays, mother seems to be waking up to the fact that women have something to do, in helping make the popular sentiment of the country; she has said more upon national affairs within the last year, than she has since my remembrance, before. But I want to talk about Raymond; I almost wish I had asked him for a private interview."

"Would you have told him your feelings in respect to the letter, Bessie, had you seen him alone, think you?"

"I'm afraid I should have shrunk from the task; I don't know as I could have said anything to him. But Clara, cousin, I am sorry I was ever jealous of him at all."

"Yet you will let him go again to a post of danger and not tell him so."

Bessie covered her face with her hands and sat silent for some minutes ere she made any reply. She then said, with apparent deep feeling, "I must become a whole Christian before I can do that, Clara."

CHAPTER XLIII.

>——"It is not best,
>That no afflictions come;
>These are the furnaces that try,
>And fit the soul for home.
>The chast'ning rod that heaven doth send,
>To teach us where to find a *Friend*."

WEEKS passed, after the incidents occurred which have been related in the foregoing chapter, and still Bessie did not relapse into that mood, the indulgence of which had brought pain to her friends as well as to herself. She was becoming strongly attached to Clara; so much so, that she was unwilling to be separated from her even for a few hours. Both the mothers of these young ladies were pleased to see this intimacy of their daughters, and both were glad, most of all, because this friendship would, they hoped, result in good to Bessie. In their anxiety for this object of their love and solicitude, they forgot that Clara was blessed even more than Bessie; yet she realized herself that while she imparted comfort to her cousin, her own heart was made better by her efforts to benefit another.

It was the earnest desire of Clara, that Bessie and Raymond should become united in heart as they had once been. She would have them united by purer, stronger ties, even, than those which had bound them, ere Bessie so ruthlessly put Raymond from her by unkindness. Bessie looked eagerly for tidings from Raymond, whenever his mother received a letter from him. She would not make inquiries herself, but she would contrive to lead the conversation in such a way, that Clara could not well avoid asking many questions about the young man, and just the questions Bessie wished to hear answered.

Mrs. Philips well understood Bessie's manœuvring, and she was well satisfied in regard to the interest she felt in the son so dear to her heart. It was no uncommon thing for Clara and Bessie to call upon Mrs. Philips, as often as once or twice a week. Clara was attracted towards this lady, by her cheerful piety, combined with great vivacity and intelligence.

"I enjoy the society of Raymond's mother so very much," said Clara, one warm day in July, "that I hardly know how to wait three days, before I call upon her again."

"Why need you wait?" asked Bessie; we can call upon her towards evening to-day, if you say so."

"Thank you, cousin; we will go then, when the heat of the day is past."

Before the hour arrived in which these cousins were to seek the home of Mrs. Philips, an evening paper was brought in, which was seized with avidity, and read by Mrs. Clement, whose interest in the war news had been great and unabated, ever after these hostilities commenced. Her heart thrilled with emotion as she read an account of the raid of General Lee into Pennsylvania, and of the excitement caused by the fear that he might, with his army, reach the capital of the State. She read this great news aloud to her granddaughter, who listened in silence with the most intense interest.

Raymond was in the army of the Potomac, and in

his letters to his mother, he had of late expressed the wish repeatedly, that General Meade would allow Lee to reach Philadelphia, and then cut off his retreat. His regiment was in that wing of the army which had been ordered to give the Southrons a fitting reception. They had met the foe, and had fought bravely. Undaunted by difficulties, each rod of ground was fought for, until it was either won from the enemy or there were not able men enough left to contend longer. Raymond was one of the bravest soldiers who honored the stars and stripes on that occasion, and his name was mentioned in the list of casualties after the battle of the second or third of July, 1863.

The news had come with electric speed. It had flashed over the wires so soon, that, when it was read by friends, it was regarded by some with a sort of stupid wonder. It was thus that Clara and Bessie felt in respect to it, as they sought the home of Mrs. Philips.

"I wonder if Raymond's mother has seen this evening's paper," said Clara, as Bessie rang for admittance when they had reached the home of Raymond; on entering the house, she looked anxiously for Mrs. Philips. That lady soon presented herself, and welcomed the young ladies with her wonted cheerfulness.

"I don't believe she has heard the sad news," thought Bessie; "I shall hate to tell her that Raymond is reported missing. I wish I knew whether she has heard about my writing that unkind letter to him. He hasn't told her, I am sure, but then that meddlesome news-monger, Miss Benson, must have informed her about it."

These thoughts passed swiftly through the mind of

Bessie; so swiftly, that a moment had scarcely elapsed, when Mrs. Philips spoke of the tidings which had come from the keystone State.

"You have heard, then, that Raymond is reported among those who are missing," said Bessie.

"I have," replied Mrs. Philips; "yet I hope that this will not long be said of him; still, he may ever be missing; yet, while I can hope for something better, I love to do so."

"But you don't know that he is not dead," said Bessie.

The tone of sadness in which these words were uttered, touched the hearts of both Mrs. Philips and Clara.

"We don't know, it is true, anything about his condition; still, it is more pleasant to indulge bright fancies than gloomy ones. I shall hope for the best, while I wish to be prepared for the worst that can come," said Raymond's mother.

"He may be wounded and be at this moment lying faint and suffering, where he cannot have suitable care. I don't believe we shall ever hear from him again," said Bessie.

Mrs. Philips strove to cheer her despondency, for she pitied her greatly. She did not know how much cause Bessie had to reproach herself, for having acted unkindly towards her son. Had this Christian mother known this, she would have pitied the poor girl more; but she regarded Bessie as one destitute of the only solace for a bleeding heart.

"I can carry my sorrows to the feet of my Saviour," reflected Mrs. Philips; "but poor Bessie has no such solace. She is still a stranger to that sweet feeling of submission to the will of a kind and holy God, which all experience, who trust in Him without reserve. I must forget my own pain, in the pleasure it will give me to comfort her."

It was beautiful to see this fond mother striving to administer consolation to another, while her own heart was wrung with that anguish of suspense, which only a mother can know. It was enough for her to know that Bessie's heart was filled with grief, by the tidings that had reached her, to make her merge her own sorrow in that of one whom she knew had long been dear to her son. Many were the words of hope and comfort which she spoke to Bessie, on that long to be remembered evening, and the poor girl left her house, at the close of the evening, with a more exalted opinion of Mrs. Philips than she had hitherto indulged, while she esteemed herself less than she had ever before done. The heart of Bessie relented at the thought that pride had prevented her from acknowledging to Raymond, that she felt she had done him wrong. She wished she had told him this, when she could have done so.

The walk home was a silent one. Albert Jenkins had been commissioned by his mother to attend them on the way. The heart of this merry lad, was in sympathy with the sadness of his family, for he loved Raymond, and, much as he blamed Bessie, he could not find it in his heart, now, to say a word that would vex her.

"How I wish I had told Raymond my feelings, when he was here," Bessie exclaimed, when she found herself alone with Clara. "Why did n't I? why did n't I?" she repeated in a tone of anguish.

"You was ashamed to tell him, you felt that you was wrong," replied Clara, who spoke very tenderly and soothingly, while she felt that she must speak the truth, if she would do her cousin good.

"Yes, it is true, I was too proud to tell him; and now he is gone; gone I fear, forever," answered Bessie. "O, I shall never want to see any one I know, but you, again, Clara. I am so wretched I can scarcely bear to live; and yet I'm afraid to die, for I know I'm not fit. If Raymond is dead, I shall never see him in either world, again."

In this way Bessie continued to talk, while she paced the floor of her room until near morning. After vainly attempting for a long time to comfort her, Clara sat silently regarding her cousin, and offering silent prayer to God, in her behalf, until the tempest of her sorrow began to subside. It was near daybreak when Bessie, exhausted by weeping and vain lamentations, came to the side of Clara, and sat down. The storm of her grief was only lulled; not one cloud had vanished, which had darkened her soul's horizon, and no star of hope would she allow to pierce the darkness; still, her exhausted nature demanded rest for a time, and would have it.

Clara assisted her to undress, and as Bessie laid her head upon her pillow, she said, mournfully, "I don't care to arise from this bed again, Clara; for why should I?"

Clara kissed the cheek of her cousin, but did not speak. She thought, however, of many reasons why Bessie should care to leave her bed again, still, she felt it would be unwise to mention any of them, on that occasion; so she laid down by her cousin, in silence, and soon fell into a sound sleep, from which she did not awake until near breakfast-time, the next morning. The first object that met her eyes as she opened them was Bessie, with her face covered with a handkerchief.

The sun was brightly shining, and Clara's heart longed to see her cousin cheered by its kindly light.

"Come, Cousin Bessie, look up and see the beautiful sun which has arisen before us this morning," said she, as she put her arms around the weeping girl, when she was ready to leave the chamber. "I don't love to go down stairs without you, Bessie; you will go with me, won't you?"

"I cannot go, Clara; I cannot bear to see the sunshine; I wish it would not shine while my heart is so sad; and it must always be so; I can never be happy again."

"O, yes, Bessie; Raymond will perhaps come again, then you will tell him that you regret what you have done, and you will both be happy. But I must not disregard this summons to breakfast, for this is the second time the bell has rung."

Clara descended to the breakfast-room with a feeling of reluctance, for it grieved her to be obliged to leave her cousin in her present condition. She had been so hopeful in regard to Bessie, that this indulgence of selfish feeling on her part, disappointed her. She could not but contrast Bessie's violent demonstrations of sorrow with the chastened expressions of grief that were made by Raymond's mother. It was the first time since Clara had been an inmate of her aunt's family, that she had appeared at the table with a troubled countenance. Her grandmother and aunt were quick to notice the cloud that was passing over her face, as she seated herself at the table. Yet this cloud was not settled there; its stay was transient; it passed away, and left the countenance of our young friend seemingly brighter than it had been before its approach.

Clara was obliged to confess that she had not slept until near daylight, and in reply to the anxious inquiries of her aunt, she was forced to reveal the truth in regard to Bessie. Mrs. Jenkins sighed deeply on hearing of the great sorrow of her daughter. She well knew that Bessie had given poignancy to her own grief, by treating Raymond unkindly, and she feared that the news which had now reached her, would be so terrible a blow that she would sink under it.

"How stern a discipline is poor Bessie's," said her mother.

"Never fear, my daughter," said Mrs. Clement; "she is in good hands, and if she only comes out of the furnace more free from dross, we shall all have reason to be grateful forever."

"But, mother, Bessie may become insane; I sometimes think she is constitutionally liable to disease of the brain."

"There is, I believe, an effectual remedy against insanity; and prevention is better than cure. I feel that entire, cheerful submission to our lot in life, is almost certain to prevent lunacy."

"But poor Bessie is not pious, mother."

"I know that, daughter; but that is not a reason that she cannot be."

"I feel and think as you do, about Cousin Bessie,

grandmother," said Clara; "and I believe, also, that she will never be united again, in true friendship with Raymond, unless she first yields the point against which she is now contending. I am aware that there is a great conflict in her heart, continually, and has been ever since I have been here. I am anxious about her, sometimes, lest she should sink, spirit weary, ere she gains the victory over self and pride. Last night she struggled hard. I trembled for her before her physical strength failed; but this morning the conflict is renewed in her soul, and I hope and fear for her alternately."

"She must need refreshment," said Mrs. Murray.

"I shall take some breakfast up stairs, and perhaps I can persuade her to eat a little," said Clara.

She did so, and by dint of persuasion, Bessie drank first a cup of coffee, and afterwards partook of a few mouthfuls of toast. She then pushed the plate upon which it was laid away from her, with apparent disgust, saying, as she did so, "I cannot eat; I will not try any more, for it seems as if every mouthful I attempt to swallow would choke me."

"Cannot you pray, my dear cousin?" asked Clara.

"I wish I could; but when I try to, that letter of Raymond's, the one I wrote to him, I mean, comes into my mind, and I cannot think of anything that I dare pray for."

"Dare not you pray for forgiveness, for doing wrong?"

'No, Clara; because I must confess my sins if I expect to be forgiven."

"That is very true, Bessie; but it is not hard to confess. Try, and see how easy it is, after you once resolve to do it. Suppose you resolve now, asking God to help you to keep the resolution, to write to Raymond, if you ever have an opportunity to write, or communicate with him in any way, to tell him you regret what you have done, and ask his forgiveness."

"I could write to Raymond, Clara, if I knew that he would not live; but it seems so humiliating, to think of ever seeing him afterwards."

"Now, Bessie, you remind me of a man who said once, he would forgive a man, towards whom he had indulged a feeling of hatred, if he died; 'but mind you,' said the sick man, 'if I get well, I shall feel towards you and treat you as I have done.'"

Bessie looked earnestly at Clara as she related this little anecdote.

"Such a way of confessing *my* foibles will not do," answered she; "I must repent from my heart, if at all."

"Certainly;" and you intend to repent thus sincerely, Bessie, don't you?"

"Oh, I cannot tell you what I intend to do; at one time I feel that I can give up this dread of humbling myself, to own to Raymond that I have done wrong, and then again I feel that I cannot thus degrade myself."

"You would not be degraded by confessing that you was sorry for a fault. It is a false view of the subject that leads you to this conclusion."

"I wish I could feel differently; you cannot know how miserable I am," answered Bessie.

Days and weeks passed, during which frequent conversations, similar to the one we have here narrated, took place in Bessie's chamber. Her mother, her grandmother, and her aunt, each in turn, tried their powers of persuasion upon this heartsick girl, still, apparently to little purpose. To her cousin Clara she became an object of intense interest. This disinterested girl knew that Bessie was gifted with powers, which, if used aright, would make her a means of great good to the world. She was aware, too, that her conflict with evil must, of necessity, be terrible, before she could triumph over the long-indulged selfishness of her heart. She saw that a conflict was already raging, which she prayed and trusted would result in victory over the pride which had long oppressed her better judgment.

Bessie saw and felt that Clara had probed her character to its utmost depths, and she knew that she was thoroughly understood by her cousin. She suffered in her own esteem, whenever she ventured to compare herself with Clara.

"How can she love me, and seek daily to promote my happiness, when I treated her so very unkindly when she first knew me. It was very foolish in me to be jealous of the interest Raymond felt in her; yet she seems to have forgotten my conduct, though *I* can never forget it. I hope she won't go home with grandmother, for I should not know how to get along without her, now; still, I am ashamed to ask her to stay longer."

Bessie, however, did entreat Clara very earnestly to remain with her, while Mrs. Clement and Mrs. Murray went to the home of the former, a spot sacred to the other as the home of her childhood and youth. Clara had long anticipated a visit to the home of her mother's girlhood, but as Bessie was anxious to have her stay longer with her, and she might hope to do her good by setting aside her own wishes, she did so cheerfully, and devoted herself more constantly than ever to the task of illuming, by her smiling countenance and playful sallies, the gloom which seemed to be settling upon the life of Bessie.

CHAPTER XLIV.

"When I came hither to transport the tidings,
Which I have heavily borne, there ran a rumor
Of many worthy fellows that were out."

"No mind that's honest,
But in it, shares some woe; though the main part,
Pertains to you alone."

WEEKS passed, after the battle at Gettysburg, and still no tidings from Raymond reached his home. Hope still lingered in the breast of his mother; still, its influence was at times scarcely felt. She was about resigning herself to the loss of this son, who had been her greatest earthly comfort, when a letter was brought to her one evening, which had been postmarked at Annapolis. Mrs. Philips could not recognize the handwriting, and took the missive from its envelope, with a feeling of dread.

As her eye glanced over the first few lines, she found that the letter, though it had been directed by her son, had been penned by a stranger. Raymond had been wounded again, and was now a prisoner of war, in addition to being a sufferer from two wounds, which he had received on the day previous to that on which the forces of General Lee had been routed by the Union Army. One of these wounds was in his neck, the other in his leg.

Raymond had been paroled, and had been as kindly treated as one could expect. A friend, whose wound had been but trifling, compared with his, had exerted himself to do for him all that the circumstances in which they were placed would admit of his doing. This letter was short, yet it came opportunely, and the intelligence it contained was less trying to this mother's heart, than the suspense she had so long endured. She had reason to think that Raymond had suffered more than he would care to have her know.

No mention was made in the letter of his feeling the want of anything; still, she feared he was obliged to live upon scanty rations, if the many reports which had reached her were true, in regard to the high prices of provisions at the South.

"I will try and do something for my noble son," said Mrs. Philips, after she had indulged herself in shedding a few tears; "but first, I will go and acquaint Bessie with the contents of my letter."

In less than an hour after the letter was placed in the hands of her to whom it had been addressed, this lady sat by the bedside of Bessie, and perused it.

"I thought I would bring you his address at once, Bessie," said this friend; "so I came immediately; but I must n't stop, for I wish to send something to Raymond as soon as I possibly can, for I fear he may be destitute of some of the comforts of life."

Having said this, Mrs. Philips took leave of Bessie, and in her haste failed to notice the perturbation that was becoming visible in Bessie's manner.

"I am glad she did not stay longer," said Bessie to Clara, when Mrs. Philips had gone, "for I could not have disguised my feelings, had she spoken to me about writing to Raymond. She would think it very strange if I should tell her it was not my intention to write to him, because she does n't know that I should be obliged to write such a letter as could not well go unsealed."

"But, Bessie," said her cousin, "don't you know that you will be obliged to write such a letter as you speak of, to Raymond, and that you will never get well until you have written it? You will not, it is true, be obliged to send it unsealed to the parole camp; and the sooner you write it, the sooner your heart will grow light, and you will be well again. I have, my dear Bessie, wished to say to you, before this, what I will ask you to allow me to say now."

"What is it you would say, Clara?"

"I would tell you I feel that your lying here, brooding over your trials, is a sad waste of time. You will never find comfort in this way; your physician affirms that it is your mind that affects your health; and now, Bessie, if you love your mother, and care to give her comfort, say to the evil spirit, which is whispering words that make you shrink from doing right, 'Get thee behind me Satan.' Resolve to think first of your obligations to your heavenly Father; then of your duty to others, which grow out of these relations. Change the subject of your thoughts but for one day, and I venture to predict that a favorable change in your health will be the result."

"You think I must determine to do my duty, let it be ever so mortifying to my pride."

"Yes, Bessie; let it bring whatever reproach it may upon us, we must all come to this point before we can see the face of God in peace, or even have peace in our own hearts."

"A hard truth this, if indeed, it be truth, which I

suppose it must be. I wish you could help me, Clara."

"I would, if I could, gladly; but no power on earth can help you."

"I cannot do this myself, Cousin Clara."

"But you can do some one thing which you know is duty, and then you can talk about the rest."

Bessie was silent for a short time, then raising herself to a sitting posture in bed, she asked Clara to bring her writing-desk to her.

"I am going to write to Raymond this very hour, and then if he does not live to receive my letter, I shall have done all I could, in this respect."

Clara gladly brought the writing materials, and encouraged Bessie to perform this duty she had so long dreaded. She laid a sheet of paper upon the desk before her, and placed an inkstand and pen near by. Then she sat down at a little distance, and busied herself with her work, yet ever and anon she cast a glance at the face of her cousin, as she traced the lines which would probably some day gladden the heart of the far-off, suffering prisoner. The expression of Bessie's countenance changed, as she wrote; a light gleamed from her eye upon the page before her, and when she had finished writing, a smile of ineffable sweetness illumed her features.

"I have done it, Clara; I have been enabled to conquer self, and I am so glad," said she, exultingly.

Clara ran to the bedside, and clasped her arms around Bessie; yet her heart was too full for utterance; she could only kiss her cousin, while tears of joy ran down her cheeks. Well might this young

Christian be joyful, when she had reason to believe that angels in heaven were, at that moment, rejoicing over this repentant one. Bessie was the first to break this thrilling silence.

"It seems so easy to submit now," said she, "that I wonder I could have held out so long. I feel as if I wished every one to be as happy as I am now. I wish you, Clara, to take this letter, lest I should ever feel differently, and shrink from sending it; and I feel as if it must be sent to Raymond, since I have expressed all my feelings towards him, in it."

"I trust you will never feel disposed to keep this letter from Raymond, for I am sure it will be a comfort to him to read it, if you have told him all."

"I wish you to read it, Clara, and judge for yourself whether it will make him happy."

Clara took the letter and perused it, while tears of joy streamed down her cheeks.

"You will never repent the decision you have made, Bessie; all your regrets will be because you have not made it sooner. Your letter will be treated sacredly, if sent now."

"I will wait until I hear from Raymond," replied Bessie.

The change in this young lady was very visible in her outward acts; instead of abstaining from food, and yielding to despondency, she resolved to use every means in her power to recover her strength; therefore, her mother was most agreeably surprised to find at supper time on the evening of that day, that the appetite of her daughter was much improved.

"I am glad to learn that you relished your tea this evening, Bessie," said Mrs. Jenkins; "and hope you feel better than you have for some time."

"Mother, I feel better than I ever did before in my life."

Mrs. Jenkins looked surprised, for Clara had not spoken of the change in Bessie, and she wondered at her cheerful countenance; it was unlike the face she had met in that chamber, for so long a period.

"What has made you so much better, daughter?" inquired her mother, with a happy smile.

"Having been made to realize my obligations as an immortal being, I feel as if I had been sleeping all my lifetime, for I have lived, until this afternoon, without any high and noble purpose of action; thoughtlessly and ungratefully have I spent the best years of my life. Many, many precious hours have I wasted in sad, miserable repinings. I wonder at the goodness that has spared me during all these years. I hope Raymond will live to be exchanged, so that I can send the letter to him that I have written to-day."

"Have you written a letter, to-day, my child?"

"I have, mother, and the writing of it has made me happy, although it was the most self-denying act of my life. Clara has told me, more than once, that I would not feel right until I resolved to confess to Raymond that I felt I had done wrong in sending that letter to him, which Miss Benson read a copy of, when she spent the day here. How strange that she should have got hold of that letter, when she was so many hundred miles off from any of us, too. I believe this was wisely ordered, for I never could have known how hateful that letter must have seemed to Raymond, had I not heard it read by Aunt Amey. I had not courage to stay in sight of any of the family, while that letter was being read, or to appear again, after the reading of it was concluded. Still, I am glad now that it was brought here, notwithstanding, I have suffered much, in consequence."

The change in Bessie was lasting, and it was a source of comfort to all her family. Albert and Willie watched narrowly for her halting; but they were obliged to confess that their sister was influenced by something higher than mere impulse, as time passed on, and they respected her greatly. Only a few months have passed since that time, it is true; but the sincerity of the change in Bessie's motives, has been tested more than once, during that short period. Her conflict with wrong is continual, yet it is not agonizing, as at the first.

From the moment she resolved to do right at all hazards, a work commenced in Bessie's soul, which, it is believed, will never cease, until her purified soul takes its place among the ransomed millions around the throne of God. It was not long after Bessie began to realize that "it is not all of life to live," before the tidings reached Raymond, in a letter written by his mother. Bessie sent a sympathizing message to him, in the missive, which gave him great pleasure. He was suffering at the time he received his mother's letter, and it was an unexpected solace to him. Bessie had expressed a desire that he might soon be exchanged, and return home.

" She must view things differently, else she would not send me this message, I am sure, and now I can hope, she will yet be the solace of my life." Raymond's heart felt relieved of a great burden, when he read this missive, and he presented an ejaculatory thank-offering to his heavenly Father, for this mercy which had been vouchsafed to him. He was, soon after this, able to write himself, and he penned a short, but kind letter to Bessie.

This missive was not long; he could not say all he wished to, either to his mother or Bessie; still, the latter felt that she was restored to that place in the affections of Raymond, which she had forfeited by her unreasonable jealousy. Many tears were shed by her during its perusal, yet they flowed from a purer source than had those she had shed in days gone by. Her thoughts were not at this time concentrated upon herself, as they had been wont to be. Self was well-nigh forgotten, in the interest she felt for Raymond and his companions, who were suffering such deprivations, for the sake of upholding our Government.

One sentiment expressed in Raymond's missive to her, was much in her mind. It was this: "If our country was worth our efforts to save it, two years ago, it is thrice worthy of all we can do and suffer for it now. Don't," he continued, "think I regret what little I have done; I am ready, still, to do all in my power for the Union. Perhaps I said too much when in prison, in missives, to allow me to hope for the safe passage of my letters, some of which failed to reach home; but somehow it is not easy for me to be non-committal, on any occasion."

Raymond then entreated Bessie to remember the brave boys who were confined with him. "None can be too grateful to these men, who have foregone everything desirable, to help save the blessings of freedom for us. Think of them, when you, with my mother, prepare another box for me. Don't forget that the well-being of the loyal soldier should be the interest of all."

Raymond did not need to repeat his request that his companions in suffering should be kindly remembered. Bessie devoted much of her time, after this, to providing comforts for the gallant men who had nobly fought for our flag. Sometimes she felt a blush suffuse her cheek, when she thought of the very many precious hours she had squandered in the indulgence of selfish repinings.

"How foolishly I have acted, and wickedly too," said she to her mother one day; "how much good I might have done when I was cherishing unhappy feelings, and forgetting, in my sinful moodiness, everything that was right. I ought to do more than others for the defenders of our land now, because I have neglected my duty towards them so long. Now, if Mrs. Sedgwick would come home, we should be happy together. I used to think, she was a fanatic; but now I see that there is a vast difference between Christian duty, and fanaticism. A Christian must think of his fellow-beings; I have learned this fact from experience, yet I used to think, because they were not perfect, that all the disinterested efforts they made were put forth for the sake of praise."

"I remember you used to say this, often," said Mrs. Jenkins, "and now, daughter," continued that lady, "you must be prepared to be judged by some, as you have judged others. There are some people, who are unwilling to believe there is any such thing as disinterestedness in this world."

"Let us try, Bessie, to prove by our lives, that these people are mistaken," said Clara.

"I am willing to try, cousin, but I fear that my working for the men in our army, will not go very far to prove my unselfishness, since I cannot feel that I am not gratifying my own feelings, in all I do for them."

CHAPTER XLV.

"She hath put on
Courage, and faith, and generous constancy,
Even as a breastplate.   MRS. HEMANS.
"No studied words of sympathy
Were coldly whispered round."

WOULD that the sufferings of the noble band of loyal soldiers at Annapolis was an exception to the general order of things, at the time of which we are writing. But alas! they were only a few among the many thousands who have fought and bled for our country's weal. And shall it be that the blood of these gallant men has been shed in vain? No, never shall it be said that there was not love of country in America, sufficient to save her noble institutions from destruction, at the hands of traitors. We have brave men, and women too, in our land, who will never cease to labor and pray, until the United States of America shall become a happy and a prosperous land. More happy and more prosperous than before the dark cloud of treacherous ambition darkened the Southern horizon of this once bright land.

But we must remember that our readers are looking for incidents, and will not care to read our sentiments..

Among the brave boys who fought and fell wounded at Gettysburg, was a young man, a mere youth, who volunteered soon after the war began. His name was Lucien Brown, an only son was he, and one greatly beloved, by the fondest of parents. This youth belonged to a Pennsylvania regiment, which did duty bravely on the memorable day of that battle, which convinced General Lee that he had greatly mistaken Yankee character, when he presumed to set his hostile foot north of Virginia.

Near the close of the battle, Lucien received a musket shot in his arm. At first, the wounded limb was so benumbed that he did not realize that he was much hurt; but it was not long before he felt his strength failing, and he sought a place of safety and laid himself down, after making an ineffectual attempt to stop the life-current which was constantly oozing from his wound.

"Must I die here, alone and uncared for?" thought this young man. Then thoughts of home, friends, and the many comforts to which he had been accustomed in that far-off home filled his mind. "If I die here, my mother, perhaps, will never know what has become of me, and I fear she will be tempted to feel that the sacrifice she has made for her country is too great. I would not have her feel thus; I would so love to live, that in future years she may exult in the thought that she has a patriot son. Our boys have fought bravely to-day, but O, how many noble men have fallen. Shall I be reported among them? I hope not, yet fear I must be."

Thoughts like these filled his mind until his great weakness induced a feeling of drowsiness from which he was aroused by a fellow-soldier, who bent over him to ascertain his condition.

"You are wounded, and must not lie here, bleeding to death. It is well I came this way, for you would take your last nap pretty soon, if you should not have something done for you. I must staunch this blood, if I can," continued this stranger friend, and he took his handkerchief as he spoke and bound up the wounded arm.

"There is a musket-ball, besides any amount of your coat-sleeve in the wound, but I can do no more for you here; and as you are not a very large chap, I can tote you to yonder house, where you can have a doctor. I am right glad I came this way, for you are worth saving, I know. I have noticed you in the ranks to-day, and we can't let you cave in, yet. Heave O," said the jolly stranger, as he tenderly raised the bleeding youth in his brawny arms. "I'll not let you fall; don't be afraid; I've carried greater weights than this, many a time."

Lucien's heart was touched with the kindness he had so unexpectedly received from this rough-looking stranger. He felt that he was to be trusted, and he rested his weary head upon the shoulder of the strange man, without a fear. On arriving at the door of a house in the vicinity of the battle-field, this man stopped, and seeing through the open door a woman sitting at work, he entered the house and asked permission to lay the young man upon a bed.

"Come this way," said the lady, who went before him to a sleeping-room upon the first floor of the house. The feeling man laid down his burden tenderly, and ran immediately to call a surgeon to dress the wound of the young man. The lady, who seemed to Lucien to bear a strong resemblance to his mother, approached the bed and bent over the sufferer with a look of pity mingled with intense interest. Her eye met his, as she removed with gentle hands his clothes, which were saturated with blood, and he thought he read unusual feeling in its expression. The surgeon soon came, and looked at Lucien's wounded limb; with him, also, came the good soldier whose efforts had probably preserved this youth from an untimely death.

"Surgeon," said this man, "there is a ball in that arm, and pieces of coat-sleeve beside."

"So I perceive," replied the surgeon, who hastened to stay the effusion of blood which was fast prostrating the strength of the youthful soldier. Scarcely a word was spoken, while the wound was receiving attention, for an almost breathless anxiety was felt by each one who gazed upon the pallid features of the young man. He was then made as comfortable as was possible under the circumstances he could be, and left alone for a time to rest. Many inquiries were made respecting the patient, of this man, by his surgeon and hostess, as they all met together in an adjoining apartment, after they had done what they might for the stranger, at that time.

"He's a plucky boy," said the friendly soldier. "I noticed him in the fight to-day, and he bore his part without flinching. I did n't see him fall, but I missed him on the field with some others who I felt an especial interest for; I was looking for a cousin of mine, whose mother I had promised that I would do all in my power for her son, when I came upon this case. Of course, I could n't pass this gallant boy by; but I must hurry off now, and search for the one I have n't found. I shall try to see this brave fellow again, and I suppose I need n't ask you, madam, to be kind to him," he continued, turning to the hostess "for I see an expression of kind feeling in your countenance, that assures me he will be cared for while he remains with you."

Tears filled the eyes of this good woman, as she assured the man he had conjectured rightly, regarding her feelings towards the soldier. "*Any* loyal soldier would find a warm welcome under this roof. I should not be true to myself, if I refused to nurse kindly any brave man who has been wounded while defending my country; but I feel that this young stranger may have even a stronger claim upon my sympathy than others. He bears a strong resemblance to a sister of mine, whom I have not seen for many years; I am anxious to learn his name on this account. Can you tell me what it is?" asked she, addressing the soldier.

"I cannot, madam; but we will find out by-and-by, I hope," said the noble man; then bade both the lady and surgeon "good day."

The surgeon looked in again, upon Lucien, and then went to administer relief to other sufferers, for the number of such was large, on that eventful day.

The house to which Lucien Brown had been admitted was not the only one to which the wounded loyal men and sometimes Rebels also had been borne, sheltered, and cared for kindly, at the time alluded to. Long will the hospitality of many a worthy farmer and his wife, in the vicinity of Gettysburg, be remembered with gratitude, by the sufferers who received their ministrations in those days of their helplessness. Many then found it blessed to be cared for, when they were far from home and friends; but those who opened their homes and hearts, to comfort the distressed, found by experience that it is "more blessed to give than to receive."

Mrs. Harvey, the lady who had so kindly welcomed Lucien, did not feel that she had done all her duty, when she had given this youth an asylum in his hour of need. She would do for others, also, and she was not satisfied, until she had sent every comfort her house afforded, to the sick and wounded whom she could reach. She watched over her suffering guest with the greatest assiduity; much did she long to have him able to converse, for the image of her absent sister, came ever to her mind when she looked upon the young man.

"I have done very wrong," said this lady, mentally, as she sat scanning the features of the youth, who was lying almost bloodless before her. "I have done wrong, in not keeping up a correspondence with my sister, for I might have improved some moments by writing, when I have felt too weary to work, even if I did not love to write. However, if this youth is spared to make known his name, if I am disappointed in regard to his being my sister's son, I will write to Martha, and try to find out if her son is in the army; for it must be that some of her family have taken up arms to help the Government. She is as patriotic as myself, if not more so; yet she does not love to write, and has so many cares, that she may find it difficult to answer my letter. Poor boy," exclaimed the good woman, after she had sat some time, busy with her thoughts regarding him, "I wish I knew your name."

A smile lighted up the features of the patient, and he opened his eyes at the sound of her voice. "You have been sleeping," remarked his hostess: "I hope you feel somewhat refreshed by your nap. Here is some porridge which you must drink, before you talk any," said she pleasantly, "and then I expect you to tell me the name of your mother."

"My mother's name is Brown, and she looks near enough like yourself, to be your sister," said the youth in a faint voice.

"I have a sister named Brown," replied the other, with an animated look at the face of Lucien ; "and you bear a strong resemblance to her ; so strong, that I have thought it possible, you were her own son. Is your mother's name Martha ?" inquired the lady.

It is ; and I have heard her say she had a sister in this State, whom she has long tried to visit, but circumstances for a long time have prevented her."

"Is your name Lucien ?"

"It is," was the reply.

The youth then mentioned several little circumstances, which convinced Mrs. Harvey that it was indeed the son of her sister, who had been providentially brought to her dwelling.

"I am very glad that you have been brought to my home, Lucien," remarked the aunt.

"So am I, aunt ; yet it seemed very unlikely, a short time since, that I should ever visit you, much less come to your house, so weak and helpless as I now find myself. But where is that noble man who brought me here ? I want to thank him for my preservation."

Mrs. Harvey told Lucien that the stranger had promised to call again to see him, if he could. She also told him what the soldier had said concerning himself.

"How strange to hear any soldier praised for doing

what he came into the army with the expectation of doing. I feel ashamed, for my part, of such men as shirk their duty. At such a time as this, one ought to do all in his power, without a thought of self-interest."

"How long have you been in the army, Lucien?"

"Not but a few months; I was too young, when the war began. I was not glad to have it continue, until my age would admit of my enlisting; still, as it has lasted so long, I am glad I had an opportunity to shed some of my blood, for the sake of sustaining the right. General Lee wont be in a hurry to attack us again, I fancy; but I shall feel vexed, if our generals allow these Southrons to get back into Virginia. It will not be the fault of the men, but the officers, if they do return."

Mrs. Harvey joined heartily in the wish her nephew had expressed in regard to the Rebel general, and then cautioned him against exerting himself to converse more, until he should be better able. She wrote on that evening to her sister, acquainting her with the circumstances which had brought Lucien to her home.

"Does it not seem strange, my dear sister," wrote Mrs. Harvey, "that we should have waited for this war to come with all its horrors, ere we could find the opportunity to write to each other? What an educator is this terrible struggle of ours, for the nation's existence. I feel that my thoughts are oftener drawn from my personal cares, than ever before. My personal interest seems swallowed up in the one great interest of our country. I need not ask you to find the way to my home, now, since I have one of your treasures here; I had almost said in possession, yet this is altogether too much to say, as he belongs to the Government, and is at the disposal of the powers that be. If you hasten here, you will probably have the privilege of visiting your son and sister together."

The above is an extract from the long letter which Mrs. Harvey penned on the evening of that never-to-be-forgotten day which we have so often referred to ere this. She found she could not only find time to write, but that she had written quite a lengthy epistle, ere she was aware of doing so. When her letter was finished, she said mentally, "How true it is that no one knows what they can do, until they put forth an effort. Here, I have quite surprised myself, by writing this letter so easily, and in so short a space of time. It must be, because my heart was in the work; that makes a great difference, truly."

Mrs. Harvey's sister received this missive, which was despatched to the post-office, as soon as written, and answered it in person in less than three days from the time it was written. The meeting of these long-parted sisters would have been joyful in the extreme, had it not been for the precarious situation in which the son of the eldest sister was placed. As it was, however, their coming together was pleasant, and the manner in which it had been brought about was by them felt to be providential.

"It was not a great journey I had to accomplish in order to get to your home, sister; the distance from Portland to Gettysburg is not so great as I had imagined, and I wonder that I have so long dreaded to set out to travel it."

"How true it is, that we need a great deal of motive power, to make us act," remarked Mrs. Harvey; "yet it is true, that we need to be impelled along in the path of duty; but now as we have met, and our interests are somewhat blended into each other by the condition of our land, I trust we shall not be parted for so many years again, as we have been."

The wound of Lucien healed rapidly after the ball was extracted, and the pieces of blouse sleeve, which the bullet had taken in its way into the very depths of the wound, had also been removed.

Lucien was allowed to remain some little time at the house of his aunt, and was so far recovered before going to the hospital, that he could walk about comfortably. Returning one day from one of his short excursions in the open air, he brought news to his aunt and mother, of the capture of one of his cousins, by some of the loyal troops.

"I wonder if this can be true," exclaimed Mrs. Harvey; "I had hoped that all our friends were loyal, and shall be pained to be obliged to blush for any of our family, who have dared to assail our Government."

"But Richard may have been conscripted, aunt, and that would alter the case considerably," said Lucien.

"That is very true; and what you have said, Lucien, reminds me of the panic which the draft has created, in several places where we have friends residing."

"Has any one dear to you, sister, been obliged to go to the war against his will?" asked the mother of Lucien.

"No; those who were able to go, who were most

dear to me, I am happy to say, loved their country too well to wait to be drafted, ere they marched to drive back the foe. But there have some incidents occurred in consequence of the draft, which are really worth remembering; one I think of now, which I must relate, as it will interest you greatly."

CHAPTER XLVI.

*"And who art thou, that, in the littleness
Of thine own selfish purpose, would'st set bounds
To the free current of all noble thought,
And generous action, bidding its bright waves
Be stayed, and flow no farther?"* — MRS. HEMANS.

"ARE you afraid of the draft?" was a question asked me, said Mrs. Harvey, by an acquaintance, whose name I need not mention, the very day on which drafting was first commenced in any of the loyal States.

"Afraid of the draft? No, indeed. Why should I be afraid of it? I asked in reply."

"Don't you care if your friends are obliged to go to the war? asked this lady."

"Yes, I care a great deal about it, and am very, very sorry, that there is any necessity for a draft to be made. It does not speak well for the patriotism of some of our able-bodied men."

"But it's too bad, I think, for a man to go against his will."

"In one respect, it is, certainly," I answered; "it is bad for the Government; for men who have no heart in their work, generally fail to accomplish much."

"You are altogether too ultra in your views, Mrs. Harvey," exclaimed this lady, in a deprecating tone.

"All the wives and mothers don't feel as you do, in regard to their friends going forth to fight."

"I wish all had more love of country than I have," said I.

" But have n't you any feeling for those who go forth to battle?" asked she.

" I believe I have a great deal of feeling, for all who have entered the Union service."

" Then I desire to know how you can be so willing to let your friends go and meet the enemies of our land."

" I would not," I said to this mother, " urge a friend to go into the army; I have never done so; yet I should not dare lay any obstacle in the way of their going, if they felt it to be their duty, or if they were merely prompted by inclination, to enlist."

" Well," said she, you can do as you like, and so will I, for our country is free yet. So I'll have my son commute if he is drafted, and be sure of having him with or near me, while you trust yours to the mercy of foes who salute them with shot and shell. I believe," she continued, without giving me an opportunity to speak, "that some of the women in our country have taken leave of their senses, that is, if they ever had any. Just look at that woman, whose son, to pay a wager he lost in betting, previous to the election of President Lincoln, walked in ten consécutive days, from the State House in Boston, to the Capitol at Washington."

" I don't know this person ; what do you know of her?" I replied.

" Why, that she made herself sick over what she termed his folly, in being smart enough to fulfil his wager, and yet, as soon as this war broke out, this very son, towards whom she was feeling so tender a few weeks before, had her sympathy and all the aid she could afford him, in taking up arms and going into the very hot-bed of riot and secession, and nobody ever heard of her worrying herself sick, because he was exposed to peril in the army. Even worse than that she has done; she long since consented that her youngest and only remaining son should enter the navy. This, she thinks, is all as it should be, and she don't appear to be very much concerned about him, or about another member of her family, who is very near, and whose seat has been made vacant for two long years at the table where she was wont to sit with him at every meal. I have heard folks who know her, talk about her inconsistency. Why, it is said, she lost nearly all the flesh there was on her bones, when her son was taking this walk; yet her health does n't suffer at all, now, on account of her anxiety. I confess, I don't understand such notions. I would rather my boy should walk as many hundred miles as he chose, than enter the army, and be obliged to march at the order of others, and afterwards meet the foe, and perhaps death, at his hands. I'm consistent, at any rate, and that's more than can be said of many a woman; for instance, that one I have told you about."

Here my friend paused, and I could not but give her my idea of the inconsistency of the mother of the pedestrian whose case she had mentioned.

"I do not see any want of feeling in this mother, to whom you have referred, because she can cheerfully give up her dear ones to go to the war, and yet, could not bear to feel that a loved son was using his energies to no better purpose than to pay a lost wager. I think I understand her feelings, and I sympathize with them, too. She can feel, when her loved ones are in their country's service, that they are doing right, therefore she can commend them in prayer to that holy Being who is Omnipotent to protect them in all places, and who will preserve them alive, until their work on earth is done. But when a son was outraging the laws of nature unnecessarily, and by performing this walking feat, desecrating two Sabbath days, she could not feel the same confidence in commending him to the care of that Father, whom she felt this dear son was thoughtlessly offending. I presume this mother would tell you, if you should ask her, that her feelings have been such as I have described, and such as many mothers in our land can appreciate."

"Well, I like what I can see with my natural eyes, better than what I am left to discern by faith. I'll keep my boy at home, and be sure of him."

"Poor woman; she did keep her son under her own watch-care; what was three hundred dollars to her, compared with the privilege of taking care of him, and keeping him out of harm's way. She could, she said, sell her sewing-machine, and some of her nice clothes, and even the spoons her own sainted mother had given her, years before, for this privilege, if his father was not ready to advance the money. She would do anything to keep her boy out of danger, and she succeeded in having him commuted."

"Where is this youth, now?" asked the sister of Mrs. Harvey, who had been listening with much interest to this narration.

"He is not to be found among the living; all his mother's anxiety to save him, could not preserve him from the fell destroyer, Death. She did indeed keep him near her, and even under her watchful eye, most of the time; yet all this care was impotent to save from death, or even from danger. It was the agonizing experience of this fond mother, to feel her own helplessness, when she would have sacrificed worlds, had she possessed them, to save her darling son. She saw him thrown from a carriage, in which he was riding, and killed instantly; she saw, too, his corpse, bruised and mangled, borne into her dwelling, which he had left but a few minutes previous in all the strength and vivacity of early manhood."

"What has it availed me to keep him at home?" cried she, in all the agony of her grief. "It could n't have been much worse, had he gone to the war. O, I wish I had not tried so hard to keep him at home."

"This is not a solitary case," remarked the auditor of Mrs. Harvey; "I have heard of others, that are similar. I well know a mother, whose son went from a city in Massachusetts, to Brooklyn, and enlisted in the navy. This mother did not know what her boy had done, until he had been absent from home two days. He was not a dutiful son, far from it; the heart of his mother had often been made to bleed by the wicked acts he had committed in the vicinity of his home.

"Yet when she heard that this bad boy was where he would be restrained, and kept out of mischief, for a time she was inconsolable, until she went to the receiving ship, where he was, and protested against his staying there. She had upwards of fifty dollars to pay for his release, and she took him home with her, to pollute the rising generation, with his sinful example and influence, as he had previously done. Who dare feel that this weak woman will not regret, a greater number of times, even, than she has paid dollars for his release, that she did not allow him to remain where he could be under some restraint, for a season. The friends of this mother, especially those who live near her dwelling, regret already the return of the boy to the home where he has ever been indulged to his hurt."

"I wish this was the only case of the kind, sister; but I fear the name of such cases is legion, and the mothers, and it may in some instances be said, too, that fathers can feel quite composed, if they only see their sons, if they are exposed to the vilest of influences, in grog shops, which, at this hour, are so numerous in our land. Such parents can even bear to see their dearest sons, at times, stagger into their homes, under the accursed influence of intoxicating drink."

"Why do not such parents open their eyes, and look about them?" asked Mrs. Harvey.

"I don't know of but one reason why they do not, and that is, they greatly prefer to be blind to the evils, which, at their very doors, are threatening to engulph their sons, forever."

"Let law tolerate and protect these dens of death, moral suasion will make all right, some time," say they. "Boys will sow their wild oats, no matter if they do get a little '*tight*' sometimes. We mustn't have men forced to do right, by removing temptation out of their way. This notion is all fanatical; we prefer to have our sons manly, and take a glass occasionally, without a feeling of restraint. If a man only *pays* for a license, he can hold up his head, and put the cup to his neighbor's lips, if God, in his holy

Word, does say he is cursed for doing so. He has human law on his side; what does he care for the law of God?"

"What you say is but too true, sister. Intemperance is killing more men in our world, than the sword. In our land, it is doing a fearful work. Had I my choice, I should greatly prefer to have those dear to me slain by the sword, rather than by the demon intemperance. If they fall honorably, in their country's cause, we oft-times have hope in their death. But what hope can we entertain concerning the inebriate, who falls a victim to his own lusts? God says, 'No drunkard shall enter heaven;' while at the same time, he invites even the vilest to turn from his cups, repent, and be saved forevermore."

Amen we say to this; and we know that many voices will echo a loud amen.

CHAPTER XLVII.

"Heaven doth with us, as we with torches do;
Not light them for themselves; for if our virtues
Did not go forth of us, 't were all alike,
As if we had them not."—SHAKESPEARE.

"I WANT to get an accurate account of the casualties in the neighborhood of Port Hudson," said Minnie Granger to Mrs. Sedgwick the younger, who was once more established in her own peaceful home. This was said soon after the surrender of that place, which General Banks and his brave boys had so untiringly sought to subdue.

"I hope we shall soon hear something reliable about your brother-in-law, Minnie," replied Mrs. Sedgwick. "I saw his name in the list of casualties, yesterday, and mention was made of his having been slightly wounded."

"Slightly wounded, sometimes means considerable of a wound," said Minnie; "in many cases these trifling wounds have resulted fatally; therefore, I feel deeply anxious about Joseph."

It was not strange that Minnie should feel great solicitude on her brother's account. It was July; the weather was intensely hot, and the temperature of the climate where he was situated was much more enervating than the air of his native clime. But if a sister-in-law felt anxious, how much more so must have felt the wife, who, with two little children, had been left months before by this husband and father, who had gone cheerfully forth from his home, as a champion of the right.

Not many days after the conversation we have narrated, news came from this dear object of affection and hope; but such news, that it only made these expectant hearts more sad than before. The letter had been penned by a brother officer, who stated that Joseph was lying very low, and his condition was considered, by the surgeon, very critical.

"I must go to him without delay," said the wife.

"Certainly you must, and I must go with you," replied Minnie.

"But who can we leave with the care of the children, during our absence?" asked the afflicted wife and mother.

"I don't know certainly, but I'm inclined to think that Bessie Jenkins will consent to look after them, for a time."

"*Bessie Jenkins* look after my children! you astonish me. Why, I thought she was too much of an automaton, to trouble herself with doing anything useful."

"But you don't know how she has changed of late. I never knew any one, in whom a change for the better, was so visible, as it is in her."

"I am glad, very glad, even in the midst of my sorrow, that this is so," replied Mrs. Stetson, the sister of Minnie.

"You, Minnie, perhaps had better see her at once, and secure, if you can, her services; tell her, she will be doing a good work, and helping the distressed."

Minnie hastened to the home of Bessie, and found she had judged her rightly, when she conjectured that she would be willing to assist herself and sister, by taking the supervision of the children of the latter.

"I will do so with pleasure; I am glad you have

asked me," said Bessie. "Can I not do something to help you get on your way to-night? for you must hasten. I will go with you to your home, for I suppose your sister is with your mother now, is she not?"

"Yes, she came immediately after this sad news reached her; she started from her home, thinking I would go and see to her family while she could go and see to Joseph. But my anxiety to accompany her led me to propose asking you to stay at her house while we both should go."

This conversation took place while these two young ladies were walking hurriedly to the house of Mrs. Granger. It was a great relief to the minds of Mrs. Granger and her daughters, to feel that the children could be left in their own home, while their mother was away from them; and a most unexpected pleasure to know that Bessie Jenkins could cheerfully accept the task of watching over them.

"Your patience will be tried, no doubt," said Mrs. Stetson to her, and I shall feel very grateful for this great kindness."

"Don't speak so," said Bessie; "I have lived many years without looking at all away from my personal comfort, to do anything for the good of others, and it is a comfort to me, now, to be able to do even a little."

"It is not a little thing you are undertaking, now, Bessie," said Mrs. Granger.

"Don't talk about what *I* am to do, now, only let us do what we can, to hasten the departure of your daughters. I feel impatient to see them set off on their journey, for every hour afterwards will bring them nearer to Joseph, and I know something of their feelings; at least, I can imagine what they must be."

The two sisters left in the cars that same evening, and faithfully did Bessie redeem the pledge she had given, to care for the children of these afflicted parents; and every act of kindness she put forth was prompted by a high and disinterested motive.

"How pleasant it is," thought Bessie, "for one to feel that they are useful; and then, how pleasant it will be, to have Raymond know that I am exerting myself for the benefit of others. Yet it is not to please him, merely, that I love to do what is right; I trust I desire to please my Saviour more than I do to please even Raymond."

With such reflections as these, Bessie pursued her way with comfort, not only to herself, but to those who were entrusted to her care.

In the mean time, our travellers had sped over the long distance which spread itself between Oak Dale and the vicinity of Port Hudson sooner than they had feared, and found themselves in safety at the end of their journey. The hour of their arrival was an exciting one to the wife and sister of Joseph Stetson. Their inquiries for him were fruitless for a time, but at length they were escorted, by one of the hospital stewards, to the bedside of the sufferer. How changed was he, since they last beheld him; his eyes were closed, and his features bore the impress of great suffering, while a deathlike pallor spread over his countenance.

In breathless silence, Minnie and her sister stood and gazed upon what appeared to them as but the shadow of him who was so dear to them. They inquired of the nurse, who was a kindly man, respecting the symptoms of his patient, and their worst fears were confirmed by the information he gave them.

"Will he be able to speak to us?" asked the sorrowful wife.

"He may, but he is failing rapidly," said the nurse, in a compassionate tone.

"O, I hope he will know us," said Minnie, with a quivering lip, while tears flowed down her cheeks.

An expression of pain flitted across the face of the sufferer, while he slowly opened his eyes. His wife bent over him, while she pressed his hand tenderly in both her own.

"Thank God you have come, and Minnie too," he said, as he glanced his eye quickly towards the weeping girl. He attempted to extend his hand towards her, and she took it and held it for some minutes, ere she could articulate a syllable. For a moment or two this husband and brother was overcome with emotion, yet his feelings soon became calm, and he smiled sweetly upon the loved ones who, he said, had been mercifully sent to cheer his last hours.

"But, oh," said Minnie, "to think that, after you have done and suffered so much for your country, your life must end thus."

Mrs. Stetson was too much overpowered with grief to speak, but she regarded her husband with a look of unutterable tenderness, while Minnie gave vent to the feelings of her sorrowing heart in the words quoted above.

"That thought is not distressing to me, sister," said the patient sufferer; "what I have done and suffered is but little, in comparison with what I would like to have done. If I have done any good to the cause of virtue and humanity, which I feel is identified with the Union cause, I rejoice at the thought.

I would love to live longer, for the sake of my country; yet I feel that God can work without me. His own right hand hath gotten Him the victory here, and I would that He should use just the instruments He chooses to accomplish His purposes. Don't," said this noble soldier, after a pause of a few moments, "don't weep; it pains me much, and seems to draw me back to that world I have given up. I love you not less, but I love my God more, much more than ever before, and more even than my dear family. To His care, I commend the dear friends I am about to leave."

"My sweet babes He will preserve, for He has promised to do so, and his word is sure forever. You, my dear, dear Laura, may trust in Him, if you will; do promise me, that you will not grieve for me, overmuch, when I am gone. You may weep, but don't indulge in grief, as some do, for it is not right." The dying husband paused many times while uttering these words, which were some of the last he was to speak to the friends who were so dear to him. He lay silent for some time, and then said, "kiss our little ones for me, and tell them, when they are old enough, it was the wish of their father that they should love God, and if they live to manhood, love and serve their country, and do all in their power to make this a holy and a prosperous land."

After these last words were spoken, the sick man seemed to fall asleep. His eyes closed slowly, and he lay motionless, while the weeping wife and sister sat near his bedside, watching and hoping to catch a few more precious words, which they could embalm in the casket of memory, after this loved one should be gone from earth.

"I fear he will not speak again," whispered Mrs. Stetson, while tears streamed in torrents down her cheeks. "Yet I must not repine, but be grateful for the privilege of hearing him speak at all."

"I am thankful we came here," said Minnie.

Just at that moment the patient sufferer opened his eyes, and motioned for his wife to draw very near to him. She did so, and placed her ear close to his lips.

"I do not wish you to regret that I became a soldier, Laura; I don't regret doing so, myself. I rejoice that my influence has been exerted on the side of right, and I hope you will never reflect upon yourself, for consenting to my leaving you. Try to be cheerful and encourage others to trust their friends with God, and not hinder them from doing their duty to our suffering country."

"I will endeavor, Joseph, to comply with all your wishes; but how can I do without you, my dear, dear husband?"

"Look to Jesus, and he will give you strength. He has done all for me; love and praise him evermore."

Again he paused, as he had done before, with his eyes closed, while a sweet expression of serenity stole over his features. After he had laid some time, apparently resting in sleep, Minnie bent over him and placed her ear near his mouth, in order to ascertain if he still breathed.

"He does not appear to respire at all," said Minnie. She then placed her fingers gently upon his heart and found that its pulsations had ceased. The nurse approached the bedside, and in the gentlest possible manner examined his patient, and found that his spirit had fled.

"How gently he passed away; this change came to him like sleep to a weary infant," said Minnie.

"He was a noble man, and a lovely Christian patriot," remarked the man, who had kindly cared for this soldier since his admission into the hospital.

What a tribute to the memory of a man, in these days which try men's souls, and develop their real characters. We would rather it should be said of one dear to us, "he was a lovely Christian patriot," than that he was monarch of this whole world. How we hate to lose these Christian patriots from our army and navy; yet we will be still, and know that it is God, who removes them to a fairer clime. These are the flowers of earth, and when the odor of their virtues have perfumed, and their loveliness adorned this sinful planet for a time, these lovely beings are mercifully removed to that world "where the inhabitants shall never say they are sick," or that any blight has marred their beauty and enjoyment.

We wish, sometimes, that the number of these noble spirits who stay a few years upon earth, to bless it, was greater than it is; but it is not well this should be so, for God, who doeth *all* things well, sees it best to remove such. Mrs. Stetson and her sweet children have our tenderest sympathy, still, we feel that herself and those dear to her, have been favored above thousands of wives, mothers, and friends, who have been bereaved by this cruel war.

In the same hospital where Joseph Stetson expired, another soldier died about the same time, whose last hours bore a striking contrast to the death-scene we have, we feel, but inadequately described. This soldier had taken up arms to assist in defending the United States Government. To a careless observer, he appeared to be as brave a soldier as Stetson. His personal appearance was more imposing; beauty sat enthroned upon his bright countenance; his splendid black eyes shone with peculiar lustre, as he stood erect, accoutred for the field, and boastfully exclaimed, that he defied the Southern chivalry; that his strong right arm was ready to help chastise traitors.

He wavered not, nor shrank from duty in the camp or on the field, and it was in the performance of duty that he was wounded and laid upon a couch of suffering. The spirit of this man chafed under this trial, and he vented his disquiet in blasphemy and curses, which disturbed his fellow-sufferers greatly. When first confined, he was resolutely determined to resist every effort that was made to do him good. He would not, he said, lie down in such an uncomfortable place, and put up with such accommodations as could be provided by Government; he therefore made himself very uncomfortable, and all about him, by his impatience and imprecations.

Then, how unlike Stetson was he when his strength was exhausted, and he knew that he must die. He murmured at everything, so that it was impossible to please him. Like his fellow-soldier, he had an affectionate wife and two small children; he well knew his wife was not in a situation to go to him; however much she desired the privilege of seeing him, it was not possible for her to be with him; still, in his impatient ravings, he accused this loving wife of indifference and forgetfulness of his situation, when at that very time her heart was wrung with anguish because she could not be permitted to minister to her husband, in this time of suffering and need.

All who witnessed the departure of this young man from earth, shuddered at the thought that he had, by refusing instruction, and wilfully neglecting his obligations to God, shrouded the scene of his deathbed in darkness and doubt, if not in despair.

"How unlike a Christian this young man died," said his nurse, mentally, after he had witnessed his death-struggles, and listened to the earnest, agonizing cries for mercy, which he made to his neglected Saviour, in his last hours. Who dare say that these cries, for the mercy of an offended God, were not heard and answered? Yet, who does not tremble at the thought that fear of punishment, rather than sorrow for sin, might have prompted these utterances. All that friends can do, is to leave such cases as this in the hands of God, without presuming to sit in judgment upon the prospects of such individuals; it is enough that they are in the hands of a Being who will not do His creatures injustice.

But thoughts of those who live as if there was no God, until death stares them in the face, and then leave this world without a firm hope founded upon the Rock of Ages, leads us to long especially, that the men who compose the army and navy of our country, may be loyal to God, as well as to these United States. Then, and never until then, will the men in our country's service be, in reality, *prepared* to sacrifice their temporal life upon the altar of their country.

CHAPTER XLVIII.

"For ambition is a burning mountain, thrown up amid the turbid sea;
A Strombolic in sullen pride above the hissing wave;
And the statesman climbing there, forgetful of his patriot intentions,
Shall hate the strife of each rough step or ever he hath toiled midway;
And every truant from his home, the happy home of duty,
Shall live to loathe his eminence of cares, that seething smoke and lava."

How many loyal hearts have been filled with anxiety, much of the time since April, '63, by the state of affairs in the neighborhood of Charleston, South Carolina. We set Morris Island down as being in the near neighborhood of Charleston, because the rapid passage of war missiles seems to annihilate the distance between these places.

Last April, the gaze of the loyal North was turned confidently to the fleet off Charleston, until, with disappointed hopes, they were forced to avert their gaze, and feel that they must wait still longer, before the fort that was first desecrated by a Rebel shot should be again possessed by that Government from which it had been wickedly wrested by traitor hands. It seemed strange that this stronghold was not compelled to surrender at that time, but it is certain that it was not. The Rebel flag floated as defiantly after the attack, as before, and seemed to mock the idea of loyal men, that this fortification must be repossessed by Uncle Sam. Several times during the summer following, Fort Sumter was attacked by our forces. Its walls were sadly battered, and its flagstaff repeatedly shot away; but as soon as it fell, it was each time quickly replaced, and flaunted in its Rebel pride before the eyes of loyal men.

"Sumter shall never be surrendered to the —— Yankees," was the bold assertion of the traitors by whom it was garrisoned during all the months of the Spring and Summer of '63. With how much interest have our hearts turned towards that point, during all this time. Not that its capture would be of much consequence to our Government as far as its wealth was concerned, or its strength as a fortification, but because it would be honorable to our forces to wrest it from traitor hands, and plant that symbol of integrity, the banner of our nation, over it once more. The Rebels knew this, and so they have determined to hold the ruins of that celebrated fort to the latest possible moment.

Morris Island was evacuated by the Southrons, and other strongholds of Rebellion were made comparatively weak by shot and shell, thrown by loyal soldiers into them. Sumter was fired upon, until it was thought expedient to take the huge pile of ruins that bore that name, by storm. It was garrisoned still, though it bore little resemblance to a fortification.

"I looked at Sumter through a glass, to-day; it seems to be a ruin. One wall looks as if it might be easily scaled." Thus wrote one who was in the fleet off Charleston, at the time alluded to, and had for days assisted in pouring shell into this shattered fortification. Then came a message from the same young man, dated September 8, in which he informed his friends that a night expedition had been planned, and volunteers called for, to go to some unnamed point on the coming night.

"I have asked permission to go," said he, "for I suspect Sumter is the place to which the volunteers are to be sent, but the enrolment officer said, at first, I was too slender to join in a work so trying as the one in anticipation, yet after all the best men on board our ship had offered, and still more were needed, by asking again that I might have the privilege of using what strength I had, I was told that I might go. You, my dear mother, shall hear from me at the earliest moment, after I return to the ship."

With this letter came tidings, through the "Press," that thrilled the heart of the mother and sisters of this young man with painful suspense on account of this son and brother. The expedition was attempted, yet it had proved a failure. Among the names of those captured by the foe, was that of the Captain of the Gunboat to which Frank Eaton belonged: the first Lieutenant's name was also recorded among the casualties. The boat sent out from this Gunboat, contained twenty men, when it joined the company of boats, in which was the attacking party that approached Sumter. This boat was one of three, that came along the beach, that were reported as having been captured or destroyed by the Rebels.

"My boy must have been in one of those boats," thought the mother of Frank; "then where can he be now? A prisoner of war at Sumter, and perhaps wounded, or it may be he sleeps in death, with the dark waters, he so fearlessly trusted in life, for a covering."

How long seemed the days that intervened, ere

another steamer came from off Charleston, and then how eagerly was each paper searched, that contained any news, by the mother and sisters of our boy. A very few more names were given by the New York Herald, of the gallant men who had so bravely volunteered to do their country service, on that disastrous occasion. More names were promised by the Herald's correspondent, yet week after week passed, and these names came not to relieve the many sad hearts that were tortured by suspense.

A letter was at the end of two weeks despatched to whoever might be the commander of the vessel to which Frank belonged, and then again, cheering hope plumed her downy wings, and floated softly through the withering atmosphere of suspense, bearing the hearts of these anxious ones to a more cheering region. It was well this could be so, for O, what heart could continue to throb day after day, under the terrible influence of suspense, unless at times the torment it causes, can be lessened by the kindly touch of hope, sweet hope.

A month had passed, and yet the anxiety of these waiting friends had not been relieved by tidings from the navy boy.

"I fear greatly that it will be long ere we hear anything from Frank," said his mother to a sister of the youth, one morning towards the middle of October, a little more than four weeks after the long to be remembered eighth of September.

"I, too, am apprehensive that he is a prisoner, and we may not hear from him for many months; yet, mother, I cannot feel that Frank is dead."

"Neither can I, my daughter; yet how it could be

possible for any of the men who were in those three boats that reached the beach at Sumter, to be saved, I cannot imagine. I don't quite understand, why the other boats could not have been on hand, to aid the first division, and probably it is not best I should. I do not care to sit in judgment upon any; I desire, more than anything else, a spirit of submission to the trials which Infinite wisdom has sent upon me. I wish to trust my child with God, and to do so cheerfully. Of myself, I know I cannot bear this terrible trial, but I feel that my Father in heaven has taught me to pray for strength, also, that He will preserve my son to be a useful man in the world, and I shall feel disappointed, if the position I feel He has dictated, is not answered. I trust Omnipotence will take care of my boy, still, my mother heart will throb with anguish at times: but I will not be distrustful."

"I wish we could hear something," said the sister of Frank, in reply to what her mother had said, "for this suspense is dreadful."

On the evening of that day, the penny-post, who brought letters to the friends of Frank Eaton, entered their dwelling. It may interest some of our readers to know that Mrs. Eaton lived in the town of G——, Rhode Island, where letters were generally carried from the post office in the latter part of the day. The approach of this functionary had been looked for with great interest for several weeks, by the friends of Frank, and hope had daily whispered, ere he came, that he probably might bring some news from the son and brother, of whom they longed to hear. Missives had been brought during the time, from many correspondents, and so long had these anxious friends looked in vain, that on this day the mother felt it would be useless even to ask if a letter had been brought from off Charleston. Great was her surprise, therefore, when the penny-post told her, upon entering the room where she was sitting, and throwing down a letter upon a table that stood near where she sat, that it had been mailed at Old Point Comfort.

"And there is another mailed at the same place, and another, and yet another," said the man, placing, as he spoke, the fourth letter upon the table. Mrs. Eaton took up the letters, and found that the four had been post-marked on the same day, and that that day was October 4.

"These letters have all been written by Frank," said his sister Nettie. "I want to learn the contents of the one that was written soonest after that disastrous expedition. Shall I read it, mother? He addresses both sisters and yourself, together."

Nettie sat down and read a missive which had been penned by her brother, on the 10th of September, just two days after the attack, which, it appeared from the letter, to have resulted in great mortification to the brave fellows who had risked all dear to them, hoping it would be their privilege, by so doing, to do something worthy of the cost they paid.

"I never, my dear mother and sisters, felt so sad in my life as now," wrote Frank. "I told you of our intended expedition, which I thought was to storm Fort Sumter, in my letter of the 8th, and now I regret to tell you, that that reconnoitre was a failure. I would tell you all about this sad affair, but my spirits are depressed, and I hate to think about it. In the most quiet manner possible, our boat started at about ten o'clock on the night of the 8th. We went to the flagship, where we were joined by several other boats, and then we started for the place of our destination. We each had a revolver and ammunition given us, also a cutlass. We were told that our work was to be close, sharp work, but we were kept in ignorance of its exact nature. In silence we rowed, so still that at times we fairly held our breath, and could almost hear the beating of our hearts as we proceeded on our way.

At one time we went so near to Moultrie, that we supposed we were to storm that fortification. Yet on we went, without asking a question. No word was spoken, save that a few orders were given in low whispers, that were passed from boat to boat without a sound. At about one o'clock, on the morning of the 9th, we drew near to Sumter; when within about one hundred and fifty feet of this stronghold, we were hailed by the sentinel with, ' boat ahoy ! ' Three times this hail was repeated, ere it was noticed by our commander. He then shouted, 'Surrender, there!' It seemed as though this order was considered rather lightly by the man on the wall above us, for he called out in a loud voice, 'nary time, Johnny; you *can't* come up here.'

"Pitch in, boys, pull ahead!" shouted our Captain, and then, with a loud yell, we pulled ahead with all our might. As the keel of our boat grated on the beach, a volley of musketry was fired upon us from the ruins above our heads. Many a poor fellow was killed or wounded at that moment; many a shot whizzed past my ears; many, too, fell short of hitting the boat in which I was stationed, which was the third one upon the beach, which was only an oar's length wide. Above the beach the wall rose to a height of forty-one feet, right above our heads; to discharge our pistols, we were obliged to hold them over our heads. The enemy burned a green light, and opened six ports, throwing a glare upon us as bright as day. This light blinded us, and we were so situated that Sumter was in the background. The alarm was general, all over the harbor. The men in the fort threw hand-grenades at us, poor fellows, who were disappointed in not finding a knocked-to-pieces stone wall, as we expected, that might be scaled. Every breach that was in the wall, on the side where we landed, was occupied with sharp shooters, who fired upon us from the moment we touched the shore.

"Twenty or thirty boats, crowded with men, were nearly all huddled together. Then commenced a fire from Moultrie on the right, and also from James Island on the left, which, with Sumter in front, made a crossfire on three sides against us. The first shell from Moultrie whizzed over our boat, throwing a hogshead of water over us, wetting us all through, in passing. It then struck the Powhattan's launch, and neither this boat nor her men were ever seen afterwards.

"It was soon found that we were powerless to act against the foe, and the order was given to retire. Some of the boats had not gone in at all; the third division, when the first shot was fired, instead of dashing forward, fell back in confusion. The rams of the enemy came around the fort, and poured a heavy fire upon us; we then retired in great confusion, while the Rebs followed us as we rowed away, with a galling fire, which sank our boats and struck our men every moment. As we became confused, the Rebels became insolent, and called loudly to us, asking why we did not come on; then they called us all the Yankee sons of b—h, possible.

"That cross fire was terrible. Of the twenty persons who went into the affray in one boat, only eight could be mustered after we returned to the ship. Our Captain was missing, also our first Lieutenant. The Powhattan's loss was great; one boat had two men left out of nine. I should think we lost nearly a hundred brave souls in all. The Rebels cheered loudly, and were very exultant over our defeat. It is certain that, had Sumter been able to fire big guns, none of this attacking party would have escaped with life. The flags we took to raise over these memorable ruins were some of them captured by the foe, others were brought back in disgrace. Sumter, this morning, is as defiant as ever. I never felt so disheartened before, my dear friends, but you may be sure that it was not the fault of the men that this attack proved a failure."

Much more was communicated by this youth to his relatives, and some facts which he stated we would give to the public, but we must wait until that public is less tolerant to the degrading vice, drunkenness. We have no heart to speak of a crime which is so easily passed over by those in high places; for what is the influence of one against the host, who, without compunction, place the intoxicating cup to the lips of their neighbor. Yea, worse than that, entice those of their own households to imbibe draughts that destroy manhood, and, in many sad cases, all that is lovely in woman.

Such care not, if all the lieutenants in the navy, and army too, degrade themselves in the presence of men over whom they are placed by Government, by their thick utterances, sounding in the darkness of night, upon ears to whom the voices of the debauched man is ever abhorrent. We wonder how it is that the very victims of intemperance can bear themselves, much less how they can expect to be respected by inferiors in position, whom their own consciences must tell them are their superiors in character. How we pity the men in our army and navy, who are obliged to be subjected to the authority of wine-bibbers.

It is not the fault of the privates in our country's service, that our arms have not oftener been victorious.

We are grateful that we have some good, gallant, and temperate officers in the United States service, but we cannot but mourn over the waste of intellect, influence, and life, caused by intemperance, reports of which come to us every day. How often have our eyes witnessed the disgrace of a pair of Uncle Sam's shoulder-straps. A lieutenant, clothed in a blue uniform, staggering through the streets of one of our principal cities, uttering the unintelligible jargon of a drunkard. What a spectacle! Our hearts have throbbed with mingled emotions as we have beheld this sight; disgust, pity, and scorn, struggle in our breast for the mastery, while we reflect that real *men*, whole-souled, earnest, patriots, are subjected to military rule, under such characters as we have just alluded to.

Would that the public sentiment of our country would banish intoxicating drink from every circle; then might we expect sooner to see the sword of Jehovah sheathed, which is now scourging this nation, for this is one of the sins which a holy God is now rebuking by the horrors of war.

One incident that has occurred since our nation's woes began, is indelibly impressed upon our minds, and it shows the importance of correct habits in men filling influential stations.

CHAPTER XLIX.

"Man liveth from hour to hour, and knoweth not what may happen;
Influences encircle him on all sides, and yet must he answer for his actions;
For the being that is master of himself, bendeth events to his will.
But a slave to selfish passion is the wavering creature of circumstance.
To this man temptation is a poison, to that man it addeth vigor;
And each may render to himself influences good or evil." TUPPER.

How much a trifling incident often affects the life of a person, especially that of a youthful person. It were well if this fact was oftener borne in mind by men in high positions. In this republican land, where all are or ought to be free to act, and where example governs more sternly than any civil law, individuals should be wary, lest, by example, they injure the country they are ready to give their life's blood to save from traitorous invasion.

"What an idea!" says one; "how can my example affect this great land I live in?"

We ask any such caviller, what any country is worth without citizens? and further, who are the citizens of a land? Are they not individual men and women? Do not the acts of every individual who lives in a community, help form the character of that community? And do not communities make the nation strong or weak, as virtue or vice abounds in them? But we did not intend to digress thus, but to relate, in this chapter, the incident to which we referred in the one which precedes it.

Most of our readers, who have read the newspapers in this country since the war began, are aware that our rulers at Washington, found it necessary, a year or two since, to establish new fortifications. It will be remembered that there has been much talk about the sites of these new war conveniences. Some wished them to be in one place and some in another; so, of course, it was important that every situation that was recommended by either party, should be not only visited, but examined in respect to its advantages as a site for the contemplated public establishment. Commissioners were consequently appointed, by the powers that be, to visit these localities and then report at the nation's capital. A party of these Government agents left a city in New England, one pleasant morning, in the summer of 18—, to examine a certain place, which had been designated by some of our great men, as an excellent locality for the said establishment.

Some high in office were authorized to accompany these commissioners. We write about this affair without any personal prejudice, for we know not the names of any of this party, excepting those of one military gentleman, and one youthful friend of ours, who was taken by this gentleman to perform some little needful service. The youth referred to was very observant of the acts and manners of the gentlemen with whom he was in company, during most of the hours of that summer's day, and impressions were made upon his mind which will be life lasting. Soon after that time this youth visited his home, on leave of absence, from a post of public duty. It was amusing, so say the friends who have heard this young man converse, to hear his original description of a scene that occurred during that tour of inspection.

"Why, my dear mother, I did not know you were such a novice, in regard to the doings of great men, as to be surprised that a site for a Government work, could not be inspected by cold water men."

This was said by our young friend in reply to a remark made by his mother, in reference to the inspection party alluded to.

"I don't know how it is, mother, but men I have seen, since I have been in the United States service, are very thirsty. Now these Commissioners, I was childish enough to fancy, were men whose appetites did not crave the ardent; but lo, before they returned from their run up the river or bay, through which their path lay, one of the gentlemen procured some whiskey, and another some wine, which they brought on board our small craft. I wondered, at first, what they could want of the heating stuff on such a warm day, but I soon found out that it was the fashion, generally, for Government men to treat, and have a jolly time over any such business. Foolish boy I, not to have known this sooner. Don't look troubled, mother; your son was not slighted on the occasion, if he was n't but sixteen years old, for a very genial sort of a gentleman offered me some whiskey, which I politely declined. He then offered me some iced champagne, and when I declined this also, the man looked at me intently for a moment, and then said, "you are a good boy not to drink anything of the kind."

"I am glad, my son, that he spoke thus, as those words speak volumes in favor of total abstinence."

"I felt that the man who uttered them would have respected himself more, if he had not been a slave to a habit that is so powerful over him."

"Never touch that cup, my son, which destroys all manliness," said the mother; "rely not upon your own strength to resist temptation, but look to Heaven for help, to keep yourself clear-headed."

"The taste of liquor is not any temptation to me, mother, for I don't love it; all I have to resist, is the jeers of companions; they ridicule me at times, unmercifully, but I have learned to ridicule myself, whenever this is attempted, and now I am seldom spoken to upon the subject. Every one seems to think I will get along as well without liquor, and so I am let alone. I must say, if I am a boy, that I pity some men who are in high places, because they seem to be slaves to stimulating drink.

"One man, in particular, I wish would never again taste spirit. I was, as you well remember, under his command for a season, and he was an excellent officer when he was not stimulated; but when he was under the influence of wine, he was unlike himself. I like many traits in this man's character, yet I cannot feel any respect for him, for it is impossible for a drinking man to inspire me with such a feeling. Then think of this other man, high in the estimation of his country, offering intoxicating liquor to a mere boy. How did he know but he might be helping make me a drunkard by doing so. I hope I shall think more of my influence when I am a man."

"They had better, when cold, resort to the remedy Clarence uses in such a case," remarked Mrs. Eaton.

"Cayenne pepper is all the stimulant he ever takes, is n't it, mother?"

"It is; and no man in the army has been sick less than he has during the eighteen months he has served his country both in the camp, and in the field. As a medicine, ardent spirit is sometimes useful, but its use kills thousands more than it ever cured."

"I am persuaded that there is no need of my taking a 'horn,' as they call a glass of spirit, and I hope I shall never be left to be a drunkard."

"Persevere, in refusing to taste even a little of that which will deprive you of self-command, as well as self-respect, and you will be safe from one great evil; an evil, too, more to be dreaded than the sword, which is now slaying so many of the lovely young men in our land."

We know this young man, and we have reason to believe that thus far he has kept free from the vice of intemperance. His taste has not been polluted by more than two years' service in the ———, and though he confesses himself destitute of heartfelt respect for intemperate officers, he is still ready to serve his country faithfully, under any circumstances.

CHAPTER L.

> "Were once our vain desires subdued,
> The heart resigned at rest;
> In every scene we should conclude,
> The will of Heaven is best."

How the hearts of Mrs. Stetson and her sister Minnie turned back to the spot that was sacred to them as the earthly resting-place of their loved friend, while they were travelling back to their home.

"How sad it seems to leave Joseph behind us," said the wife, after a long and painful silence on the part of both these friends, as they journeyed homewards.

"It does, indeed," replied Minnie, "and the thought would be agonizing, could we not feel that his immortal spirit is happy with his God."

"Yes," said Mrs. Stetson, "and there is another comforting reflection beside, and that is, our belief in the resurrection of the dead, which is promised in the Bible."

"It is indeed a sweet thought that the dead shall rise again, and that in heaven we shall recognize those we have known and loved on earth."

"Were it not for the sustaining power of the gospel," replied Minnie, "the heart-burdens which this desolating war has brought upon thousands, could never have been borne."

This last remark was heard by a fellow-traveller, who stood near the sisters as they were standing together, upon the upper deck of a steamer which was bearing them from all that remained of their precious friend. It was true that their home was at the end of their journey, yet who that has been placed in circumstances like theirs, does not appreciate the feeling that filled the hearts of these sorrowing ones, and divided their interest between home and the grave of the loved one. So absorbed were these mourners in their own feelings, that they had not noticed a stranger was observing them intently, until they were addressed by the person before referred to.

"Who brought this desolating war upon our land?" asked this stranger, in a sharp, disagreeable tone, looking at Minnie as she spoke.

"The war is raging, and that is a point all are agreed upon," responded Minnie, with some spirit, for her feelings on this point were very vulnerable, and she felt that, under the circumstances, the question asked was unkind as well as uncalled for.

"You need n't be so fiery over it," said the coarse individual, who, for the sake of convenience, we came near calling a lady. "If there had n't been so much fuss," continued she, "made about the 'golden rule,' this war would n't have been brought about. Judging from what I've heard and seen, I suppose you've friends, or a friend, down by Port Hudson; and I know of others who were crazy enough to consent to their family's being half destroyed; but, thank my stars, nobody dear to me is in danger of being shot, and I don't mean they shall be, if I can keep 'em at home. Some of the women in our country act like fools. They may as well go to Congress, and done with it, as to be acting as they do at home, making men believe.

all sorts of nonsense to be their duty. For my part, I'm not a masculine woman; I don't want to have my influence go to help turn things upside down in the country, as these other women do. I am a peaceable woman, and want things to go smooth where I live, so that a body won't be obliged to pay so much for what they want. Only think on 't now, a piece of cotton cloth can't be bought without you have to pay all out doors for 't."

During the delivery of the speech we have quoted, our friends watched for a pause, during which they might escape from the presence of the speaker without seeming rude; but they watched in vain. Mrs. Grumpy was one of those women who will make you hear what they have to say, whether you will or no. Minnie, when she found she must listen to this disagreeable one-sided conversation, at first felt annoyed even more than her sister, but as her sense of the ludicrous was very strong, she was amused by the stranger's regret at the high price of cotton cloth; and when this untutored being paused, at the end of the laughable sentence last uttered, to take breath, Minnie could not resist an impulse to answer it.

"Then you are troubled by the high price of cotton?" said she.

"Troubled? yes, of course I am," replied the stranger; "who is n't, I'd like to know?"

"I'm not," said Minnie gently, yet firmly.

"You 're not? I'd like to know why you aint; perhaps you 've got a lots er cloth on hand, and so don't need to buy any now. Folks that have, don't feel so anxious to have peace brought about as I do."

"I wonder," thought Minnie, "if it is worth my

while to state my views to such a person; it seems like wasting words, to try to convince people who think as she does that they are in an error, and still, she will feel that I have not anything to say if I remain silent."

"Suppose," said Minnie to Mrs. Grumpy, "I tell you that the price of cloth is something I seldom think of, because my mind is occupied by subjects of more importance."

"It is, is it?"

"Yes."

"Then I guess you haven't had to buy any cloth very lately."

"Yes, I have."

"Well, did you have to pay a big price for it?"

"I paid more than triple what I used to pay, of course."

"You did; and you think these *enonnemous* prices all right, I suppose?"

"I think it an inconvenience growing out of the war; the price of almost every article sold is advanced in time of war, in all countries."

"But there was no need of this war, at all; I've had friends at the South, always, and I've known all along by them, that the Southerners would always have been peaceable if they had been let to have their own way a little. Of course, they wanted things to please them; they aint used to being crossed, and if the folks at Washington had only given way to 'em, 'twould 've been as calm all over the land as smooth water. I don't see the use of fighting 'em, and stirring up the country, as the folks did when the South fired that ar cannon inter that fort in South Carlina.

If they'd only kept still, 'twould all 've turned out somehow; at any rate, there 'd not have been so many deaths in the country as there has been, as things have turned out. But I'm beat, that you don't seem to care a good deal about the high prices of everything, and are not down on this war; for I suppose, by appearances, that you 've lost some friend down South there, have n't you?"

Minnie wiped the tears she could not keep back, as the recollection of the bereavement which her sister and herself had so recently suffered came over her spirits. She could not speak for some moments, but at the end of that time she spoke calmly, saying, she had lately lost a dear friend, who had died from the effect of wounds received in battle.

"Mercy on us," cried Mrs. Grumpy, "and still you want this war to go on."

"I have n't said that I did," replied Minnie.

"Well, I know you haint just them ar words, but what you 've said, amounts to that, you know, or I do."

"No, madam, pardon me for contradicting what you have said, but I have not left you to draw an inference, by any word I have spoken, that I wished to have war in our land. I would be grateful to have it cease this very hour," said Minnie, with much earnestness, "yet I should mourn to have it end so as to leave our country in a worse situation than when it begun; I love my friends, and I love my comfort as well as most people do, and this war deprives me of both friends and comfort, such as I enjoyed before it commenced, but I would not have it end unhappily for the nation, even if my own life must be sacrificed in consequence."

"You're real earnest, but you aint a peace-woman, I see," said Mrs. Grumpy.

"You or any one else can see that I am not a person who would compromise right for the sake of peace," said Minnie, "and I wish them to. I'm not one," continued she, glancing towards the crowd that had gathered around the party, attracted by the loud voice of Mrs. Grumpy, "of those who wish to have the wound Rebellion has inflicted upon our noble institutions slightly healed so that our land would be left exposed to the horrors of another and more terrible conflict than this. Justice and mercy must go hand in hand, in the administration of law; mercy alone would fail to benefit such traitors as the United States has had to deal with. The leaders in this gigantic Rebellion need hanging; it would be merciful to the South to hang them." Minnie then moved away from the little assembly of listeners who had heard in silence the conversation between herself and the self-introduced Mrs. Grumpy. She had scarcely passed beyond the sound of their voices, before various comments were made upon the views she had expressed.

"That's a bright one," said one.

"She's a noble girl," said a gentleman who had been an interested auditor, while Minnie had been speaking. "Such young ladies as she is, do a good work for our country, in her hour of darkness."

"Indeed they do," responded another gentleman, "for they do much to sustain our young men in the field, by their influence; and the influence of woman is always powerful, either for good or evil."

"I suppose such a girl as she is must have a beau in the army; but, if she hasn't, she helps other girls' **beaux to be brave**," said a fourth speaker.

"My opinion of the matter is," remarked a fifth speaker, "that women ought n't to have anything to do with public matters in any way. I reckon they're out of their place when they talk about the affairs of the country, and give their opinion as this young lady has done, in this public place. I want my daughters to mind their own matters of dress, visiting, and the like, and not get their brains turned topsy-turvy about the country they happen to live in. There's enough folks to see to war matters without them."

Mrs Grumpy happily coincided with the views of this speaker, and we left these two selfish ones engaged in a cosy chat about the meddlesome qualities of some women of the present generation, who really are so stupid as cheerfully to bear their part of the great burden now laid upon our bleeding country, for the sake of right.

Our friends, while they remained on the steamer, after this, took care to keep aloof from Mrs. Grumpy, for their thoughts were too full of sad thoughts, to admit of their engaging in unnecessary conversation, without pain. The sight of the steeples of their own town was hailed with pleasure, as they approached their home; still, this pleasure was qualified, because they had been obliged to return, leaving in a distant grave all that remained of their almost idolized husband and brother.

"When I think," said Mrs. Stetson, just before the travellers alighted at the home of their mother, "that Joseph will no more sympathize in our joys and sorrows, I don't know how I can live; then we shall miss his letters so much, too. Oh, how sad it all is."

"Yes," said Minnie, "if we allow our thoughts

to dwell upon the dark side of the picture; but there is a brighter view to be taken, and Joseph wished us to look upward, where he is now, rejoicing in his heavenly home."

"I thank you, sister, for reminding me of this, just at the time when I most need support. See, there stands our mother in the door, and she can with difficulty restrain her tears, even now. Let us look upward and cheerfully trust in God.

CHAPTER LI.

>———"Who, that bears
> A human bosom, hath not often felt,
> How dear are all those ties which bind our race
> In gentleness together; and how sweet
> Their force; let Fortune's wayward hand the while
> Be kind or cruel!"

"How has Bessie got along with my children?" asked Mrs. Stetson, soon after she arrived at the home of her mother. Ere Mrs. Granger could reply, Bessie entered the house, accompanied by her little charge. The youngest child clung to her fondly, while the other walked by her side, until he saw his mother and aunt. He then bounded towards them, with an expression of childish delight, encircling the neck of each in turn, and declaring, as he kissed them, that now he had a mother and two aunties, for Bessie was just as good as his Aunt Minnie.

"I love Auntie Bessie, too," lisped little Walter, the baby of the whole family.

"What has Auntie Bessie got to say about my little fatherless boys, I wonder," said the mother of the children.

"That they have given me less trouble than I anticipated when I volunteered to look after them, and that I am very glad I have been able to stay with them during your absence from them."

"You have conferred a favor upon me, Bessie, as well as upon my daughter, by caring for these little ones, because I should have felt that I must have them with me, if you had not, and my health has not been adequate to such a task."

"I have known, Mrs. Granger, that you were not well, and this knowledge determined me to avoid troubling you about many little matters that concerned the children, which I should have run to you about, had I felt it would have been right. I have learned that I can rely upon myself now I have been obliged to, so I feel that I ought to thank you for the experience I have had, rather than accept thanks from you."

"Is this Bessie Jenkins?" asked a lady who had entered the room where the friends were assembled, unobserved, and unintentionally had been a listener to their conversation.

"Why," Aunt Amey! exclaimed several voices at once.

"You are surprised to see me, I suppose, because you supposed I was absent from the place, but you might have known I could not stay away from any of this family, when any part of them are afflicted in any way. I sympathize with you, deeply, if you don't believe Aunt Amey is susceptible of much feeling. But never mind anything about that, now; only tell me, if it is really true, that Bessie Jenkins took care of these little ones, when their mother was away."

"It is true, Miss Benson," replied Bessie, "that I have taken care of them, during the last fortnight and longer."

"How much help did you have?" inquired Aunt Amey, doubting somewhat the correctness of the statement Bessie had made.

"Only my woman of all work, Aunt Amey," said Mrs. Stetson.

"Well, then, wonders are farther from ceasing nowadays, than ever, I am obliged to say. Why, I shouldn't have been any more astonished, if I had been told that Mrs. Abraham Lincoln had come from Washington, to look after these little boys, during their mother's absence. Bessie, how changed you must be. I must say what I feel, for I am too glad to conceal my feelings. Another startling case has occurred, recently," said Aunt Amey.

Bessie laughed outright, as Aunt Amey said this.

"You seem to imply, Miss Benson, that my having taken care of this friend's children for a short season, is something startling."

"I confess that it is so unlike any act of yours that has ever come to my knowledge, that I was startled at hearing what you had done," replied Aunt Amey.

"Then what do you think of what Lilian Grey has done of late?" asked Bessie.

"That is no more for her, if as much, as for you to bring your ideas down to tending children. I thought you didn't use to love children, Bessie."

"I didn't, but my feelings are very different towards them, from what they were a few months since."

"What of Lilian Grey? tell us about her, for we have not heard," said Minnie, speaking for her sister, as well as for herself.

"Why," said Aunt Amey, "all there is to tell about her is, that she has been getting cured of her aversion to meet strangers, or to push herself forward under any circumstances. You probably know how diffident she has always been."

"Yes, I know," said Minnie, "it was out of the power of any one to persuade her to take the lead in anything, she was always sure to shrink back, when with a party of ladies she was entering some public place, and would be found in the rear when she went into a church or hall."

"Every one who knows her, has noticed this trait in her character," said Bessie.

"Well, we know now, that folks can do things sometimes that are against nature," remarked Aunt Amey, "since Lilian Grey went to Annapolis, alone."

"She must have been prompted by some powerful motive," said Mrs. Stetson.

"Affection and sympathy were stronger feelings at the time than diffidence, probably, else she could not have overcome her diffidence, so as to have done this," said Mrs. Granger.

"That is true," said Aunt Amey. "It was a sight worth seeing, one day in August, when news was brought to her home, that an only brother of hers, who had been wounded at Gettysburg, and had been in the hospital at Annapolis some time, was in great danger, from a disease which was becoming prevalent among the wounded soldiers. The family were about assembling around the dinner-table, when the tidings was brought from this absent one, who was dear to them all."

"Lilian, after a moment's reflection, determined to go to her brother, and try to get leave of absence for him, if she should find him able to be carried to his home. This determination she at once expressed to her family."

"You cannot go, Lilian," said her father; "you will be sick if you do."

"But who will go if I do not? you, father, are not

able, and I feel that some one of us must start this very hour. Don't discourage me; I can bear some hardship, as well as Lucius—a great deal; think how he has suffered, and how trying it must be to a youth like him, only eighteen years old, to be situated as he is, without a friend near him."

Her father said no more, and that same hour Lilian set out on her journey from Landville to the place where her brother was suffering, a distance of several hundred miles. Circumstances had separated Lilian from this brother, for some years previous to the time when he enlisted, and he had so changed that she did not recognize him when she found him. The meeting of this brother and sister was most interesting. Lilian remained several days at Annapolis before she succeeded in procuring a furlough for Lucius; but she did succeed, and took him home with her, where he was permitted to remain some little time.

"Where is Lilian, now?" inquired Minnie.

"Here in Oak Dale, stopping with her friends, the Delmots; she left her brother at home when she came from there, a few days since."

"These friends of hers, I hear, are greatly afflicted," remarked Bessie.

"They are," answered Aunt Amey. "I have just come from the house of Mrs. Delmot, and it is true that Clarence is a prisoner at Richmond. His wife and mother both feel distressing apprehensions of his suffering, if not dying from starvation, in the hands of his Rebel captors."

"Their present trial is greater than mine," remarked Mrs. Stetson, while tears ran down her cheeks. "My loved one suffers not, but is sweetly resting upon the bosom of his Lord and Saviour, while this husband and son is enduring the horrors of a captivity such as has seldom, if ever, been experienced, even in barbarous countries."

"Has Mrs. Delmot had a letter from Clarence since he was captured?" asked Mrs. Granger.

"She has, and she read it to me this morning. Clarence says he should not have been captured, had he not been deceived by the blue overcoats which were worn by the Rebels. Supposing them to be Union soldiers, he got within a carbine's length of several of Stuart's cavalry, when three of these guns were, in a moment, pointed at his breast, and he could do nothing but surrender. He stated that there was some disputing over his horse, as to who should have him, but that he was allowed to take from his saddle-bags anything he wished, which, he remarked, was a privilege granted to but few."

"What does he say of his situation and eatables?" asked Bessie.

"He did n't speak of his food at all, but said he was confined in a room forty-two feet square, with a hundred and fifty-six prisoners; that all these had to be marched two by two, daily, to one small stream of water, where all were permitted to wash their faces and hands. No farther ablution was allowed, neither could they wash their clothes on any occasion; he stated also, that the dirt and vermin were intolerable, in the prison where he was confined."

"I hope Clarence is not in the Libby prison," said one of the company, and all present echoed this hope.

"He is not," continued Aunt Amey, "but is in the Laundry prison, and that is n't a fit place for cattle even, much less for such gallant men as are incarcerated there."

"Clarence said in his letter that he looked through iron grates and thought of home," said Bessie. "It seems very hard that so brave a fellow as he has been should be shut up in such a terrible place; a common prison-house would be awful, but these dens, where traitorous men shut up loyal soldiers, are intolerable. I feel indignant when I think of these Rebel barbarities."

"So do all, who are friends to humanity," said Mrs. Granger.

"Clarence is the right kind of a man to get along with disagreeables, without hurting himself by chafing his spirit about them," said Minnie; "he has always abstained from the use of intoxicating liquors, also from the use of tobacco; consequently, he has more strength to endure now, than most of his fellow-prisoners."

"*That is true*," said Aunt Amy, speaking in an emphatic tone; "and some, who sneered at his use of cayenne pepper, would now be glad of some of the strength he has saved by resorting, in times of exposure, to this stimulant instead of ardent spirits."

"Clarence Delmot has been a faithful soldier," said Minnie, "ever since our troubles began. He is unpretending, but he is fearless and valiant; once his horse was shot under him; once he lay concealed through one whole night and day, within a few rods of the foe, in order to escape capture; yet now, after having been unharmed by shot and shell, which has seventeen times been poured upon him by the Rebels, he is incarcerated in a loathsome prison."

"These things are harrowing to dwell upon," said

Mrs. Granger, while a tear bedewed her cheek, "yet we must obey the injunction, 'Be still, and know that I am God,' that Being who will make this terribly cruel war to cease in his own good time."

CHAPTER LII.

"O, what men dare to do! what men daily do! not knowing what they do!"—MUCH ADO ABOUT NOTHING.

"Why art thou cast down, O my soul? and why art thou disquieted within me?"—DAVID.

"To talk about God's having anything to do with the diabolical actions that have disgraced our land for the last four years is nonsense," said Aunt Amey Benson one day, soon after the temporary triumph of the Southrons in Tennessee, in the autumn of 1863. This eccentric lady was finishing her visit at Mrs. Granger's, which she had begun months before. The home of this niece was considered by her a convenient stopping-place, while she was going the adjacent country over in search of those who were remotely connected with herself, or any of the relatives whom she had once visited. She fancied sometimes that ties of relationship existed between herself and people who cared not to recognize her as an acquaintance, even.

It would not be doing Aunt Amey justice to say that she was coarse in her undue familiarity, for this was the reverse entirely, with her. She had a way of saying things unlike any one else. She would sometimes, when angry, use very unbecoming expressions, yet from her lips they fell upon the ears of those in her society with less of coarseness in the sound than as if another had uttered them. Miss Benson professed to be a Christian, and would have been very angry with any one who should have expressed a doubt of her piety; still, she would often find fault with the administration of the world's Sovereign. The expression with which this chapter commences is one of the mildest she was wont to indulge in, for there was something in the manner and life of Mrs. Granger, which often restrained her, even when she had opened her lips to utter a harsh, unwomanly speech.

She remained silent for some little time after she had spoken the sentence before quoted, seemingly waiting for some one to reply; but as no one answered immediately, she went on.

"I grow madder and more mad every day; the men at Washington act like a pack of fools. They're afraid the Rebels will get hurt; and if the Union army whips them ever so little, the Government gives them sugar plums to keep them from feeling the hurt any, and while this is going on at the capital, our young men are being slaughtered by thousands all over the land. For my part, I don't know where the overruling power is, that some folks talk about. There is Mrs. Saunders, who has just heard of the death of her son, Albert; what can comfort her, I ask?"

"The grace of God can console even her sorrowing heart, Aunt Amey," replied Mrs. Granger.

"Well, I'd like to know how, for I can't see any way in which the loss of that son, upon whom she was dependent for her support, can be made up to her."

"Mrs. Saunders laid Albert upon the altar of her country; he did not go without her consent. She had probably counted the cost, ere he left her; indeed, I am sure she had, for I have heard her say so, and, as she is a Christian, she will weep over her fallen son, without murmuring, and, I think, with a feeling of gratitude, that he has so nobly finished his work on earth. Albert loved his Saviour, God, and his mother can feel that he is now resting from the labor and turmoil of earth, in the society of 'the just made perfect in heaven.'"

"But, Minnie Granger, you haven't heard all the particulars in regard to poor Albert Saunders, else you would n't feel that his mother could be comforted."

"I must, Aunt Amey, ever believe, that 'earth has no sorrow that heaven cannot heal;' still, I feel that the circumstances connected with the death of some friends we are called to mourn is deeply aggravating." .

"Aggravating, indeed! that word does n't express half the terrible meaning of some of the reliable accounts that reach us from those who have had friends imprisoned on Belle Island. Albert Saunders was one of the sufferers in that abominable, filthy, devilish, tormenting place."

"Seems to me you abound in superlatives, auntie," said Minnie; "I feel very much indeed for the Union prisoners who have lately been brought to Annapolis; my heart bleeds at thought of them; but it will not better their condition to apply hard names to persons or places."

"Well, you can handle the Rebels and their hellish holes tenderly in talking of them, if you like, but I believe as John Randolph, of Roanoke, once said he did; that it is best to call spades, spades, and corruption, corruption. When anything is devilish, I am determined to call it so; and you, young Miss Minnie, can talk about superlatives as much as you please, it won't alter my mind at all."

"Aunt Amey," said Mrs. Granger, "let us call on Mrs. Saunders to-day. Will you go this afternoon?"

"Perhaps I shall say something you won't like, if I go with you, Minnie, for it appears your daughter does n't like my phraseology."

"Don't lay this expression of my taste up against me, will you, auntie?" expostulated Minnie. "I had better have kept silent than said what I did to you just now, you are so many years my senior, that it was n't a bit pretty in me to speak so."

"Well, well, child that you are, I suppose I shall forgive you this time, and a great many more times beside this, for we never do agree in matters of taste, unless it is in respect to flowers, which we both love."

Mrs. Granger, accompanied by her aunt sought the dwelling of Mrs. Saunders at an early hour in the afternoon of that same day. They found this afflicted mother sorrowing deeply, yet she murmured not. "The Lord gave, and the Lord hath taken away, and blessed be the name of the Lord," said she, when refering to the great loss she had sustained in the death of Albert. "I should not have chosen the suffering for my loved one, which he was obliged to endure," remarked she meekly, while speaking of his incarceration in prison, "but I left everything concerning my darling to God, and I am satisfied with what He has chosen for me."

"You don't mean that you are reconciled to the thought that your son suffered from hunger, do you? if so, you are destitute of a mother's feelings for a child, I am sure," said Aunt Amey.

"I don't mean that I love to think that he suffered at all, when I look only to the fact that he was a sufferer. The contemplation of suffering always distresses me, even if the victim is a stranger. I am not without maternal feelings, Miss Benson, but believe me, there is a power that can enable even a mother to triumph over the doting fondness of her heart, in cheerfully sacrificing the dearest object of her love, when duty calls."

"I confess," responded Aunt Amey, "I don't understand such lofty logic, it is altogether above my limited powers of comprehension; still, I think I have quite an amount of sense that is common."

"You style yourself a Christian, aunt," remarked Mrs. Granger, "and you, too, depend upon your good works for salvation. This last is what I cannot do, yet I am not puzzled at all by the views expressed by our afflicted friend. Like her, I feel that the assurance given us by God, is to be relied upon in any emergency. When I read the consoling promise He has made in the words, 'My grace is sufficient for thee,' my spirit becomes hopeful; it is only when Christians forget that God is the immutable rock of their strength, that they despond."

"I have learned by experience that what you have said is true," replied Mrs. Saunders. "When the news reached me of the death of my Albert, it came like a thunderbolt. I knew before, that he had been sent a prisoner to Richmond, and that afterwards he had been removed to Belle Island. I received one letter from him, after he arrived at that dreadful place, it did n't surprise me that this letter was short. The spirit of this missive was more cheerful than I could have expected, though it was evident that it had been penned by a trembling hand. He assured me, in the few words which he then wrote, that God was the 'strength of his heart, and his portion forever;' 'then,' added he, 'why need I fear what man can do unto me, since I can trust, and not be afraid, even of the wrath of our erring, God-forgetting brethren at the South.'

"The accounts in respect to the suffering of our prisoners have been so contradictory, that they have inspired hope and fear, alternately. I did at times fear that my darling son might experience the horrors of starvation; still, I would not indulge such a feeling for a moment. That he would become an invalid, during the remainder of his life, I thought very probable, for I cannot see how any of the half-famished men who are held captive for even a few weeks by the Rebels, are to recover the strength, wasted by living as they are obliged to live in those loathsome prisons. I have always dreaded imprisonment for Albert, more than the balls or shells of the enemy."

"So have I," said Mrs. Granger.

"And I have also," remarked Aunt Amey, "but at this moment I am anxious to hear all that Mrs. Saunders has to say of her son. I am reminded forcibly by what she has already said, of my loved and fallen nephew," and Miss Benson wiped her fast-flowing tears as she spoke. "I know your story must be a sad one, and it will pain you to tell it; still, it will interest me, and, I doubt not, my niece also."

"I need not assure Mrs. Saunders that I feel the most intense interest in regard to her loved son; she has long known that I feel deeply for every loyal soldier, whether they suffer much or little; then how much more must I feel for this interesting young man, who is so dear to my friend."

" I know, Mrs Granger, that the last message sent to me by my noble boy, will delight you. It was this. 'Though I shall die probably without seeing you again, my dear mother, I hope you will thank God that you had a loved son to give to your bleeding country. My soul is stayed upon God, my Saviour, and I am strong to endure; I trust you to His care. My bodily strength fails, so I must say farewell for a little time. We shall soon meet in the presence of Jesus, my Redeemer, my King, my all in all.'

        'ALBERT SAUNDERS.'"

November, 1863.

When the reading of this note was concluded, Mrs. Saunders looked up and perceived that her auditors were both weeping with her.

"What a priceless legacy your son has left you," said Mrs. Granger, in a voice that trembled with strong emotion.

"That is true; a world, in comparison with these few lines, would be valueless to me," said Mrs. Saunders.

"He appeared to be carried above his situation by his faith in God," said Aunt Amey. "I must confess that I am a stranger to such faith as is manifested in that dying message; I wish I had even a little of it."

"You and I may have it, for the asking," said the weeping mother.

"Then it must be that you have asked for it, for it seems that you are held up, now, by a kind of faith I have never exercised;" and Aunt Amey looked down as she spoke, and seemed to be taking views of herself, which brought a feeling of sadness to her heart, for she sighed deeply ere she spoke again. She then remarked, "I will try and read my Bible without prejudice, in future. I have always been bound up in the belief I was taught in infancy, and supposed those who believed God was a Sovereign were gloomy persons; but I find this is not the case with many."

"Were it not for my belief in the universal control of that Being who notices even the fall of the little sparrow, I could not be comforted now," remarked Mrs. Saunders.

"Then you are comforted, although your earthly dependence is gone?" said Aunt Amey.

"Yes, I am comforted; for I am enabled to lean upon the bosom of that Saviour to whom my darling trusted me in his last hours. Those hours were, I believe, brightened by the presence of that Almighty Friend, whom he loved and served in life. The letter written me after Albert's death, in which the little missive I have read to you was enclosed, contained a few sentences that are invaluable to me. After acquainting me with my great bereavement, the writer remarked, —

"Your affliction is great, my dear madam, but you have consolation in this trial, such as few are blessed with. Your son was a whole Christian; he sank from exhaustion into the arms of death; but he never murmured, never seemed to feel that he was hardly dealt with. Could you, my dear Mrs. Saunders, witness the suffering I have seen since we came to this place, and see the difference between those who are Christians, and those who are not sustained by the hopes the gospel affords, you would be incited to great gratitude, by the knowledge that your son was supported by the promises of God, until his spirit returned to Him who gave it.

"Here have been endured the sharpest of earthly sufferings by the brave men and boys, who have been prisoners on Belle Island, until almost starved. I blush for the men, at the South, who have been guilty of this monstrous crime. Some have died literally from starvation, some have died from the effects of trying to eat, while their stomachs were unfitted by long fasting to receive food, and some poor sufferers have died with food before them, which they could not eat. One dear youth, a mere boy of sixteen, was made insane by hunger, and his agonies cannot be described. Strong men that were, writhed in agony, after they were brought here, and died from the effect of the savage treatment they had received at the hands of those by whom they had been held prisoners of war. In contemplating these terrible results of man's depravity, one is led to ask what has made the difference between the moral acts of the North and South during this war. Why are the Southrons barbarous in their treatment of all over whom they have power? This question is forced upon every reflecting mind, and must be answered, yea, it answers itself.

"I have ever been pro-slavery in my views, yet glaring as broad daylight, do I see that the peculiar institution of the South has been a curse to my Southern brethren, by producing in them a hardness of heart, which is fast carrying them back to the humiliating barbarism of the dark ages. Please excuse me, dear lady, if, out of the fulness of my heart, I have written of that which does not personally concern you. I would write more of your brave and manly Albert; with pleasure I state the fact, that he was gently dealt with at the last, by his heavenly Father, in comparison with most of his fellows, and also that he has left his patient image in the memory of many a man who saw him on his death couch. I am unfit to attempt to offer you comfort, other than this letter will afford. But God can, and will, I trust, bind up your broken heart."

Very respectfully, your servant,

R. M. J.——

"He need not have said that which implied I have not a personal interest in the sufferings of all my loyal countrymen, for I feel that I suffer in sympathy with all such."

"I'm sure I do," said Mrs. Granger, "and I agree with his views in regard to the effect of, the Southern institution alluded to. I pray God daily, to rid my Southern friends from the scourge. My heart bleeds at the thought that mortal man can be guilty of such acts, as the Rebels have been guilty of towards the loyal men who have fallen into their hands. Well may humanity weep over their atrocities. What motive can influence them to keep men whom they could easily parole until they are reduced to such a lamentable condition?"

"It cannot be any better motive than to please their old master, his Satanic Majesty," replied Aunt Amey, "but after seeing you all so kindly disposed towards these tenfold murderers, I am beginning to feel that it is perhaps better to pray for them, than to curse them, as I always have done, so I'll try to forgive them, if it is possible, far enough to ask the Lord to give them better hearts."

"Our Saviour prayed for His own murderers, and said they knew not what they did; we can say this of our Southern brothers and sisters too," said Mrs. Saunders, "and Miss Benson," she continued, "I want you to feel that the great and holy Being to whom you expect to trust your soul throughout eternity, is worthy to be trusted with the management of the affairs of even this great nation. We must not ask to see his plans; we have proof upon proof that he is 'too wise to err, and too good to be unkind.' I trust I feel this, and am not afraid that I shall ever want anything necessary for my highest good."

"Amen," said Mrs. Granger, but Aunt Amey was obliged to say, "I believe I should be happier, if I could say amen to what has been said by this child of affliction."

We hope the day is not far distant when not only Miss Benson, but every son and daughter of our country, can from the heart join in one hearty amen; when it shall be said throughout our land —

"Sound the loud trump o'er the wide-spreading sea,
Jehovah has triumphed, our country is free."

CONCLUSION.

Now, kind reader, you and the writer are about to part. We have been together through various scenes which have occurred since our country's woes began. We have looked upon life as it is in this land at the present day.

The writer would be glad to be enabled to inform her readers that Raymond Philips had been exchanged, and that he and Bessie had met again; met, too, under happy auspices, such as we trust they will some day be blest with, on meeting; but we may not finish their history, for our story is not a romance, although a degree of novelty has marked the pages of our work. Bessie has sent the letter to Raymond which she at first was so afraid would not be treated sacredly by the hands through which it must pass, to reach the friend to whom it was addressed. The reception of the letter has filled Raymond's heart with joy.

Mrs. Sedgwick is helping her husband, though he is now at Chattanooga and she at home. She aids him by her cheerful letters, her patience, and her prayers. She has never repented having consented that he might serve his country; neither has his mother, who very recently, in a letter to a sister, wrote: "If my son shall fall, I will bless God that he has been worthy to suffer and to die in the cause of liberty and right."

Who will not bless God that our loved Union has many mothers like Mrs. Sedgwick? Such women as she is, will read this book through without passing over any of its pages with disgust ; we are confident of the sympathy of such as she, and we would love to linger in their company ; but we have written as many pages as our publisher desires at this juncture. But if our readers give us a pleasant hint that they would like to hear more of Bessie and Raymond, and some of their friends, we may be induced to offer them a sequel to our story.

We have redeemed our pledge to our readers now, and offer them just the work we promised, while we crave for ourselves their kind indulgence.

www.ingramcontent.com/pod-product-compliance
Lightning Source LLC
Chambersburg PA
CBHW022113290426
44112CB00008B/659